A Spanish Woman in Love and War

Constancia de la Mora

T0385691

A mi madre

A Spanish Woman in Love and War
Constancia de la Mora

SOLEDAD FOX

sussex
ACADEMIC
PRESS
Brighton • Portland • Toronto

Published in association with the
Cañada Blanch Centre for Contemporary Spanish Studies

Cañada Blanch Centre
for Contemporary
Spanish Studies

2 4 6 8 10 9 7 5 3

First published in hardcover 2007, reprinted in paperback 2011, in Great Britain by
SUSSEX ACADEMIC PRESS
PO Box 139
Eastbourne BN24 9BP

and in the United States of America by
SUSSEX ACADEMIC PRESS
920 NE 58th Ave   Suite 300
Portland, Oregon 97213-3786

and in Canada by
SUSSEX ACADEMIC PRESS (CANADA)
90 Arnold Avenue, Thornhill, Ontario L4J 1B5

British Library Cataloguing in Publication Data
A CIP catalogue record for this book is available from the British Library.

Library of Congress Cataloging-in-Publication Data
Fox, Soledad.
[Constancia de la Mora in war and exile]
A Spanish woman in love and war : Constancia del la Mora / Soledad Fox.
p. cm.
Originally published under title: Constancia de la Mora in war and exile. 2007.
Includes bibliographical references and index.
ISBN 978-1-84519-447-5 (p/b : alk. paper)
  1. Mora, Constancia de la, 1906–1950. 2. Spain—History—Republic, 1931–1939. 3. Exiles—Spain—Biography. I. Title.
DP264.M7F69 2011
946.081092—dc22
  [B]

2010045630

Typeset and designed by Sussex Academic Press, Brighton & Eastbourne
Printed by TJ International, Padstow, Cornwall.
This book is printed on acid-free paper.

Contents

List of Illustrations   vi

Foreword by José Álvarez-Junco   viii

Acknowledgements   x

List of Abbreviations   xii

Introduction   1

  I   Old Spain: Portrait of a Family   5

 II   The War, 1936–1939: Fighting Fascism from the Press Office   32

III   Mission to New York: Propaganda and Diplomacy   84

IV   Refugee Crisis: From the White House to the Blacklist   106

 V   Mexico, 1940–1950: Exile   134

Epilogue   171

Notes   178

Bibliography   203

Index   208

List of Illustrations

Illustrations, pages 50–57 and 112–119. The author and publisher gratefully acknowledge the following for permission to reproduce copyright material:

1 Prime Minister Antonio Maura giving a speech, Bullring of Madrid, April 1917. D-28 Fondo Gráfico Fundación Antonio Maura.
2 Primer Minister Antonio Maura and King Alfonso XIII, Calle Alcalá, Madrid. 1918. C-86 Fondo Gráfico Fundación Antonio Maura.
3 Three of Antonio Maura's daughters: Margarita, Estefanía, and Constancia Maura (Constancia's mother), 1900. C-63 Fondo Gráfico Fundación Antonio Maura.
4 Portrait of Constancia in Paris, 1923. A-49 Fondo Gráfico Fundación Antonio Maura.
5 Portrait of Constancia, 1925. A-50 Fondo Gráfico Fundación Antonio Maura.
6 Portrait of Constancia and Luli, 1929. A-51 Fondo Gráfico Fundación Antonio Maura.
7 Ignacio Hidalgo de Cisneros, *c.* 1939. Comintern Archive (RGASPI), Moscow.
8 Ignacio Hidalgo de Cisneros (profile), *c.* 1939. Comintern Archive (RGASPI), Moscow.
9 Constancia and her cousins arriving at the trial of Migual Maura, March 21, 1931. Courtesy of the Hemeroteca Municipal, Madrid.
10 Jay Allen, *c.* 1939. Courtesy of Michael Allen.
11 Jay Allen (close-up), *c.* 1939. Courtesy of Michael Allen.
12 Constancia. Photo by John Condax, Philadelphia, Summer of 1939. Courtesy of Kate Delano Condax Decker.
13 Constancia with Laura Condax (with her back to the camera) and friends, Philadelphia, Summer of 1939. Courtesy of Kate Delano Condax Decker.
14 Luli (back row, sixth from left) with Dolores Ibarruri's daughter Amaya (back row, eight from left) and other children at a summer camp in the Soviet Union. Date not known. Archive of Dolores Ibarruri.
15 Luli and friend in the Soviet Union, *c.* 1943. Archive of Dolores Ibarruri.

16 Constancia, Anna Seghers, and Ludwig Renn, *c.* 1944. Archivo Teresa Miranda. Photo by Hans Gutmann.

17 Constancia in Mexico with the First Secretary of the Soviet Embassy, *c.* 1943.

18 Portrait of Constancia in Mexico. Courtesy of Eladia de los Rios.

19 *Mexico is Theirs* advertisement from the Modern Age catalogue. Courtesy of Kate Delano Condax Decker.

20 Luli, *c.* 1945. Comintern Archive (RGASPI), Moscow.

21 Constancia and Lini de Vries. Constancia's house, Cuernavaca, December 1949. Courtesy of Constancia Moreno.

22 Ignacio in exile in Poland, undated. Courtesy of Maria Sanchez and Juan Haro.

23 Ignacio with Sanchez Arcas family, Rafael Alberti, Pablo Neruda and other friends, undated. Courtesy of Maria Sanchez and Juan Haro.

24 Ignacio and Pablo Neruda in Poland, undated. Courtesy of Maria Sanchez and Juan Haro.

The publishers apologize for any errors or omissions in the above list and would be grateful to be notified of any corrections that should be incorporated in the next edition or reprint of this book.

Foreword by José Álvarez-Junco

Today, in 2006, we celebrate the 100th anniversary of the birth of Constancia de la Mora. Her dynamic career is, like all careers, marked by chance and hasty decisions. Nonetheless, everything that happened in it seems logical and exemplary. Few twentieth-century Spanish biographies illustrate like hers the conflicts and paradoxes that beset society at the time and which culminated in the Spanish Civil War (1936–1939); few give so many insights into the tremendous changes that occurred in Spain and the world in that recently concluded century.

Constancia de la Mora was, first of all, a woman, and her gender conditioned her entire existence, destined as it was from the start to occupy a submissive role of wife and mother. She was, secondly, an aristocrat, granddaughter of Antonio Maura, the most successful conservative politician during the reign of Alfonso XIII, and her cultural environment prepared her for life with rules of conduct and an interpretative world view originating from the limited scope of a traditional Catholic upbringing. However, the demands of her own environment and the circumstances of her historical epoch would ultimately lead her to clash with that entire world.

Her family wanted to give their daughters a sophisticated education, so, as a child, she was assigned an English-speaking tutor, and was later sent to Cambridge. That contact with British life influenced her rebellion against the inanity of the feminine world in Spanish high-class society. When she returned to Spain with her English education in the early 1920s, her role in life was reduced to attending parties and gatherings, to parade herself and eventually arrange a marriage of "convenience." However, she was terribly bored by the young people of Spanish high society, criticizing their poor intellectual interests and abysmal sexual education using reflections similar to those of Stefan Zweig. And her desire for independence, just when it was time for her to submit and get married, led her to the first confrontation with her parents. As a way of affirming her will, she opted to marry someone of her own choosing. This turned out to be a big mistake that would mark her life, because her husband was an unscrupulous dowry hunter whose only intention was to cheat her and her family in order to get hold of their fortune.

Constancia's rebellion took a giant leap forward when, faithful to her principles of independence and moral rectitude, she decided to separate from this husband. This was the moment her personal history became part of national history: during the years 1930–31, after the fall of the dictator Primo de Rivera and later of King Alfonso XIII himself, with the proclamation of the Republic. Constancia not only held hope in the new regime, but also took advantage of the recently passed divorce law to liquidate her marriage with the intention of marrying another man, the aviator Hidalgo de Cisneros (later general of the Republican Air Force). Constancia had become, to the scandal of her family and social circle, a "Republican". And her commitment to the new government was such that, when the Spanish Civil War began five years later, she devoted herself intensely to the Republican cause and eventually joined the Communist Party. The epilogue of her book, from New York in July 1939, ends with "Long Live the Republic!"

The rebellion of this personage is, as such, triple: as a woman destined to be an obedient daughter and wife, she decided to choose her husband by herself and later get divorced; with a traditional Catholic upbringing, she refused to distribute alms and scapulars with other ladies of high society in order to support Republican anticlericalism; and as an aristocrat and landowner, she chose to hold a salaried job and, during the Spanish Civil War, aligned herself with the Communists.

In 1939, the cycle had run its course. Constancia de la Mora had, as an old aristocratic friend once reproached her, "betrayed" her family, and her grandfather Maura. She had lost, as she herself confessed, all of her friends from her childhood and youth. As the title of her autobiography, *In Place of Splendor*, suggests, she gave up privilege and tradition and instead committed herself to living *on her own terms*, as she once put it. That was a real revolution for a Spanish woman of her time. Among other things, it meant to defend the Republic.

MADRID, April 2007

Acknowledgements

Many people have helped me at the various stages of researching and writing this book. In Spain, the United States, and Mexico, numerous individuals have been immensely helpful and kindly shared their personal stories, contacts, and/or papers, and answered many questions:

J. C. Michael Allen
Aurora Arnaíz
Tobyann Berenberg
Eileen Bransten
Lourdes Caraballo
Santiago Carrillo
Kate Delano Condax-Decker
Fanny Edelman
Germán Escrivá de Romaní de la Mora
Moe Fishman
James Kahn
Tony Kahn
Alvar Haro
Juan Haro
Cindy Hawes
Charlotte Kurzke
Paloma Lagunero
Teodulfo Lagunero

Ignacio Luque
Mario Mengs
Teresita Miranda
Constancia Moreno Cedillo
Tamara Pascual
Eladia de los Ríos
Amaya Ruiz
Dolores Ruiz
Paul Quintanilla
María Sánchez
Sol Sender
Ramón Sender Barayón
Edelgard Skowronnek
Pola Tomas
Renata Von Hanffenstengel
Susan Wallis
Georgia Wever
Milton Wolff

Various scholars and archivists have been indispensable in helping me locate materials, sources, and generally offering advice and suggestions:

Candy Entisne (Archivo General de la Guerra Civil Española, Salamanca).
Sebastiaan Faber.
Gijs Kessler (International institute of Social History, Amsterdam).
Daniel Kowalsky.
Gail Malmgreen (Tamiment Library/Wagner Labor Archives, New York University).
Ignacio Martínez de Pisón.

Pelai Pages.

Alfonso Pérez Maura (Fundación Antonio Maura, Madrid) and Carmen Rivera.

Victoria Ramos (Archivo Histórico del Partido Comunista, Madrid).

Svetlana Rozental (RGASPI, Moscow).

Policarpo Sánchez.

David Wingeate Pike.

My gratitude also goes to the excellent staff at the Franklin D. Roosvelt Library, the Hemeroteca Municipal de Madrid, the Rare Book and Manuscript Library at Columbia University, and Rauner Special Collections at Dartmouth College.

I would never have been able to embark on this research project without the combined support of a Fulbright Senior Research Grant, and the Williams College Class of 1945 World Fellowship Program, and most certainly not without the encouragement of my colleagues in the Department of Romance Languages.

Elizabeth Kolbert and John Kleiner gave me insightful feedback on my book proposal, Mark Donen has read and helped me improve countless drafts of the manuscript, and Anthony Grahame, Editorial Director at Sussex Academic Press, has guided me through the publishing process with patience and thoroughness. I am very grateful for their contributions. Any errors in the present text are entirely my own.

Finally, I would like to thank Paul Preston for his constant encouragement and generosity.

Abbreviations

CEDA	Confederación Española de Derechas Autónomas
PCE	Partido Comunista Español
MAE	Ministerio de Asuntos Exteriores
NKVD	People's Comisariat for Internal Affairs
PSOE	Partido Socialista Obrero español
POUM	Partit Obrer d'Unificació Marxista
SRRC	Spanish Refugee Relief Campaign
SERE	Servicio de Evacuación de Refugiados Españoles
JARE	Junta de Ayuda a los Refugiados Españoles
JAFRC	Joint Anti-Fascist Refugee Committee
JSUN	Junta Suprema de Unión Nacional
CP	Communist Party
UME	Unión de Mujeres Españolas

Hay tantos muertos en mi corazón
Pretenden vivirme
Tantos muertos y tan primaverales
He visto sus raíces arrancadas
Sus blandas alas sin sangre dulcemente
Esos muertos prometiendo siempre que van a morir.

Germán Bleiberg, "Hay tantos muertos en mi corazón," *Selección de Poemas 1936–1973* (London: Grant & Cutler, 1975), p. 78.

Introduction

¿y qué se hizo . . .
de Hidalgo de Cisneros
Constancia de la Mora . . .
Qué se hizo
de tanto fantasma lejano?
Manuel Vázquez Montálban

Constancia de la Mora, who had once been the spokesperson of the Spanish Republican government, was killed in a car crash in Guatemala in January 1950. Her body was flown to Mexico to be buried near her house in Acapantzingo. She had left Spain in 1939 and never returned. The funeral was attended by some of the most prominent Spanish Republicans in exile, as well as by a few watchful FBI agents. Pablo Neruda delivered the eulogy. De la Mora had died on the eve of her forty-fourth birthday, and immediately after her death she was revered as a beloved comrade, and a martyr for the Spanish people. Neruda vowed to keep her memory alive.

The compelling story of her life, as presented in her memoir *In Place of Splendor*, seemed to guarantee that she would not be forgotten. She had been an aristocrat turned Republican, a celebrated author, and an international political figure who had known Stalin, Eleanor Roosevelt, Ernest Hemingway, Tina Modotti, Vittorio Vidali, and Anna Seghers among many others. Milton Wolff, the last commander of the Abraham Lincoln Brigade, remembers:

> Constancia was big news when we were doing the fighting, there being so few from her social milieu . . . who remained loyal to the elected government; it did take a lot of courage to do so. And inspiring for the men in the trenches, Spaniards and brigadistas alike. In Place of Splendor is one of the best books on the war and the times, I don't know why it isn't in print.[2]

In the 1940s, people went to Mexico to meet her. A few veterans from the Abraham Lincoln Brigade even named their daughters Constancia.[3] A famous blacklisted Hollywood couple, Ben and Norma Barzman, named their daughter after Constancia's: "We named our daughter Elizabeth . . .

although we knew already we were going to call her 'Luli' after the daughter of Spanish aristocrat Constancia de la Mora, who joined the loyalists (those loyal to the democratic republic of Spain)."[4]

Yet, instead of remaining one of the most famous heroines of the Spanish Republic, Constancia de la Mora somehow faded from history. The tombstone that marked her grave in Mexico has disappeared. Her name is absent from the majority of memoirs and archival collections in which one would expect it to be. Even her husband, Republican Air Force Chief Ignacio Hidalgo de Cisneros, wrote very little about his wife in his two-volume autobiography *Cambio de Rumbo*. When one occasionally finds a reference to her, it is often inaccurate. For example, one recently published study of the VI Congress of the Spanish Communist Party says that she was in Prague, in December 1959.[5] By 1959, she had been dead for nine years. Some of those who knew her, said she was a fanatical Communist, highly placed in the party's hierarchy, and perhaps also a KGB agent[6] who had been involved in the most sinister aspects of Stalinist purges within Spain. Santiago Carrillo, who was Secretary General of the Spanish Communist Party in exile from 1960 to1982, and a communist since 1936, has little to say about Constancia. He claims that he had no idea she was ever in the party, and that the only important thing she did was to write *In Place of Splendor*. For others, she was a dilettante who had merely worked in the Ministry of Foreign Affairs during the war, and who was certainly not a heroic figure.

During the civil war, De la Mora rose to the prominent position of Director of the Republican Foreign Press Office. However, it was her 1939 *In Place of Splendor* that created her celebrity. The book was one of the first personal accounts of the war to be published. It was appealing and persuasive because her life story closely paralleled the upheavals in Spain from the turn of the century to the Republican defeat. Constancia, who was the granddaughter of the Spanish Premier Antonio Maura, had betrayed the conservative allegiances of her family and had fought to defend the Spanish Republic from Franco and Hitler. It is for this book that she is most remembered today.

In Place of Splendor recounts how she rejected money, privilege, and social conventions. She took the unusual step, for a woman of her background, of working. She also got one of Spain's first divorces. She and her second husband, Hidalgo de Cisneros, became one of the most well-known couples of the Republic. When the government was finally forced to flee Spain in 1939, De la Mora went to New York to gather support for the Republic. The book was written in the United States in English in order to reach out to an American audience. She hoped to convince Americans, through her own story, that Franco's so-called victory was illegitimate and a crime against Spanish democracy. *In Place of Splendor* opened doors for de la Mora, including those of the White House. She became a friend of Eleanor Roosevelt's and for nearly two years lobbied her on behalf of the Spanish Republican refugees.

It was the fact that a woman from her background had chosen to fight fascism that created De la Mora's legendary reputation. Her memoir casts everything that she did in a purposeful light. However, although it appears candid, it glosses over details which would have shown who she really was. She was more complicated than the person portrayed in her book. Surprisingly, only a year after her great personal and commercial success in the United States, Constancia was blacklisted and obliged to spend the remaining years of her exile in Mexico.

The key fact omitted from her book is that she and Ignacio Hidalgo de Cisneros were members of the Communist Party, and it is against this background that her decisions during and after the war must be understood. Furthermore, her part in writing *In Place of Splendor* was quite limited. While the book is based on her story, the author Ruth Mckenney in fact wrote it. While Mckenney gave the memoir its form, research has led me to believe that the majority of the historical information, especially the review of political events leading up to the war, was provided by the war correspondent Jay Allen. It was his idea to use Constancia as a figurehead in order to rally aid for Spanish Republicans.[7] Allen lived in Spain in the early 1930s and was an expert in Spanish politics; Constancia was too young and inexperienced to have the kind of knowledge reflected in her memoir. Moreover, she had not been in Spain between 1932 and 1935 because she was living in Rome where Ignacio was Military Attaché to the Spanish embassy.

In Place of Splendor is still studied and quoted both as an account from the Spanish Civil War, and as one of the best examples of twentieth Spanish women's autobiography. The book was re-published in 2005 in Spain, generating interest in the press and selling an impressive number of copies. However, because De la Mora's life has never been fully examined, more than sixty years after it first appeared her memoir continues to be taken at face value. My objective is to complete the portrayal of the woman in *In Place of Splendor*.

The year 2006 marks the hundredth anniversary of her birth, an appropriate time for more facts of her life to, finally, be made known. Scholar Shirley Mangini has called de la Mora "a ghost of history". She points out that she "in fact disappeared from political life after the war and spent her remaining years in exile in Mexico, though no one to date has published an account of her life and death there."[8]

The chapters that follow fill this gap by offering new perspectives on her life, drawing on interviews, archival materials, correspondence, and unpublished memoirs collected from Mexico, the United States, Spain, and Russia. These materials shed light on the period of her life covered in *In Place of Splendor* (1906–1939) and tell, for the first time why and how the book was written. The story of her exile (1939–1950), during which she worked on behalf of the Spanish refugees while hoping she and the Republican government would return to Spain, is reconstructed.

In the end, the significance of *In Place of Splendor* is that it left a partial but impassioned account of a political struggle that would otherwise have been completely forgotten. The enigmas imposed by the book – how it was written and why, what it fails to say, and what became of de la Mora – are what this study attempts to resolve. Though she was a more difficult person than she seems in her memoir, she nevertheless remained concerned for Spanish Republicans long after they had been forgotten by most others, even while she was in exile struggling to create a new life for herself.

Constancia de la Mora was a powerful character who was part of a movement that made great personal sacrifices to fight fascism in the 1930s. Western governments were unwilling to engage in this fight, and these early antifascists, many of whom found their calling through the Spanish Civil War, were unfairly ostracized for decades. Jay Allen's son reflects on his father's experience, which parallels Constancia's and that of so many other supporters of the Republic:

> *My father and his friends were all "premature Anti Fascists." . . . That is they warned us all of the danger of Fascism long before the West was prepared to see the danger, while the western elites were supporting Hitler. And my father and his friends all paid a high price for their integrity. They all suffered many defeats. Harsh defeats.*[9]

1
Old Spain
Portrait of a Family

Before *In Place of Splendor* had even arrived in bookshops, the book's advertising campaign in the *New York Times* set in motion the creation of a legend: that of Constancia de la Mora. The publicity headline read: "Ernest Hemingway, Vincent Sheean, Leland Stowe have hailed this amazing book: Constancia de la Mora's *In Place of Splendor*."[1] What captivated her American fans was not so much that Constancia had been an eyewitness to the events in Spain between 1936 and 1939, nor that she had worked for the Republican side, and not even that she was a woman involved in a civil war. What hooked them was that she came from a grand aristocratic background and that she had foresaken her lifestyle and family to devote herself to defending democratic ideals. The publisher's blurb describes Constancia as " a wealthy aristocrat of the old Spain, a citizen of the Spanish democracy, and . . . now an exile from Fascist Spain." Hemingway called her "a legend", and Stowe compared her story to that of the Grand Duchess Marie's, but added that "this blue-blood of Spain" wrote with "far deeper perception" and was "one of the noblest women I've ever met."

One would have expected that what made Constancia de la Mora appealing was her departure from her origins, and not her patrician lineage. Yet *In Place of Splendor* spends one hundred and twenty-three pages on Constancia's conservative upbringing and marriage in the chapters entitled "Childhood in Old Spain" and "Marriage: The Life of a Spanish Woman," and another hundred on her transition from politically ignorant, bourgeois wife to militant Republican divorcée in "Spanish Awakening". In total, her memoir devotes more space to her pre-war experiences than to the war itself. It seems that Constancia's elegant childhood and youth were emphasized for the sole purpose of crafting a dramatic story. The American reader who approached the subject of the war in Spain may have been sympathetic to democracy, but would have been wary of Communism and the violent anti-clericalism that was rumored to have swept through Republican zones. Therefore, a heroine who was from a good catholic, aristocratic family was an ideal and disarming spokesperson for the Republic.

It may never be possible to entirely separate truth from fiction in the first three chapters of *In Place of Splendor*, nor is there any need to review in detail the first thirty years of Constancia's life as recounted in her autobiography. However, it seems that her memoir casts her entire life in a purposeful light with one goal, that of swaying American public opinion in favor of ousting Franco's regime and reinstating the Republican government. Constancia's story was employed as a means to this end: Spain's history was much more appealing when packaged as the dramatic enlightenment of an aristocratic heroine. Though many of the plot ingredients are indeed based on her memories and are fair enough representations of her life in Spain, they are artfully woven together to create the tale of an almost mythical heroine. According to *In Place of Splendor*, Constancia was from a young age foresighted enough to see beyond the cruel and selfish ignorance of her family and their class; furthermore, she was selfless and renounced her privileges and comforts in the name of the Spanish people. The idea, of course, is that Constancia's personal story showed the justness of the Republican cause because she gave up so much in order to join the fight. Keeping in mind that she was from an exceptionally powerful family and had, compared to most Spanish girls, many social and cultural advantages, might it not have been precisely her background that gave her the nerve to be different? On the one hand, she had a great deal to lose, but on the other she was very spoiled and unafraid of risks; it was inconceivable to her that something she adamantly believed in could fail.

Since she had done more or less as she pleased throughout her life, she became a militant Republican because it appealed to her. This does not mean that she did not come to care sincerely and passionately for the Republican cause to which she would devote many years of her life, but her retrospective justification of her supposedly longstanding political vocation seems too good to be true. It is more plausible that Constancia's political conscience was gradually awakened when she began to live on her own in 1931, a period of her life that coincided with the beginning of the Second Republic. And there is no doubt that her political ideas and personal commitment to Republicanism developed most intensely only after she met the seductive and politically engaged pilot who became the great romance of her life: Ignacio Hidalgo de Cisneros.

The first chapter of her memoir, "Childhood in Old Spain," emphasizes the grand and somewhat cold lifestyle in which Constancia grew up. The portrait of her family also exaggerates their social pedigree. Her grandfather, Antonio Maura, was the prime minister of Spain, and it was his position alone that was the source of the family's prestige. When Constancia was twelve, in 1918, Maura was called upon by the king to "save the country" by forming a national government, and he was hence known as "the savior". His popularity soared and Constancia said that she and her younger sister Marichu "spent an intoxicating winter with our noses in the air and out necks out of joint, lording it over the rest of our school friends who were distinctly not the granddaughters of a savior."[2] Antonio Maura was a self-made man, an anomaly for the Spain of the time. His middle-class family was from Mallorca, where they ran a small tannery in Palma. He was said to be the brightest of the family's ten children, and was sent off to Madrid to study law and make something of himself. When he arrived in the capital, he only spoke Mallorquín and one of his great accomplishments was learning Spanish not merely fluently, but well enough to be considered later as one of the greatest political orators in Spain's history. Though the king bestowed an honorific title on him in recognition of his work, Maura would not accept it. However, his son Gabriel, eagerly took the title, Duke of Maura, for himself and used it in combination with his other recently acquired title of Count of Mortera (through his marriage to the Countess of Mortera, the heiress to a Cuban brewery fortune). On the ambitious snobbery of her mother's brother, Constancia commented: "My grandfather, for instance was offered a title over and over by the Crown – but he disdained a title so new, preferring to be the most famous statesman of Spain. His heirs were not so finicky. My uncle was the Duke of Maura before my grandfather was decently dead."[3]

These two recently acquired titles of Constancia's uncle were the only connection to the aristocracy in Constancia's family, which was otherwise middle class on her mother's side, and upper middle class on her father's. Therefore, the following comment is misleading: "Our family differed from the rest of the aristocracy of Spain only in my grandfather's exotic disdain for a 'dukedom'."[4] In fact, her family, though powerful and well off, differed from Spain's aristocracy because it was simply not aristocratic. Her grandmother on her father's side had invested in land around Segovia, and it was there that Constancia's father built a house during her childhood. The house and the land, known as La Mata del Pirón, were not part of an ancestral estate.

Constancia knew perfectly well that her family was not aristocratic, and it seems that her only goal in applying this gloss to her background was to impress American readers. After all, the dramatic story of an aristocratic young woman becoming a Republican is more gripping than the political awakening of a *bourgeoise*. Gabriel Maura's titles are worked into the memoir in a very calculated manner, which is only too apparent in the line: "These rolling Latin titles perhaps sound very elegant in English. At least I think they always impressed the young women who came from Ireland to bring up the embryo dukes and countesses and baronesses."[5]

The beginning of *In Place of Splendor* also tells the story of a young girl who could not fit in with her family's expectations of her. She did not feel naturally pretty or feminine, and loathed the many hours spent in her convent school devoted to embroidery and needlework. Constancia is portrayed as a tomboy, sheltered, and surprisingly snobbish. This comes across clearly from her reaction to being forced to live with other "lesser" pupils at school. At the age of twelve her parents temporarily enrolled her in convent school as a boarder. Their goal was to shield her from the facts of life. She was not supposed to know where babies came from and her mother's pregnancy (with Constancia's little brother) was becoming visible. This short period spent outside her family circle and in the company of girls of inferior social status is described in terms of the arrogance of youth:

> *They welcomed me, of course, as a diversion in their horribly dull lives. They were mostly girls from provincial towns, daughters of rich families. The boarders wanted to know why I had been sent away from home and since I couldn't answer because I didn't know, I wept and raged at these sad little girls whom I considered provincial and beneath me.*[6]

Some surviving childhood letters to her grandparents in Madrid from La Mata in Segovia, suggest a girl who seemed quite happy at her family's country house, and who, as the eldest, organized her own comings and goings and those of her younger siblings. The tone of the letters is very affectionate, and their style is conventional. In a letter written when she was fourteen, after apologizing for being lazy and not writing more often, she says that she and her siblings spent mornings studying with a governess, followed by handiwork, and that afterwards they played and went horseback riding, and then to confession. She also reports that they were all making great strides in tennis and photography, and that though her sisters were looking forward to spending the rest of the summer at St. Jean de Luz, she was enjoying La Mata so much that she would have been happy to stay.[7]

In October of the same year the children again spent several months alone. Though they had servants, Constancia seems to have been in charge. Her parents were abroad in Berlin and the children were back at La Mata, taking walks and playing more tennis and riding.[8] In November, Constancia wrote to plan their return to Madrid but a few weeks later, in December, her parents cabled her to tell them to wait at La Mata until further notice.[9]

The only other available letters to her grandparents are from four years later, when her parents allowed Constancia to study at Saint Mary's Convent in Cambridge, England for three years. In her memoir, this experience is described as "the one happy period of my life my parents gave me."[10] It is to these years in England that she ascribes her budding independence of thought. For the first time she lived without a maid, a chaperone, and had her own money and time to spend as she pleased. In an early letter from her time in England, she wrote that she was learning to work with leather and that she had sent her first piece to her mother. She added that "it is completely worthless, but I am just so proud when I think I made it all by myself."[11] Her younger sisters Marichu and Regina were also at Saint Mary's, and stayed on after Constancia had finished and moved into a flat on her own in Cambridge. She remained until December 1924, and claimed that she wanted to stay on in order to visit "her nuns," and that the Mother Superior had recommended that she extend her time in England. By then, Constancia was eighteen, and she had no real interest in returning to Madrid. She said that her parents did not seem to mind either way, so she preferred to stay in Cambridge "a thousand times" over returning.[12] She even toyed with the possibility of taking a job in a shop, but her mother quickly put a damper on that plan. Constancia finally went back to Spain under pressure from her mother, but also lured by the idea of her debut and her friend María Isabel's invitation to spend the summer at her palace near Bilbao.[13]

Despite her experience in Cambridge, and her taste of independence, once she was back in Spain, Constancia settled back into her family's way of life. A trip to Paris transformed her from ugly duckling to chic swan, and she soon became a social success. By the mid twenties she was in the society pages of the conservative newspaper *ABC*. It was reported that she played in a foursomes golf tournament at the exclusive Puerta de Hierro club,[14] and she was seen in a "red dress with black and red embroidery" at a wedding reception at the elegant Tournier.[15] At sporting events and cocktail parties, she was on the same guest list as King Alfonso and dictator Primo de Rivera. Of the latter's professed "feminism", she observed that he could "only understand two classes of women: beautiful girls to whom he could throw a compliment and have an interchange of spicy conversations, if nothing else; and staid matrons with large families and Catholic and conservative ideals."[16] In between social events, Constancia devoted her time to charity work that was arranged by her mother through the Catholic Sisters of Charity. According to *In Place of Splendor*, it was her experiences with the poor of Madrid, especially of young widows with children, that first showed Constancia how the other half, the majority of Spaniards in fact, lived. If living in England had, according to her, awakened her independence, working with the poor gave her a social conscience:

All that Winter I was swept by passionate feelings of shame and remorse – remorse for I knew not what crime. I felt bitterly ashamed of my own empty and luxurious life. But I was taught by my mother, by the Sisters of Charity, in fact by everyone I saw or talked to, to find justification in it by the few hours a week I gave to works of charity . . . I was subtly made to think by my mother that the people I met on my weekly visits were not the same kind of people we were, that the unfortunate poor were the products of something unknown, for which we were not in the least to blame. But I could not find this explanation really satisfying . . . Sometimes I made some comment, or sometimes I could not help the tears coming into my eyes at the injustice I saw. "She has a heart of gold," my parents said.[17]

Within this existing system of charitable work, in which poverty was simply taken for granted, she saw no way of solving the problems of the poor and grew restless. Thus despite her heart of gold, Constancia soon began to wonder just how she was going to spend her time. Charity work, sports by day, and parties by night were not enough to satisfy a twenty-year old girl eager to become more independent and leave her parents' home. In 1920s Spain the only way for a young woman to create an adult life, aside from entering a convent, was marriage:

In 1926 I was twenty – and not married. I began to worry. Of course I had plenty of beaux – what we called "flirts." But the kind of man who had money and social position and health, and who asks your hand in marriage from your father – this kind of man was slow in turning up in my life. And I was becoming more and more bored. Life had absolutely no meaning. I was tired of parties and tired of "good works." My mother and I quarreled more every day. In this state of mind, uneasy, restless, almost desperate, I met the young man whom I was to marry.[18]

This young man was Germán Manuel Bolín y Bidwell, a *señorito* from Málaga. Constancia must indeed have been desperate, because she became engaged to Manuel Bolín only two days after meeting him.[19] The only positive comment made about him is that he was tall. Despite her differences with her sister, eighty years after this ill-starred marriage, her sister Regina still rues the day Bolín entered Constancia's life.[20] He was a dissolute fortune hunter and seemed determined to humiliate Constancia and take advantage of her family's resources and patience. Bolín was sure that his in-laws would keep the young couple on a generous allowance ensuring the lifestyle she was used to.

From her parents' perspective, Bolín was a provincial nobody. They were horrified at her engagement, yet their protests only made her decision to marry him firmer. It is possible that if sustained their pressure would have prevailed, but on December 13, 1925 Antonio Maura died and the family's attention was absorbed by their role in what became a nation-wide event. There was a three-day wake, which everyone, including the King and Queen, attended to publicly give their condolences to the family of Spain's most famous statesman. Huge crowds followed the funeral procession and the family's "sorrow seemed forgotten in the deluge of artificial pomp."[21]

Bolín took advantage of the family's grief to ingratiate himself with the de la Mora – Maura clan. He made himself indispensable to Constancia's mother, and she no longer made any protests about the upcoming wedding. The society pages of *ABC* reflect the conventional stages of the couple's quick steps towards the altar. On February 9, 1926 the engagement of "the charming Constancia de la Mora y Maura" granddaughter of the "unforgettable statesman" was noted in the society page.[22] On April 27 *ABC* announced the upcoming wedding of the "most beautiful *señorita* Constancia de la Mora" and that the ceremony would take place in the strictest privacy due to the recent death in the "illustrious Maura family". 23 On May 17, 1926 Constancia and Bolín were married in the fashionable Los Jerónimos church in Madrid.

The marriage was a disaster from the beginning. Constancia and Bolín spent their wedding night at La Mata, and there she realized that she had made a grave mistake: "In the great silence and quietness of La Mata my marriage proved to be very different from what I had expected. I knew before morning that I did not, and never would, love my husband."[24] We cannot imagine what transpired, but the next morning they left as planned for their honeymoon which was to be a grand European tour. Constancia was so upset and lonely throughout their trip that she bought an expensive bulldog to keep her company.[25]

On their return to Spain, the couple settled in Bolín's native Málaga where Constancia quickly discovered that the men in the Bolín family were all in the same business: that of marrying rich women.[26] Nevertheless, nine months after their marriage on February 26, 1927 Constancia gave birth, in Málaga, to her daughter Constancia María Lourdes Bolín de la Mora, or "Luli" as she would be known.

Soon after Luli's birth, the couple decided to move back to Madrid, but things did not improve in the capital. Though his powerful father-in-law made sure that Bolín was given a succession of well-paid jobs, Bolín had no interest in them. According to *In Place of Splendor*, Constancia was too ashamed to live off the income her parents gave her and decided it would be better to find a job herself. It was at this point that she met a woman who would have a great influence on her outlook: Zenobia Camprubí.

Zenobia's background and lifestyle must have seemed quite exotic in Madrid. She was married to the poet Juan Ramón Jiménez and her mother had been half American, making Zenobia both bicultural and bilingual. She was infinitely more modern than any of the young women Constancia knew and was happy to help Constancia find work. Enterprising and pragmatic, Zenobia ran a shop in Madrid called Arte Popular where she sold artesanal objects collected from around Spain. She also bought, redecorated, and furnished flats which she then rented to visiting Americans. When the two women met, Zenobia was about to go on a trip and she immediately hired Constancia to look after her furnished apartments. Constancia was delighted, though the one and a half pesetas (roughly ten cents) she was paid an hour could hardly have made a dent in her usual expenses.[27] Zenobia also introduced Constancia to two Americans who wanted to learn Spanish and she began giving private lessons as well.

Soon afterwards, Zenobia's partner in Arte Popular left and Constancia took over. Her new identity, certainly not radical but nevertheless exceptional for the Madrid of her time, gave her a thrill:

> A de la Mora, the granddaughter of Maura, a clerk in a shop! Even a fine shop, owned by two society women! The hours were long and the pay very little, but I found having a real job for the first time in my life entirely absorbing. My parents found it horrifying. The scandal was terrific.[28]

Constancia stuck by her guns and defended her new independent, quasi-bohemian lifestyle. Her financial situation, however, was by no means penurious. Though by 1929 she had taken a smaller apartment and dismissed Luli's expensive trained nurse, she managed to keep two servants in addition to a Swiss nursemaid for her daughter.[29] Bolín was starting yet another job, this time at the Chrysler Motor Car Company. Again, he had been hired only because of Constancia's family, and yet again he was fired within months.

The Awakening

By the end of the summer of 1930, which she spent with her in-laws in St. Jean de Luz, Constancia decided that the marriage had no future. Her old friend María Isabel made a surprise visit and urged Constancia to drive back to Spain with her and stay, as she had for years, at her palace at Arriluce near Bilbao:

> I sat quietly in the car driving back to Spain. And all at once I knew I was finished forever with the absurd and painful life I had been leading. All my childish ideas of staying with Bolín no matter how miserable and unhappy he

*made me, evaporated. I was a woman, a woman of energy and with, I had begun
to think, at least enough brains to make her own living. I had no thought of
divorce and remarriage for I was a Catholic and besides, divorce was illegal in
Spain. I only wanted to live my own life with my child, free of the man who had
made me so unhappy for the last three years.*[30]

Pressured by her in-laws to give the marriage one more chance,
Constancia spent part of the fall and Christmas of 1930 with the Bolíns in
Málaga. In the meantime, her husband had gone to Paris to try and make
a living there. Instead, he spent the money he had taken with him and wired
his parents to bail him out, blaming Constancia for his failure. These experiences reinforced Constancia's idea that she had to start a new life, and by
January 1931 she was back in Madrid with Luli and got a legal separation
from Bolín.

*Most women of Spain in similar circumstances in those days would have been
forced to swallow the bitter pill. What else could they do? I thought it over carefully, with a certain sensation of fear. And then I knew my mind was made up.
I did not love my husband; indeed I regarded him with contempt. Even more, I
had discovered that work gave me much more satisfaction than idle amusement.
I valued my independence, I decided, more than anything else except my child. I
was not afraid of the future. I knew that I was violating every canon of the society
I had been brought up in – Spanish women of my class accepted sorrow submis-
sively, as the will of God. To break free of the family was a profoundly terrible
act. But I was ready, at long last, to burn my bridges . . . So finally I packed up
my clothes, took my Luli, and departed for Madrid – and freedom. I was twenty-
five years old, and ready to begin my life once again. As my train came into the
station at Madrid, I was filled with a sensation of strength and happiness.*[31]

Constancia arrived in Madrid in March, 1931 and went back to work at
Arte Popular with Zenobia. Her separation from Bolín quickly became old
news as the social world was now more interested in the political chaos that
had been fermenting for months and was now taking over Spain.

The Primo de Rivera dictatorship, in power alongside King Alfonso
since 1923, had always been unpopular and had steadily gained critics:

*The whole country groaned under a vicious and oppressive government. During
the dictatorship, real wages fell and hours rose in the mines and factories – Primo
de Rivera's gift in kind to the industrialists and foreign bankers. During the
dictatorship, the peasants saw their wretchedness increase even though that hardly
seemed possible, so wretched had they been before . . . Newspapers were mercilessly
censored. Men went to jail for a whispered word against the King or Dictator.
Hundreds were driven into exile.*[32]

There were several failed uprisings against the dictatorship and, unexpectedly, Primo de Rivera was finally brought down by the military. During an internal struggle amongst prominent generals, it became clear to the King that Primo de Rivera had hardly any support in the Army and Alfonso dismissed him, replacing him with General Berenguer from Morocco. In the ensuing chaos, the various Republican parties, which had previously been divided, united and proposed a democratic Republic which they hoped would win the elections that were expected to be called by the King. In August, the Republic selected a political committee that included many future leaders: Alcalá Zamora, Azaña, Casares Quiroga, and Prieto. An alternate committee included Constancia's uncle, Miguel Maura. Until Constancia herself became politicized, Miguel was the only member of her family with Republican sympathies.[33] But the King stalled for time and many Republicans suspected that General Berenguer was there to stay. As a reaction against the politically stagnant situation, a group of Republicans planned a revolt against the monarchy. One of the leaders of the revolt was Ignacio, who Constancia did not yet know, but who would soon become her second husband. The December 1930 revolt is described with a certain pride in her memoir:

> On December 15, the republicans tried to revolt against the Monarchy. The plans had been made very carefully. The Air Force, which unlike most of the Army was officered by many Republicans, was to back up the trade unions. The planes were to rise over Madrid as the trade unions declared a general strike. As the morning of December 15 broke, the Air Force revolted according to plan. The Republicans in the force gave the Monarchists a choice: either they joined the revolt or submitted to being locked up. Ignacio Hidalgo de Cisneros, a young man born to the purple of Spain who had long since left the comfortable confines of his family's opinions, was one of the leaders of the Air Force uprising.

However, the general strike that was supposed to have cleared the Madrid streets had not materialized. The pilots, who had intended to bomb the Palacio de Oriente, seeing streets filled with civilians, turned around and flew out of Spain into exile.

By the time Constancia returned to Madrid in March 1931, the elected Republican political committees had been betrayed and undone by police spies. Their members, including her uncle Miguel, had been arrested and were awaiting trial. The Republicans attracted many sympathizers, but so did the Monarchy, and Spain had become radically divided. According to *In Place of Splendor*, Constancia had spontaneously sided with the Republic without really realizing it. She simply supported what she generally understood the new government represented: democracy, land reform, freedom, an end to ingrown corruption, and so forth. Her uncle Miguel was to become one of her first political heroes. The trial of her mother's younger brother was set for March 21. Constancia's family already began to show the polarized positions taken by so many Spaniards in the 1930s. Ironically, as Miguel awaited trial in prison for his anti-monarchical activities, his elder brother Gabriel, the Duke of Maura, had been appointed Minister of Labor by King Alfonso. Constancia was determined to go to Miguel's trial, she "wanted to find out why men were ready to give up everything, even their liberty and lives if need be, for the Republic."[34] When she learned that the passes for the trial had already been given out, she had an idea. In a gesture indicative of her resourcefulness and privileged lifestyle, she convinced her cousin, the Duke of Maura's daughter, that they should both go to the trial in the Duke's official car. The police promptly cleared the way for the official car, but when the two young ladies emerged, the press went wild. Unruffled by the attention, Constancia displayed a delighted and triumphant smile in the photographs printed in the evening papers. At the end of the trial the Republicans, including Miguel, were released. Constancia was "one of the hysterically shouting crowd that moved out of the court room to the street with the triumphant defendants."[35]

Through Zenobia, Constancia inadvertently made another important connection to someone completely unrelated to her family's world who would become an important part of her future: Jay Allen. While Constancia made her final attempt to live in Málaga with the Bolíns she arranged, through Zenobia, to sublet her own flat in Madrid to the American correspondent Jay Allen and his family. Now that she had definitively given up on her husband, Constancia was faced with the prospect of telling Allen that she needed the flat back immediately for herself and her daughter. Not only was he gracious and understanding, but Jay would soon become one of the most influential people in Constancia's life.

Jay Allen knew much more about the political situation in Spain than most Spaniards. He had been a foreign correspondent for the *Chicago Daily Tribune* in Europe from 1926 to 1934 when he was fired for "alleged insubordination".[36] From 1934 to 1936 he lived in Madrid, doing historical research on Godoy as well as participating, somewhat inadvertently, in revolutionary activities. Allen, who was well connected in the political and press world in Spain and the United States, was one of the staunchest and most effective international defenders the Spanish Republic would have.

Constancia was jubilant when just weeks after her return to Madrid elections were held, the first free elections in decades, and the Republic was victorious on April 14, 1931, forcing the King into exile. *In Place of Splendor* portrays Constancia and Zenobia as spending their days at Arte Popular engrossed in political developments. The society women who used to come to the shop just to see the granddaughter of the great statesman as shop clerk stopped coming once the Republic had won:

> *One of the first reactions of the aristocracy of Madrid to the new republic was to withhold money from circulation – a very effective way of sabotaging the demo-cratic government. And as time went on and they had to buy food and such necessities, they decided that at least they could go without glass, pottery and embroideries, rather than buy them in a shop run by Republicans!* [37]

Constancia remembers that she was much too excited by the reforms the government was putting in place, such as new free schools and the separa-tion of Church and state, to worry about the decline in business. In April she says she was only concerned with building the new Spain. However she may have been slower in distancing herself from the aristocracy and the right wing than she admits. For as late as June she was still seeing her aris-tocratic friend María Rúspoli Caro, Countess of Buelno and daughter of the Duke and Duchess of Sueca, on a regular basis. Not only was María Rúspoli a socialite, but in June 1931 her husband, Mariano del Prado O'Neill, Count of Buelno, became a candidate for the extreme right-wing Catholic party Acción Nacional in the constituent elections of Jaén. This party, founded by Gil Robles and later known as Acción Popular, was the central component of CEDA (Confederación Española de Derechas Autónomas).

In reality Constancia's Republican transformation was not as clear cut as she claimed. María Rúspoli's letters show that while her husband was cam-paigning in Jaén, María wrote to him frequently to report on her activities in Madrid. As late as mid June she seems to have spent almost every day with Constancia, who she and everyone else called "Connie". On June 18, for example, she and Connie had lunch at a German restaurant in the Ventas neighborhood of Madrid, then went back to Connie's, in their chauffeured car, to rest in preparation for the arrival of a large group of friends coming to play bridge and have tea. Two days later they were all having lunch again at the house of another friend, Carmen Alonso, and spent another afternoon playing bridge. María was relieved to report to her husband that she had luckily been at the easy table with an inexperienced Englishman and a Turk. Connie, on the other hand, was with the serious players.[38]

In June it seems that Constancia's attitudes were still in keeping with those of her upbringing. In fact, despite what she says in *In Place of Splendor*, at twenty-five she was far behind the vanguard of the burgeoning women's movement of Spain. While Constancia played cards with CEDA supporters, there were outstanding and eloquent Spanish women playing central roles in the democratization of Spain's political and social systems. Along with extremely well known figures such as the communist Dolores Ibárruri or the anarchosyndicalist Federica Montseny, Victoria Kent (Radical Socialist Party), Margarita Nelken (Socialist Party), and Clara Campoamor (Radical Party) were members of parliament. Many other outspoken women, such as the writer María Lejárraga García, ran for office and wrote about the issues facing Spanish women in 1931. There were important political organizations for women, lobbying for women's right to vote and to divorce. These interests were reflected in the Republic's agenda for reforms.[39]

Constancia would eventually become a radical, but the early days of the Second Republic did not galvanize her into action. She was brought into politics through Ignacio. In June 1931 their relationship was just beginning, and as it intensified, so did her political commitment to the left. Ignacio was, by all accounts, an extraordinarily charming man. Her sister, Regina warned Constancia before introducing her to Ignacio: "You will fall in love with him, Constancia . . . Everyone does. His men worship him and so do all the women he has ever met."[40] By the time Constancia met him, he was enmeshed in Republican political life and his idealism and passion transformed her life.

Ignacio

Ignacio Hidalgo de Cisneros y López de Montenegro was born in Vitoria in 1894. His family was aristocratic and *carlista*. The Carlists were an ultra-conservative faction that had wanted Fernando VII's brother Don Carlos to inherit the throne, rather than his daughter Isabel. In fact, Ignacio's father had known Don Carlos well and kept up a friendly correspondence with him. Ignacio came from a long line of military officers and sailors, one of whom had been the last Viceroy of Spain in Argentina, Baltasar Hidalgo de Cisneros. Though Ignacio's childhood passion for planes and flying would lead him to follow the family military tradition and become an air force officer, in every other respect he rebelled against his family's long established values.

In 1931, Ignacio was a bachelor and stationed at the Cuatro Vientos airbase in Madrid. It was from here that the failed revolutionary attempt to establish the Republic had been made in December 1930. At the time that this revolt was being planned, Ignacio was still a gentleman revolutionary. He participated, as he recalled in his memoir, not from any militant feelings, but out of good sportsmanship. Essentially, he felt that the other pilots counted on him:

I started to worry that the other pilots, who assumed I was committed to their ideals, would think that when the moment of truth came I was a coward ready to abandon them to face the danger alone. I saw that because of some misunderstanding, my friends were counting on me and that if I did not come through I would be judged harshly. These thoughts were stronger than any logical reasoning. The latter would have led me to conclude that it was absurd to get involved in such a risky enterprise, especially one that I did not particularly support. In a word, I decided to join them and go to Madrid.[41]

After the failure of the revolt, the pilots immediately changed course and flew in opposite directions towards France or Portugal hoping to cross the border as quickly as possible, before being brought to justice for this botched coup.

Ignacio spent several months in exile in Paris, along with other pilots and important Socialist leaders such as Indalecio Prieto, with whom he became very close. It was during this period that he became politically engaged. When the Republic won the elections in April, the exiles returned to Spain by train, unsure if they would be imprisoned once they crossed the border. Ignacio certainly did not anticipate the welcome they were given:

We finally got to the border, where thousands and thousands of people, with countless bands playing music and hundreds of red and republican flags, welcomed us enthusiastically. I saw the republican flag for the first time, I hadn't even known there was a republican flag, and for the first time I heard people yell "Long live the heroes of Cuatro Vientos!" I got goose bumps when I heard those cries, and I was embarrassed to be called a hero. It would never have occurred to me that the uprising I had participated in unexpectedly, and under pressure would be considered a heroic act. In fact I had been worried by the poor execution, and ultimate failure, of our attempt.[42]

In Madrid, Ignacio's life began to change. When he was not near the air base in Alcalá de Henares, he spent most of his time with Prieto, who had been made Minister of Finance for the Republic. At his house Ignacio first met Juan Negrín, then a well-known professor of physiology, and the Socialist minister Fernando de los Ríos. Ignacio also went to gatherings at the Lion d'Or Café on the Calle Alcalá where he met the famous bullfighter Ignacio Sánchez Mejías, the poet and publisher Manuel Altoalaguirre, and Federico García Lorca. He regularly saw a group of Socialist intellectuals including Negrín, and others who were all to become important Republican political figures: Julio Alvarez del Vayo, the future Minister of Foreign Affairs; Luis Araquistaín, the future ambassador to France; and Marcelino Pascua, the future ambassador to the Soviet Union. It was during this period that Ignacio began his enduring friendship with Rafael Alberti and his wife, María Teresa León, who had become communist party members in 1931. Through them he met another poet and intellectual who would also become a lifelong friend: Pablo Neruda. Though Ignacio had taken part in the Cuatro Vientos uprising without clear political ideas, the fallout of that experience had converted him. By the summer of 1931, he was a committed Republican, and his faith would never waver:

> At the Albertis' house we used to talk about literature, art, and other intellectual matters. But the priority was given to political issues and what was happening in Spain was considered to be of the greatest importance. Their approach to political problems seemed to me to be both rational and revolutionary. Bourgeois or aristocratic notions had been completely eradicated from their language. They seemed even closer to the people of Spain than the leaders of the workers associations I had met. To my surprise, I felt much closer to them than I did to my friends who were professional politicians.[43]

Thus, when Constancia and Ignacio first met at the end of April, he was already a revolutionary while she was still a society bridge player. Her political transformation would come very quickly after they fell in love.

"The Bolsheviks"

Ignacio was impressed by Constancia's independent spirit. For him it was quite unusual that she had chosen to work and live in her own flat, rather than stay cloistered in the luxury of her parents' house. Though Constancia was not self-sufficient by any standards, she seemed exceptionally independent and modern to Ignacio. He had never met a woman from their background who had left her husband, taken a job and had her own flat, who was sympathetic to the Republic, and who even spoke English and French.

Ignacio and Constancia became inseparable, and their friendship with Zenobia and Juan Ramón Jiménez flourished. In the meantime, their relationships with their families began to deteriorate. On August 10, 1932 one of the military's most famous generals, José Sanjurjo attempted a coup against the Republic in Sevilla. Though the coup was a fiasco, its aftermath had a polarizing effect on Spaniards:

> In Seville, both communists and anarchists declared a general strike, and several upper-class clubs were burned. Sanjurjo was persuaded to flee to Portugal. Apprehended near the border at Ayamonte, he was brought back to be tried with

150 others, mostly officers and including two scions of the house of Bourbon. The first rising against the republic thus ended in the discomfiture of its opponents.[44]

Tensions increased when the properties of the conspirators of the highest ranking Spanish nobility, the grandees, were seized. It was in the midst of this escalating political tension that Constancia and Ignacio announced to their families and lifelong friends that they were going to be married after she divorced Bolín. She was counting on the Republic's divorce law to make that possible. The family reaction to the news was one of horror, and from Ignacio's point of view, utterly hypocritical. It would have been acceptable to have a discreet affair, people said, as long as the couple kept up the appearance that they were only "friends". The charade did not even need to be convincing, it was simply the tribute that had to be paid to the conservative Catholic society they inhabited.

Ironically, Ignacio and Constancia's more honest plan of divorce to be followed by a civil marriage was perceived as social and moral treachery, a prejudice that immediately put an even greater distance between Ignacio and his family:

As soon as anyone even hinted that there was anything questionable about my behavior, or ideas, I sent them to hell. I was never the intransigent type, but the contempt their words and actions showed for anything to do with the Republic was so offensive that I could not take it. This attitude, now displayed so impudently, was not new. They had always felt the same way about the Spanish people. It was an attitude they were born with, but had not felt the need to show with such great insolence until the people had brought about the Republic and were finally able to hold their heads up.[45]

During the fall of 1932 and early 1933, as Constancia became more important in his life, Ignacio engaged in an uncharacteristic letter writing campaign. First, he contacted many of his powerful friends in Republican political circles hoping their pressure would help expedite Constancia's divorce. When a date was finally set, Ignacio notified Indalecio Prieto, then Minister of Public Works. Prieto immediately alerted the Minister of Justice, Alvaro de Albornoz, who Ignacio had also contacted.[46] Constancia wanted the divorce as quickly as possible, and a guarantee that she would have full custody of Luli. In the complaint presented by her lawyer, Constancia petitioned for divorce on the grounds outlined by the "fourth cause" in the new Spanish laws: unjustified abandonment of his family. Since September 1930, when the couple had separated, Luli had been living with her mother, and her father had contributed no financial support towards Luli's living expenses or education. Furthermore, her petition stated that even before the separation Constancia had been forced to seek employment because her husband did not work, and moreover spent all her money, this being the cause of the separation. Constancia was determined not to let Bolín have custody of Luli, which she was sure he wanted only to secure an allowance for himself.[47] Today, the arguments Constancia presented are standard, but it is important to keep in mind that her situation was unprecedented in Spain. After many delays, Constancia was finally granted a divorce, one of the first of the Second Spanish Republic, and custody of Luli.

Only days after the divorce Ignacio began to plan their wedding. The civil ceremony was held in Alcalá de Henares on January 16, 1933 and the witnesses included a small, but elite representation of the Republic's foremost political and intellectual figures: Prieto, Marcelino Domingo and Juan Ramón Jiménez.[48] Nobody from Constancia's family was present.

As newlyweds, the couple spent their honeymoon hiking and touring rural Spain, and going to concerts. Back in Madrid both Ignacio and Constancia were deeply impressed by two Russian films they saw. While Ignacio describes how influential the first exposure to Soviet ideas was on them, Constancia omits this episode from her memoir. It might not have been appealing to the potentially anti-communist audience her story was intended for:

> For the first time I saw a Soviet film. It made a profound impression on me. I think it was called The Path of Life . . . it was about the civil war in Russia. We left the film deeply moved by the realism with which the terrible tragedy was depicted. The second Russian film we saw was Battleship Potemkin, which affected us even more . . . I remember how much we discussed these films amongst our friends. These conversations made me think seriously for the first time that there was a country in which a revolution had completely changed the order of things. It is incredible that an event as important as the Russian Revolution was barely spoken of in Spain . . . Despite my lack of knowledge about Russia, my ignorance of what those enigmatic Bolsheviks thought, wanted, or did, people were starting to call me "the Bolshevik". My sister's friends used to ask her "What is your brother the Bolshevik doing?" The same thing started to happen to Connie. Several people asked her if it was true that we were Bolsheviks . . . I found it amusing that anyone could think that I could have any connection to those distant revolutionaries.[49]

In the wake of the scandal of divorce and a civil wedding, not to mention their growing reputation as revolutionaries, both Constancia and Ignacio thought it would be a good idea for them and Luli to leave Madrid for a while. When Ignacio heard that the post of Military Attaché in Mexico had become available, he wrote to Marcelino Domingo and requested that the position be assigned to him:

> I would like to make a request that, if fulfilled, would resolve my current situation. There is an opening for the position of Military Attaché at the Spanish embassy in Mexico, and I would like to take this post. But since we returned from Paris, I have had no contact with politicians aside from you and Don Indalecio ... Since I have finally mustered up the courage to request something for myself, it would be very disappointing to be turned down. I thus appeal to you, who know me well. If you think I could do the job, I hope you will put my name forward, as I am sure that coming from you the suggestion will be approved.[50]

Domingo immediately contacted Prime Minister Manuel Azaña to intercede on Ignacio's behalf.[51] Ignacio seemed confident that with Domingo's help he would be able to secure the post, but the ministry had other plans for him. After a few weeks of waiting for a response, Ignacio was called to Prieto's office and informed that he had been assigned a diplomatic post, but not the one he had requested. To his surprise and dismay, he had been appointed air attaché to Rome and Berlin.

Fascism

The first stop on this assignment was Rome. Ignacio and Constancia and set off together, and Luli joined them as soon as they had found a flat. In his typically modest and bemused tone, Ignacio reveals that:

> I had never been to Italy, nor did I know the first thing about Fascism ... I had no idea what an embassy was either. However, what was most extraordinary then and still strikes me today, is that I left Spain for Rome without knowing just what I had been hired to do in Italy. Nobody had bothered to fill me in regarding this small "technicality".[52]

The ambassador in Rome was Gabriel Alomar, a professor and friend of Azaña's. According to Ignacio, Alomar suffered from an acute inferiority complex, not a desirable quality for Spain's new Republican ambassador to Fascist Italy. Ignacio's first impressions of the Spanish embassy in Rome are perceptive and show the repercussions Spain's political tensions were having on its diplomatic staff, who were

> offended at having to represent a government that had had the nerve to abolish the king and "those poor little infantitas"; and that had appointed common, vulgar nobodies to positions that had always been held by the right kind of people.

> *These diplomats were like the servants of a grand aristocratic house, who had suddenly been brought down to serve a mere bourgeois. They felt demeaned, despite the fact that their new bosses treated them with more respect and consideration than the aristocrats.*[53]

The pro-monarchist tendencies amongst the diplomats were clearly evident at a reception Ignacio and Constancia attended at the Spanish embassy to the Vatican. The ambassador's[54] wife was blind, and thus failed to notice when midway through a reception the priest with whom she had been chatting got up to leave. He was replaced by Constancia, who had taken his chair. Constancia was shocked when this lady turned towards her, thinking she was still addressing the priest, to talk about Alfonso XIII's daughters who were living in Rome: " I think it would be wonderful to go visit those poor little *infantitas*, and my only regret is that I cannot go see them myself."[55] It was thus made clear to Ignacio and Constancia what kind of people were representing the Republic in Italy.

In Rome, the couple befriended a young German woman who invited them to visit her family's estate near Munich. Constancia and Ignacio had a frightening experience during their first evening in Germany, which they spent in Friedrichschafen. They were having dinner in the hotel restaurant when a dozen Nazi military officers arrived "with their brown uniforms, high boots, and red arm bands with swastikas. These were the first followers of Hitler I had laid eyes on."[56] The men stared at the couple threateningly as they talked loudly about them. Ignacio, who understood no German, stared back. The presiding officer at the table finally got up and went towards the reception desk of the hotel, apparently to find out who Constancia and Ignacio were and if they were Jews. On his return, neither he nor the others paid any more attention to them, but the experience scared Ignacio, who was normally unruffled in the most dangerous situations:

> *This scene, which may seem anticlimactic, was extremely tense, and I think it could have ended very badly for us. During that time in Germany, cowardly aggressions against Jews had intensified. Connie's appearance, and the shape of my nose must have led them to think we were Jewish. If the head officer hadn't been surprised by my attitude and gone to ask who we were, I think things would have turned out very differently.*[57]

Without referring to this experience, Constancia does point out how happy they were to leave Germany, "which seemed more oppressive every moment."[58]

In the fall of 1934, while they were in Italy, the political tensions in Spain were escalating. A faction of monarchists met with Alfonso in Rome hoping to organize a Mussolini supported coup.[59] In the meantime, reactionaries in Spain were paradoxically "moving briskly ahead with their plans to put the clock of the nation back a hundred years." The Republican government had not yet been able to put most of its land reforms into effect, and in Constancia's words the "CEDA, the organization of Spanish right parties, was determined to wipe out even the theory of land for the peasants, wages and unions for the workers."[60] Constancia's views had changed radically and quickly. Only three years earlier she had spent her days playing bridge and organizing lunches and dinners with her close friend María Rúspoli Caro, the wife of a CEDA candidate.

Ignacio was apparently the only genuine Republican employed by the Spanish embassy in Rome, and he was reluctant to work in his office because he was sure that it was full of Fascist spies.[61] In response to the CEDA takeover of key cabinet posts under Prime Minister Alejandro Lerroux, a former leftist who had turned conservative and who for many was a traitor to the Republic, general strikes were called in Madrid, Barcelona and Asturias. Catalonia then declared itself an independent Republic. The strikes in Barcelona and Madrid only lasted a few days. In Asturias, however, the people united firmly against CEDA. In response to their resistance, the right unleashed a systematic and brutal repression of the strikers, who were attacked by the air force, navy, and army. This disproportionate military reaction to the Asturian strike was a clear harbinger of the nationalist reprisals that were to come during and after the Civil War:

> *A harsh and extensive repression ensued throughout Asturias in which General Franco, as* de facto *head of the war ministry, deployed both Moroccan troops and the Foreign Legion. Constitutional guarantees were suspended across Spain. The impact on the left was catastrophic. Thirty thousand of them were imprisoned and many of them tortured.*[62]

Unable to bear being trapped in Rome with the Fascists while the Republic was being threatened, Ignacio decided to fly back to Spain. Constancia, alone with Luli, was anxious that he return quickly and safely. Ignacio's friends, María Teresa León and Rafael Alberti, turned up to keep Constancia company on their way back to Spain from a writers' conference in Moscow. This was the first time she had met the Albertis and she liked them immediately. They stayed with her because they had no money left to return home, and in any case felt safer abroad. The Albertis had heard that their house in Madrid had been searched and the police were awaiting the chance to arrest them. Rafael Alberti had been a communist since 1931, and there is no doubt that the attractive intellectual couple, on their way back from the Soviet Union and full of praise for what they had seen there, made a great impression on Constancia, especially in the context of the recent events in Spain and her experiences in Italy and Germany. [63]

In Spain, both Ignacio and Jay Allen, Constancia's American friend and former tenant, were involved in ensuring the physical safety of Republican leaders in the wake of the strikes. Allen, who was in Madrid, later remembered how:

> *During the Republican-Socialist-Catalan rising 1934 (called Asturias rebellion because it was only effective there – and only for a time) {I worked} for The Chicago Daily News. Facts: morning after rebellion began. It was already going badly in Madrid. Negrín, {Alvarez del}Vayo, Araquistain showed up at my flat . . . Unable to get thru to Barcelona they wanted me to get a message to Azaña there . . . Over radio I heard that my artist friend Luis Quintanilla had been arrested, then that he had escaped, then that he hadn't been arrested or anything but was being sought [64] . . . I knew that the police, if really looking for him, would eventually come to me. I thought the others should leave and it was agreed that they would – next morning.* [65]

Quintanilla, still on the run, showed up at Allen's apartment. Allen thus ended up harboring four major revolutionary figures: Alvarez del Vayo, Araquistain, Negrín, and Quintanilla. He says that "they had simply shown up uninvited,"[66] but the fact that they turned to him when under threat shows how much they trusted him. "Trigger happy" *guardias civiles* arrived at Allen's building the next day, and in their excitement to find him, shot his neighbor, who had no political involvement at all. The fugitive Republicans had left by the time his apartment was raided. Nevertheless Allen was arrested and held until the United States ambassador Claude Bowers came to his rescue.

Ignacio was also in the thick of the aftermath of the Asturias uprising. His mission was to move Prieto, who the *guardias civiles* were desperate to arrest, safely out of Spain. Constancia tells how Ignacio borrowed a car with French number plates and hid Prieto in the boot in order to drive him across the border undetected:

> *The plan worked splendidly at first. The Civil Guards saluted as they saw an air force major passing. Prieto, one of the best-known figures in Spain, was out of sight. But half way to the border, Prieto exploded. The cramped quarters were killing him. He straightened up and rode on the back seat. Next, he got hungry, and insisted on stopping at the house of a friend whom he described as absolutely reliable, for dinner . . . even Ignacio got nervous before he spotted the French border – with Prieto in plain sight for all Spain to see, riding along in the back seat of his car.* [67]

Prieto and Ignacio were met by another driver who took him safely across the border after dark. The story of Prieto's escape proves how reliable Ignacio was politically, and gives us clues about Constancia's hostile feeling for Prieto. She calls him a "fat, bearded gentleman" and describes him in childish and ridiculous terms. Since Prieto had her fired from the press office during the war, Constancia had come to despise him, and the references to Prieto throughout *In Place of Splendor* reflect this retroactive antipathy.

The events of October 1934 further polarized many Spaniards, and Ignacio and Constancia, although living in Rome, were very worried. The Italian press covered up the atrocities in Asturias, but the couple was in contact with many exiles who kept them informed. Ignacio had also returned to Rome with first-hand news:

> *Gil Robles and CEDA had turned Spain into a bloody prison . . . The new Chief of Staff, general Francisco Franco, brought Moorish troops ino the Spanish mainland on their first mission of war in Spanish history . . . Few stories in history are so terrible as the dreadful happenings in the Asturias after the Moors had conquered . . . children and women were arrested and tortured with fire and steel whips until they told where their fathers and husbands were hiding. Thirty thousand were put in prison. Thousands of others hid in the hills.* [68]

The discrepancy between what was actually happening in Spain and what the Italian press was reporting made Constancia aware, perhaps for the first time, of the powerful political effect the press could have abroad. Seeing the truth repressed and distorted in the newspapers gave her a taste of the right-wing propaganda she would struggle against during the civil war.

Although eager to return to Spain, Ignacio waited patiently to be officially recalled. Resigning would mean abandoning the army, which he did not want to do. His political sympathies made him an outcast at the embassy. When the staff put together a list requesting donations for the widows and children of the Civil Guards who had died in Asturias, Ignacio was incensed and put out his own request, on Embassy letterhead, asking for contributions for the families of the miners killed during the repression. He started the list with his name and gave a month's salary.

In early 1935, Ignacio was asked to make his first official appearance in Berlin. Though he had originally been posted to Rome and Berlin, all of his work had been Italy and his only exposure to Germany had been the holiday he and Constancia had taken a year before. This new assignment seemed very much like a diplomatic comedy of errors. When they arrived, he and Constancia were given a surprisingly enthusiastic reception. Somehow, the Germans had not been informed that Ignacio was a loyal Republican. Instead the Nazis were convinced that he was an envoy of

General Franco or CEDA leader Gil Robles. Not realizing their mistake, they spoke freely to Ignacio about their plans. Inadvertently, he found himself in the position of a privileged spy. After his initial bewilderment, the Nazi's revelations began to sink in. The Germans wanted aerodromes in Morocco and the Spanish Sahara, permission to build bases for their Zeppelins in Spain and the Canary Islands, and to create a vast radio network throughout the country.[69] In exchange, they would provide all the necessary materials and aircraft to completely modernize the Spanish air force.[70] It became apparent to Ignacio that the Nazis and Spanish politicians on the right had been in dialogue for some time, and were conspiring against the Republic. What upset him most was the fact that the Germans were convinced that Spanish generals, including Franco, could easily and quickly organize their own air force equipped by Germany.[71] It was clear that many officers were ready to betray their government.

After Berlin, they met with Prieto in Paris and Ignacio reported what he had learned about Nazi plans in Spain. As Constancia recalls, Prieto was not impressed:

> *It was not Ignacio's fault that his country was not prepared when the time came to resist a Nazi invasion. "Don't get so excited," Prieto said . . . Ignacio bit his lips – but he said nothing.*[72]

The couple spent a restless spring and early summer in Rome until Ignacio was summoned back to Spain. In September 1935 Ignacio and Constancia at last moved back to Madrid.

Prelude to War

During the autumn, the couple went through the motions of going back to the life they had left behind in the early days of the Republic, but it was impossible to ignore the changes in the political situation. Constancia went back to work with Zenobia at Arte Popular, but most people were more concerned with the ever deepening political tensions than with home decoration.

Everything seemed to have changed in their absence. Ignacio met a former friend and ally from the Cuatro Vientos revolt, the aviator Ramón Franco, whose behaviour indicated to him the direction political power was taking. In 1926, Ramón had become a hero by flying across the Atlantic from Spain to Argentina. Unlike his brother, the future dictator Francisco, he had been a Republican.

While in Italy, Ignacio had heard rumors that Ramón had become close to Lerroux and that he had cut himself off from the left, but he refused to believe them. When he finally saw Ramón, by chance, he was shocked to realize that the rumors were true:

> *He spoke to me with a cynicism that left me stunned. I felt that the man speaking to me was a true fascist. I have never forgotten his last words: He said, "Listen, Ignacio, if the choice is between being forced to drink castor oil, or making someone else swallow it, I prefer the latter."*[73]

Ramón's cynical grasp on the situation reflected the point of view of many Spaniards, and was indeed prescient. Castor oil purges would be a staple method of his brother's torture program for decades. This would be the last time Ignacio saw Ramón Franco.

In November, Prieto was smuggled back into Spain across the French border. Ignacio and Constancia were going to hide him in their house in Madrid, but found an alternative place because they were afraid that seven-year-old Luli might say something and give him away. The fact that Ignacio was the first to be contacted and entrusted with protecting Prieto, who was returning to try and overturn the CEDA rule, is proof of his central position within the Republican political hierarchy.

At the end of 1935, the CEDA began to fall apart, and a weak and makeshift centrist government was put in place. Pressured from all sides, President Alcalá Zamora decided in early January to dissolve the *Cortes* and call for February elections. Constancia's description of these elections is key to understanding the basic argument presented by *In Place of Splendor*. The election line-up was the "reactionaries with their frank program of fascism and back to the Middle Ages" against the "people with the Popular Front program of democracy and mild liberal reform."[74] The Popular Front was a coalition formed by the Left Republican Party (Azaña), the Republican Union (Martinez Barrio), the National Republican Party (Sánchez Román), and the Catalonian Left Party (Companys). The reason why the aims of the Popular Front are so carefully outlined is obvious: many Americans and British had been convinced by Francoist propaganda that had portrayed the Republic as a radical communist government, and *In Place of Splendor* provided a unique opportunity to set the story straight. The Popular Front was not revolutionary, but democratic, and had put forth a program of mild reforms that were a continuation of the policies the Republic had started in 1931 which had been interrupted by the *bienio negro* (two black years) of the CEDA takeover.

Despite her involvement in Republican politics, Constancia's parents had accepted her civil marriage, and she and Ignacio now saw them regularly. Ignacio's charm and solidly aristocratic background must also have been a factor in their renewed good relations. However, the cordiality was short-lived. Constancia's father, Germán, summoned the couple one day to tell them he was dividing up his land amongst his children before the Agricultural Reform Bill was passed. In so doing, he would not be forced to sell any land, and Constancia and her siblings would have their full share. Constancia refused, flatly, to support any kind of circumvention of the Republican law. Her rejection of his offer put an insuperable distance between herself and her father, of whom she had been very fond in the past. Her relationship with her sisters had also deteriorated beyond repair. Regina, who had been her favorite, considered Constancia an embarrassment. In the meantime, her young sister Marichu had gone over to the opposite political extreme. Though married, she was allegedly having an affair with Primo de Rivera, the son of the former dictator and the young leader of the Falange. Constancia was quick to condemn this relationship, and said that Primo de Rivera

> *drove her into this vicious organization. I could not help but add that I knew the pattern well, I had seen it abroad: a wealthy, idle, ignorant young woman, married for money to a man she dislikes, seeking sensation, any antidote to boredom – this was the ideal fascist.*[75]

Politics were eroding most of Constancia's former ties. Even her friendship with Zenobia began to cool. Zenobia was politically neutral and had refused to vote in the elections. She had made new friends while Constancia had been abroad, and now "stubbornly refused to 'take sides.'"[76] Only a few years before, Zenobia had seemed a pioneering and outspoken feminist to the sheltered Constancia. Now, her predominate concern for her business made her seem like a classic bourgeois, ready to support anyone who would protect her interests.

When the Popular Front won the elections, Constancia and Ignacio had a mixed reaction. Their relief was overshadowed by the knowledge that the right wing would not give the new elected government a chance to govern peacefully: "I do not remember a night or day we were not hurriedly told of some secret plot against the Republic. The reactionaries, having lost at the elections, obviously intended to win at the point of the bayonet."[77]

Gunmen paid by the Falange were killing anyone associated with the Republic, from officers to Popular Front newspaper vendors.[78] The Popular Front itself was then, of course, vocally blamed by the right wing for destroying law and order. Ignacio begged President Azaña and Casares Quiroga, who was both Prime Minister and Minister of War, to act. He knew that if they did not take measures against the army and the Falange, the Republic would soon be attacked. But in an echo of Prieto's response in

Paris to Ignacio's report of Nazi plans for Spain, Azaña and Casares Quiroga were not impressed by Ignacio's insistence, which they viewed as alarmist.[79]

As the summer began, the situation grew worse as right-wing plans to stage a Nationalist military revolt against the Republic solidified. There was a snag in the plan when on July 11, a group of nationalists who had got their dates mixed up seized the Valencia radio station. Realizing they had acted too soon, they retreated in embarrassment, but not before tipping off anyone who cared to know that a coup was imminent.[80] Ignacio was momentarily relieved because he thought that with this evidence the government would inevitably take action. But by the night of July 12 the government still had no plans to act and Ignacio was desperate: "Any idiot would know what to do. Arrest Franco. Arrest Mola. Arrest the whole dirty lot of them. Act now and explain later, try them six months from now if you must – but arrest them now, *now*, while there is still time!"[81]

In Place of Splendor attributes Constancia's Republicanism to a series of factors, including social boredom, exposure to a different way of life in England, her independent streak, and her work with Zenobia Camprubi. Constancia does not credit Ignacio with her transformation, but the chronology of events makes the impact of his influence clear. It is ironic that Constancia repudiates Marichu for being influenced by her lover José Antonio Primo de Rivera. Constancia would have her readers believe that her own Republican sympathies were something she was born with. She does not reveal how much Ignacio had to do with her discovery of her own capacity for courage, commitment, and her ability to work tirelessly in desperate conditions.

Ignacio's experience as a revolutionary combined with his Republican and Communist connections and his inside knowledge of the air force and military made him a unique mentor for Constancia. Political life at Ignacio's side was exciting because the couple usually seemed to know, even before higher-ranking politicians knew, what was coming. Yet their lives were also haunted by a demoralizing pattern of surprise and frustration because despite their foreknowledge, they were powerless to prevent the growing right menace against the Spanish Republic.

What gives Constancia's experience before and during the war such a poignant perspective is how much she knew, thanks to Ignacio's insider information, yet how little either of them seemed to be able to do to change their country's future. When in 1935 they informed Prieto of the German plans for Spain they had heard of in Berlin, he did not take them seriously. Casares Quiroga thought that Ignacio was an alarmist when he warned of the impending military plot in February 1936. Despite many frustrating experiences such as these, Constancia would spend the war trying to convince foreign democracies, as Ignacio had tried to convince Prieto and Quiroga, that the Republic desperately needed their help and support. She and Ignacio were right on every count: the disloyal military officers, the role of Germany and Italy, and the unfair and devastating effects "non-intervention" would have for the Republic. She believed that once the United States and Britain knew, with irrefutable evidence that she could provide her foreign journalists, that Italy and Germany were attacking the Spanish Republic they would come to the rescue. It was to this end that she would dedicate the three most important years of her life.

II
The War, 1936–1939
Fighting Fascism from the Press Office

*Jay Allen came in to see me yesterday ... He is outraged
over our embargo on munitions of war to Loyalist Spain. He thinks,
and I agree with him, that this is a black page in our history.*
The Secret Diary of Harold L. Ickes[1]

However unconventional or strong-willed Constancia de la Mora may have seemed in her youth, nobody could have ever predicted that the convent-educated granddaughter of Spain's renowned conservative Prime Minister Antonio Maura would end up having dinner with Josef Stalin at the Kremlin. Her metamorphosis, though radical and remarkably quick, is perhaps not so surprising if we take into account the specific circumstances of her experiences.

Constancia was thirty years old when war broke out in 1936, and until then her life had seemed destined to closely mirror the changing political landscape of Spain. From 1923 to 1930, coinciding with the dictatorship of Primo de Rivera, she had felt stifled by the social norms of her oppressive family and by her unhappy marriage to Bolín, a politically conservative, socially ambitious and dissolute playboy who embodied the worst qualities of what Constancia refers to as the "old Spain". The legal and social changes brought about by the Republican government from 1931 onwards had benefited her directly, as the new laws enabled her to finally divorce Bolín and remarry the left-leaning Republican pilot Ignacio Hidalgo de Cisneros. With Ignacio at her side, Spain's political situation became the dominant focus of her life, and she was intent on furthering the progress towards freedom and equality she and her country had belatedly achieved. By the time the Nationalist uprising took place in July 1936, Constancia was a well-informed and militant progressive, and the brutal experience of the war quickly radicalized her even more. The beginning of the war also brought about a complete break with her family. Her parents were in Paris in July 1936. Their convenient absence heightened Constancia's suspicions that her father, whose electric company was connected to Nazi Germany, had played a role in the preparations for the military plot.[2] They sent her a telegram from Paris to make sure she was safe, and to inform her that they would try to get back to their country estate in Segovia via Portugal. This was, as Constancia points out not without a certain defiant pride, the last direct word she ever had from her parents.[3]

Tracing the appearances of her name in the Spanish press offers a superficial, but telling, portrait of the dramatic changes in her life. In the 1920s she is mentioned only in the context of high society in the conservative newspaper *ABC*. The paper announced her engagement, her taking part in a golf tournament at the Puerta de Hierro country club, and her marriage to Bolín.[4] However, by 1938, with Spain at war, Constancia appeared in a completely different context and with her new husband, Ignacio. The Republican paper *Frente Rojo* reported her donation (200 pesetas) to the "Comité Nacional de Mujeres Antifascistas"[5] and attendance at a farewell ceremony in Córdoba in honor of the president and secretary of the "Sección Femenina del Comité de Ayuda a España Republicana." Here she was no longer in the company of debutants, but of other left-wing female political leaders such as Elvira Taborda, Dolores Ibárruri (better known as La Pasionaria), Matilde Campos, Margarita Nelken, and Irene Falcón.[6] A few months later *Frente Rojo* published a letter to the wives of the *Guardias de Seguridad y Asalto* from the wives of the Republican Air Force Commanders inviting them to join the Commission of Women's Aid to the Ministry of Defense (*Comisión de Auxilio Femenino del Ministerio de Defensa*). The Commission's purpose was described in the following words:

> *Our thoughts are with those who have fallen on our fronts, assassinated by Fascist barbarity, heroes and martyrs to the universal cause of peace and democracy . . . we will bring fraternal spirit to the hospitals . . . we'll work so that the children of our combatants and the orphans of our heroes can have bread and affection. We want to help the workers who are struggling in our factories to supply the fronts. We will do everything we can to sweeten the dark and anguished lives of the evacuees . . . Each one of us . . . can achieve great things . . .* [7]

Fifteen women signed the letter. The name at the top of the list is Constancia de la Mora's.

As Mary Nash points out, for many Spanish women the anti-fascist fight was the most exciting experience of their lives, and what they faced allowed them to reach unprecedented prominence in the public sphere.[8] When the Republic was faced with the military uprising in July 1936, Constancia responded immediately and her energy, education, and outgoing personality made her a dynamic part of the Republican struggle.

While she collaborated in many ways, her most important role was to be in the Foreign Press Office.

The aim of this chapter is to provide both background and a counter-point to the version of events Constancia gives in her memoir *In Place of Splendor*. What episodes did she either change or leave out of her re-telling of the period between 1936 and 1939? Were her activities during the war in fact as significant as she says, or were they recast in a heroic light by her memoir? Or conversely, did she have more power, especially within the communist party, than she admits? Both Republican and communist offi-cials placed great trust in her, as demonstrated by the fact that she was eventually made the Director of the Foreign Press Office, which put her in charge of an essential part of the Republican war effort: propaganda. Her job was exceptionally challenging because of what Herbert Southworth describes as the special make-up of correspondents in Spain:

> *the press that covered the Spanish War was more diversified in its actors and its interpretations than the press that reported on the Second World War; thus the field open to propagandists during the Civil War was large and varied . . .* [9]

In his memoir *Cambio de rumbo*, although Ignacio says remarkably little about Constancia, he does emphasize the enormous responsibility she had and how well suited she was for the job:

> *After . . . Guadalajara . . . I went to Valencia to set up our General Air Force Staff. There was Connie, full of optimism and very happy with her new job in the press office, which had been arranged for her by Manuel Sánchez Arcas (the prestigious architect and one of the most cultivated, modest, and honest people I have known). This new job was perfect for Connie as she was enthusiastic, eager to work hard, and spoke four languages; and the combination of these qualities allowed her to make a huge contribution to the propaganda mission. Given the circumstances of our war, propaganda was of the utmost importance. Interaction with foreigners who came to see what was happening in our zone and with the correspondents sent by the world's leading newspapers was not easy. If one was not tactful, among other things, the visit could backfire. Connie overcame whatever difficulties she faced, and according to those who saw her on the job, both Spaniards and foreigners, her work in the press office was extremely useful to the Republican cause.* [10]

The last part of *In Place of Splendor* recounts the period from July 1936 to February 1939 from her point of view within the press office and is enti-tled "Widows of Heroes Rather than Wives of Cowards", a phrase borrowed from one of Dolores Ibárruri's speeches. She also includes obser-vations passed on from Ignacio, who had been named Commander in Chief of the Air Force. It is no surprise that in this chapter Constancia's story becomes increasingly political, and her involvement in the public sphere more prominent. From the very first pages of her narrative of the war, her agenda is clearly directed to the American reader:

> *I did not know, nor did Ignacio at the War Office, nor did the people of Spain know, that even as we all awoke and went to work that morning of July 19, 1936, in Berlin and Rome two dictators were giving the orders for the invasion of Spain by fascist troops, airplanes, cruisers, transports, technicians, Army officers, ammunition, guns, and money. The unequal battle – Spain against Germany and Italy, with England and France and the United States handcuffing my country's fighting arms – had already begun. But we did not know it.*[11]

She openly criticizes the United States' policy of non-intervention and the embargo on Spain, and points out how this position was to be responsible for the defeat of the Spanish Republic. She also blamed Britain for abandoning and denigrating the Republic in its press from the beginning. Constancia saw the British newspapers as willfully misrepresenting the Spanish government in order to justify their non-intervention:

> *In the meantime, the wobbling, timid, conservative Republican Government of Spain had already been dubbed "red" by British newspapers. Although it was, and has always been, perfectly clear to anyone with the slightest degree of common sense that the Spanish Government was a mildly liberal democratic government, England's largest newspapers were already calling the Giral government "communist". In July we were all amazed by the sudden deluge of lies. Attacked at home by the fascists, we found ourselves betrayed abroad by the newspapers of a friendly democratic Government.*[12]

Though not her official title, Constancia soon came to be known as the "head of public relations" for the Ministry of Foreign Affairs (*Ministerio de Asuntos Exteriores*) and was involved in many aspects of promoting Republican Spain's image abroad. Aside from vetting articles for military information and arranging visits and interviews for correspondents, she was also involved in the preparation of films shot by foreign crews during the war. Filmmaker Thorold Dickinson remembered her as a "splendid linguist and a tireless worker"[13] who was responsible for choosing and organizing the locations and introducing the crew to the prominent figures of the Republican zone, including Dolores Ibárruri.[14] Under Constancia's supervision, the filmmakers shot what was to be a documentary entitled "Spanish ABC" on cultural development in Republican Spain during the war that highlighted adult education, and the increasing number of theaters and libraries. Though most of the footage was devoted to these cultural and/or educational images (i.e. soldiers in the trenches studying trigonometry, young actors bringing theater to the soldiers) they also shot newsworthy political material such as a captured German plane, proof of the intervention of the Axis powers in Spain.

The reports on Constancia in *Frente Rojo* and accounts of her work such as Dickinson's confirm her own characterization of her contributions to the defense of the Republic. However, other sources suggest that her activities were perhaps more complex than she reveals. In 1936, Constancia became a communist, and this fact appears nowhere in her apparently frank memoir. Just as she had removed inconvenient information from the articles approved by her Foreign Press Office, she omitted any mention of her communist affiliation from her own story.

In Place of Splendor could have offered a unique perspective on the role of many other Spanish communists during the war, but Constancia carefully left out the names of her many important friends and collaborators. Again, this was largely done to avoid having her own name associated with the communist party, but also probably out of political discretion as her memoir was written so soon after the end of the war. Irene Falcón, for example, wrote her autobiography decades later, and remembers Constancia fondly: "Constancia and I had met before the war in the women's movement. We were close friends", but Constancia makes no reference to Falcón or other prominent women in her autobiography. There is not even a mention of Irene's sister Kety who worked with Constancia in the press office. Another example of her style of dissembling is her treatment of Dolores Ibarruri, the legendary *Pasionaria*. Constancia knew *Pasionaria* well, but in her book she describes her as a heroic leader whom she admired only from afar. She calls *Pasionaria* the "great woman deputy to the Cortes" and describes how her speeches moved crowds but plays down her own role reducing herself to a distant, anonymous admirer.

Throughout her narrative, Constancia portrays her contributions as humanitarian rather than political. Her first job in the war was running the children's colonies in Madrid and Alicante. It is indeed ironic that her initial enthusiastic involvement on the Republican side of the war so closely echoed the charity work foisted on her by her socialite mother years before. But there were important differences. First, by this time Constancia was more mature and politically engaged, and second, the children were even worse off in 1936 than they had been under Primo de Rivera because they had been used as political pawns. Since the early 1930s, the poor children and orphans had been abandoned by their former conservative benefactors in order to teach the Republic a lesson: "one of the first steps the rich Monarchists and fascists took under the Republic was to refuse to support the orphanages and pauper schools they had always kept up before. Let the Government do it, they said cynically."[15] So, in the late summer of 1936, Constancia and a group of other young Republican women, including wives of pilots and Indalecio Prieto's (then Minister of Air and Marine) daughter Concha, took over running the orphanages and schools. She and her "regiment of women" cleaned up the children and the filthy buildings they lived in and made sure they had food.

In September, when the bombings started in Madrid, she evacuated the children to Alicante. She found abandoned houses and converted them into adequate shelter for the 650 children who were by then under her care. As Madrid became more dangerous, the government evacuated as many children as it could, and Constancia found herself with her hands full trying to set up housing and supplies for this mass emigration of children. In keeping with her desire to practice the democratic ideals to which she subscribed, she placed her daughter Luli in one of the children's homes where she reportedly "thrived". Food was scarce and thus Constancia and her colleagues in Alicante were overjoyed at the arrival of a Soviet ship, the *Neva*, which had brought food and supplies. She points out that it would have been even better if the ship had brought arms, but the Soviets were obliged to comply with the British-led Non-Intervention Pact.

Many Republicans were happy to welcome the Soviets, because the democratic countries that should have been helping them resist the Nationalist uprising were not providing any support. The hard line the rest of the world had taken thus far in the war had given the Soviet aid, even if it was only in the form of butter and canned meat, a symbolic importance for many Spaniards. Constancia described how moved people in Alicante were by the arrival of the *Neva*, and how "we all felt most embarrassed to discover that the stevedores loading the ship in Odessa had worked night and day to finish their task, contributing their wages to buy more food for Spain."[16] She described the townspeople of Alicante weeping with joy in the harbor at the proof that at least the Soviets had not abandoned them. In her description, Constancia states defensively that the Soviets brought nothing but food and aid to Alicante, and that "No 'agents of Stalin' roamed the streets."[17] She seems to be anticipating the reader's suspicion of her glowing account of Soviet influence in Spain, and wanted to ensure that the Soviets were seen to have been providing much needed aid and support, but not meddling in politics. She wants her audience to conclude that Soviet help did not mean communist intervention, and that butter did not come along with Stalinist agit-prop.

However, the truth was slightly different. Along with food, the Soviets had already begun to send over supplies of propaganda materials that were circulating around Spain, in a campaign would reach its height between December 1936 and October 1937 when "thousands of Soviet books, pamphlets, and journals, and hundreds of different posters, musical recordings, and films" were shipped to Spain.[18] As early as the fall of 1936, celebrations of Soviet aid to Spain were taking place all over the Republican zones. Constancia's future colleague in the press office, English journalist Kate Mangan,[19] remembers the spectacular celebration of the Soviet Union in Barcelona in November:

> *I stood and watched the procession to celebrate the anniversary of the Soviet Union. It took four hours to pass, and everyone was in it, that is more people were in it than watching. There was a first detachment of child refugees, the 'pioneros de Madrid' with cropped heads and those striped pinafores that make Spanish boys and girls alike, who loudly cheered. There were Red Cross nurses holding out sheets for pennies, ambulances painted with scenes of blood-transfusions. There were all the political parties and organizations including the POUM, very high-brow with banners written in Russian. There were endless trade unions carrying the tools of their trades and some of those embroidered silk banners that look like those in churches.[20]*

Though Constancia clearly supported a Soviet role in Spain, the fact that she would obscure her own communist affiliation in her memoir is, of course, not surprising. She was trying to make a sympathetic case for the Spanish Republic against the Franco regime to the American public. The force of her argument was that she had no political agenda aside from "truth" and "democracy". But it is precisely her defensiveness that makes the reader suspicious, and it is easy to find evidence of her political allegiance elsewhere. An official Comintern document confirms both her party affiliation and the fact that she worked on behalf of the communist party in Spain during the civil war.[21] Ignacio's memoir likewise confirms that they had both already joined the party before the arrival of the *Neva*. Ignacio, whose post had kept him in Madrid, had gone to see Constancia in Alicante and his visit had coincided with the arrival of the Soviet ship, an event so exciting it nearly made him forget to tell his wife the following important news:

> *I had forgotten to mention to Connie the fact that I had joined the communist party. As I was getting ready to leave . . . she said that she had to tell me something, something she had done secretly and that she wasn't sure I would approve of. Her face became serious as she told me she had become a member of the communist party. She started to explain why she had joined: how much the communists*

had helped, how they were the best people she had worked with, etc., etc. In short, she gave me all the same arguments I myself had made when I decided to join. I cut her agitprop short, and when I told her that I had also become a communist her expression . . . was a mix of surprise and joy, and we embraced happy and moved by the wonderful coincidence."[22]

This is corroborated by Burnett Bolloten who interviewed the couple in Mexico in 1940, when they both gave the same reasons for joining the party that Ignacio would later give in his book: " . . . he joined the communist party, as did many other Socialists, quite early in the war because of its discipline and efficiency and the help received from the USSR."[23] Irene Falcón, who was *Pasionaria*'s personal secretary and closest collaborator, also remembers that:

Both of them (Constancia and Ignacio) had aristocratic backgrounds, and as she confided to me, they each became communists separately. When he, somewhat apprehensively, confessed to her that he had become a communist, she replied, "That makes two of us". In the midst of war, one day Hidalgo de Cisneros asked his chauffeur how he could become a communist, to which his chauffeur replied that he could do it right then and there since he was a member and could get him a party card.[24]

It was Constancia's communism that would make many people wary of her during the war and in subsequent years. It is important to keep in mind that it was not only the right wing that feared communism, but also many potential liberal allies in Spain and the United States. Furthermore, if being a male communist was bad in the eyes of many, being a communist woman was worse. Even female Republican friends found de la Mora's activism extremist and reprehensible, and distanced themselves from her because of it. Predictably, not many other women from the upper crust of the bourgeoisie became radicals. De la Mora's heartfelt engagement quickly alienated her from friends she had assumed to be politically like-minded. This was the case with Zenobia Camprubí, who had been her great friend during the years of the Republic. According to Hidalgo de Cisneros, they were "very close friends. Connie could always count on Zenobia for understanding and affection at the most difficult times."[25] However, in Camprubí's *Diario*, it is clear that their friendship withered once de la Mora became politically engaged. Camprubí and her husband, the writer Juan Ramón Jiménez, left Spain in August 1936 and though Zenobia kept in touch with de la Mora for a short time, their political differences soon dampened her feelings. In 1937, from her exile in Puerto Rico, Camprubí wrote about her disapproval of extremism and revolutionary ideas:

There is no doubt that I was not born to be a revolutionary. I would prefer to make the best of what there is, rather than turn everything upside down, knowing that the new experiment might fail. The problem is that I am skeptical about all these grandiose political programs that are supposed to redeem humanity.[26]

Late in 1937, Camprubí wrote in her diary that she had spent an afternoon discussing "Connie M." and that she was still fond of her. However, she was upset by "her narrow fanaticism in political matters."[27] At the beginning of 1938, she was surprised to discover, through a mutual friend, that Constancia had become a communist:

I ran into Marinello and after trying to get him to talk, he finally told me that Connie had joined the communist party, and that she was an active member . . . He had also heard rumors that Ignacio was going to lose his command. But why would Ignacio, a socialist, have problems? Perhaps he changed after I left . . . I feel completely lost in terms of politics in Spain. For me it may as well be ancient Greek.[28]

In contrast, it is interesting to note Constancia's changing view of Camprubí. Though she knew that her friend had left Spain because Jiménez's health was frail, she could not forgive Zenobia for having put her husband's well-being before that of their country, and was clearly eager to go on record with her criticism:

We had all been disappointed and hurt when my friend Zenobia and her poet husband, who at first had helped us run homes for children in Madrid, had suddenly packed their trunks and left Spain. We considered it something of a desertion. Spain needed her poets. Zenobia might have been useful. She was needed. And yet Zenobia and her husband, like many Spanish intellectuals who thought themselves too delicate and too sensitive to stand the horrors of war, had gone abroad.[29]

Constancia was equally upset when Republican Air and Marine Minister Indalecio Prieto decided to send his daughter Concha, her collaborator, out of the war zone:

I had a great shock. Concha got a peremptory note from her father. The military situation was tense. He could not work in peace with his daughters in Spain – in danger. They must leave. I could hardly believe my ears. The women of Spain were fighting beside their men, building barricades, and cooking food while the guns roared. We were comparatively safe, doing work, however unromantic, that was absolutely necessary. Why should the Minister of Air and Marine consider his daughters above the women of Madrid?[30]

Concha Prieto was very involved in her work with Constancia and apparently at first refused to leave. She and her father had a tug of war that lasted for several days, but finally he whisked her away in the middle of the night, along with Blanca Prieto and Azaña's wife. Afterwards, Constancia did not hold a grudge against Concha, but this event gave her a pretext to lash out against Prieto because of the impact his personal decision had had on Republican morale:

> *And from the three women leaving Alicante in the morning . . . the cook and the children and the townsfolk had drawn one conclusion: if the Minister of Marine and Air (sic) called the Civil Governor to force his daughter to leave Alicante, it must be that we were all in terrible danger . . . I tried to quiet the children and the town. I did not like to tell the truth about Prieto, and tried to explain that he was just a very doting father. But while I tried to go about calmly, inside I was filled with rage. That a responsible Government officer could behave in such a way . . . I have never believed that because a man has power in the Government he should not share the suffering of his country. Women and men of Madrid wept over their children, dead from the fascist bombs, but Prieto could not leave his daughters in Alicante!*[31]

Constancia's critics would later see this and other attacks on Prieto in her memoir as having come from a partisan motivation on her part. Prieto's hostility towards the communist party was well known. Later in the war he would have Constancia temporarily fired from the press office and she never forgave him for this.

In 1939 the average American reader of *In Place of Splendor* could have easily accepted Constancia's self-portrait as a liberal Republican and antifascist without suspecting that she was a communist. Her emphasis on her aristocratic background also provided an effective foil. However, in hindsight, it is easier to read between the lines. What is telling is that just as Constancia had nostalgically described the glorious arrival of the *Neva*, everything to do with the Soviet Union is praised in her narrative. Her admiration was evidently sincere because in December 1936 she sent her nine-year-old daughter Luli to Odessa. Luli would remain there, without her mother, until 1945. Though many Republican children were sent to Russia, most were sent considerably later in the war. Luli was one of the first children to leave Spain, an indication not only of her mother's faith in the Soviet system, but also of how well connected she was in communist circles. Carmen Dorronsoro de Roces, who worked with Constancia in the Foreign Press Office, remembered that Luli was considered special because "she didn't go on a collective trip like my daughter, she went alone, with two other girls, and they had been invited by the Soviet government; one of the girls was even invited to live at Voroshilov's house."[32] According to Constancia's version, Luli sailed to the Soviet Union on a food ship with just one other child, "Charito", the daughter of an unidentified Air Force pilot. Constancia remembers saying a sad goodbye to Luli at the ship's gangplank, and her well-trained daughter bidding her farewell without shedding tears and with a brave *"Salud!"*.[33]

Luli arrived in the Soviet Union before the many official children's homes that were being set up for Spanish orphans or refugees had been prepared. She spent the early period of her stay at the home of Corps Commander Uritsky, chief of the Red Army's Intelligence Directorate. Having Luli in his house made Uritsky curious about her father Ignacio.[34] Uritsky took advantage of a visit to Moscow from the well-known American correspondent Louis Fischer, who was covering the war in Spain, to ask him about Ignacio:

> Uritsky: *Do you know the head of the air force?*
> Fischer: *Lt. Col. Cisneros?*
> Uritsky: *Yes, his daughter is with us.*
> Fischer: *I know him. I think that Cisneros is a devoted man. His wife runs a children's home, a beautiful woman, from an aristocratic family. I got to know her in April. She was my translator. And I also got to know him then. She said that she rarely got to see her husband, because he slept in the aerodrome, because he was afraid every day and night that there would be a revolt by the pilots. So he was on guard, then, and he was on the side of the Republican government.*[35]

This dialogue gives a clear indication of Constancia and Ignacio's appreciation of the instability of the air force during the first months of the war. It also shows that the couple was well connected in Spain within the communist party, or they would neither have been able to send Luli to the Soviet Union nor have her stay with someone as powerful as Uritsky. On the other hand, neither Constancia nor Ignacio had made their political reputations yet and were clearly new names to high-ranking Soviets.

By New Year's Eve 1937, Constancia felt that she could do no more for the children and convalescents in Alicante and she decided to leave to see Ignacio. Her friends Rafael Alberti and María Teresa León drove her to visit him at the army encampment at Albacetel. On the way, the couple convinced her to apply for a job in the Government Foreign Press Office (by then in Valencia). In fact, her friend the American correspondent Jay Allen, had already suggested the idea. The Albertis argued that Constancia's knowledge of foreign languages, especially her fluent English, and her experience abroad, would make her extremely useful. They talked her into working in the press office "all the way to the Army encampment where [they] . . . were to speak that night."[36] Constancia followed their advice and went to the Foreign Press Bureau, which was part of the Ministry of Foreign Affairs headed by Alvarez del Vayo, to meet with the office's Chief Censor and Head, Luis Rubio Hidalgo. In her memoir, Constancia does not mention that the Albertis were also communists, and that María Teresa was powerful within the party and surely had her reasons for recommending that Constancia apply for this new job.

Louis Fischer remembered that in January 1937 Constancia asked that he speak to Alvarez del Vayo to recommend her for a job in the Foreign Press office. In fact, Fischer intervened repeatedly with del Vayo on her behalf: " Del Vayo is a gorgeous human being, but he often procrastinates, and I talked to him several times, and also to his wife Luisy, urging Constancia's appointment. Finally, he appointed her."[37] In the end, she was officially hired by Ignacio's friend Manuel Sánchez Arcas.[38]

Was Constancia prepared for the Foreign Press Office post she was taking? Her first impressions of her new job make her seem quite naïve. She says she even had trouble finding the building where she was to have her interview. If she felt shy and self-conscious before arriving, her encounter with Rubio Hidalgo in his lugubrious office only made her feel worse:

> *Señor Rubio . . . lived like a mole in the middle of the Foreign Press Bureau. His office was practically pitch-dark. All the shades were drawn. The only daylight leaked in from cracks in the door . . . A shaded dim desk light made an eerie pool of green in the gloom. In the midst of this darkness sat Señor Rubio, partly bald, with a tiny mustache, pasty-colored face, and dark glasses. Dark glasses in the midst of all the gloom!*[39]

Rubio Hidalgo and Constancia did not hit it off. She was initially asked only to censor the articles of the English and American foreign correspondents. Her instructions were to make sure that the stories were free of messages in code, wild rumors, or any military information that could strengthen the enemy's position.[40] Though she claims to have been quite daunted, she flourished in her new position. She eventually transformed the office's atmosphere completely, bringing about close contacts between government officials and foreign correspondents. In the process, she soon overshadowed Rubio Hidalgo and edged her way into the most powerful position in the office. She though that reporters should be treated as well as possible and given good access because, she reasoned, if her office could help them write the truth, it could help the Republic win the war. Of course, not everyone on the Republican side agreed on just what the truth was at any given moment, but this does not come through in Constancia's account. According to her, the foreign correspondents were simply given access to the facts and she was surprised that they did not always accept these facts.

> *I knew, as all of us did – that the cause of the Republic depended on the world knowing the facts . . . At first, I was not a little puzzled at the way correspondents shied at simple facts that were presented to them to make their work easier. I soon came to take into account this healthy, though somewhat paralyzing fear of "propaganda" that is a part of every good reporter's nature. And so I accented my work towards helping them to find out the facts for themselves by giving them whatever facilities we could scrape together for their work . . . I came to admire terribly this passion for fact . . . I came to see that this, after all, was the way to get the facts into print, to have the men who sent them convinced of their accuracy because they themselves had got them. I have to smile when I hear stories of how we "influenced" the foreign correspondents. And now, of course, as one looks back over their coverage, one sees that if they erred it was on the side of understatement.*[41]

It is nearly impossible to read Constancia's description of her position within the Foreign Press office without feeling sympathetic to her struggle to show the world how the Republic was caught between the arms embargo on one side, and the Nationalist and international attacks on the other. Everyone had to know that Spain was being invaded not just by Franco, but also by Hitler and Mussolini. This was information that she desperately wanted the American, British, and French governments to react to, yet they repeatedly refused to respond.

Most of the journalists who worked with her remembered her fondly afterwards because she "was a brilliant success. She knew languages and the psychology of foreigners, and the correspondents liked her."[42] If one takes her version at face value, along with the glowing accounts of her work from the foreign correspondents and International Brigade veterans, she was a Republican heroine. However, the idea that her office had no interest in propaganda or influence of its own seems disingenuous.

Kate Mangan observed that women like herself and Constancia, who spoke languages, were rare and therefore very valuable in wartime Spain:

> *I found that women were very much at a premium in Spain, particularly those who could talk to foreigners in their own language. It must have been ideal for female spies. For no good reason, everyone seemed very trustful, and just because I had been seen with one person who was 'de confianza' I was accepted as alright by everyone without further enquiry – though, of course, there was plenty that was concealed from me. It was assumed that I was politically sound and well intentioned, 'valid' but naïve and untrained. This was true, but I was even more ingenuous than people thought.*[43]

Like Constancia, Mangan emphasizes her complete ignorance and how ill equipped she was to start propaganda work in Republican Spain. Though both women may have, to some extent, exaggerated their political naïveté in their memoirs, the Republican propaganda effort was by necessity filled with amateurs, especially at the beginning of the war. When we take into account what was at stake, it is rather sobering to think how haphazardly people were chosen to be in such crucially important positions:

> *I made friends with a man . . . with whom I could only communicate in bad French. For this reason, perhaps, he did not seem to doubt that I had the political and professional background to undertake propaganda newspaper work. I had nerve enough to undertake anything and was canny enough not to give away my ignorance to him, while busy poring over Marxist literature in private. There were so many sets of letters in use that I felt it quite dangerous if one casually mentioned any combination of the ABC without learning the significance of this new alphabet. The PSUC, the POUM, the UGT, the CNT-FAI, the JSU, were only some of them. It seemed as if all the banners in town were bristling with mysterious initials. I wore a hammer and sickle badge – such badges were sold on the street and one could join anything one fancied for a few cents. I wore a red kerchief round my neck and a red ribbon round my hair.*

Mangan briefly returned to England for Christmas and then came back to Spain for a new job as correspondent for the *Christian Science Monitor*, and with a letter of introduction to the correspondent of the *Daily Express*.[44] But soon after establishing herself in the Hotel Inglés in Valencia, her American roommate Louise told her to go meet Liston Oak for a job as secretary and translator at the press office.[45] Liston Oak was, at the time, in charge of English propaganda for the Republic. It is easy to see why having an educated American influencing how the American and British public would see the war was important. Unfortunately, Oak was a poor choice:

> *Liston Oak, like most of the people Louise introduced me to, was not really a friend of hers. She probably did not know him any better than she knew me . . . He was a tall, distinguished-looking, middle-aged American with glasses and curling grey hair which he wore rather long at the back. He generally wore a large-sized floppy beret. Some Spanish ambassador abroad had decided that, to get the right kind of publicity in English, an American was the thing needed, and Liston Oak had impressed him. Liston was a chameleon kind of character. I always felt he was unreal and a faker though I did not know until afterwards what he was up to. Poppy[46] told me later that he had been an actor and a schoolmaster and an organizer for some charitable society and that he was really an all around failure.*

He was not bad to work for except when he had fits of thinking he had to be busi-
ness-like in the American style. We did not know about his politics though I
thought he took rather an interest in FAI and POUM, but he said he did it to
be fair. When I discovered his second wife had left him I assumed that he had
come to Spain to forget about it. Many of the odd people who turned up had some
such reason.[47]

Thanks to Oak, Mangan was introduced to Kellt,[48] the former head of
the foreign department. In the meeting, Kellt urged Mangan to keep her
eyes and ears open at the press office claiming that it was full of "very bad
people" and that the director, Rubio, was too clever, and that Selke[49] was
not to be trusted. Mangan writes that all these warnings "seemed rather
odd afterwards as the person we all should have been warned against was
neither Rubio nor Selke but Liston himself."[50] Oak, a figure that
Constancia notably avoids mentioning in her own memoir, ended up
leaving the press office for Barcelona. He left Spain just before the May
uprising. According to Mangan,

It seeped through that Liston was consorting with the POUM a great deal in
Barcelona. He left shortly before the May rising in that town, in haste, we heard,
with the police on his track. It was much later that we heard from America that
he had been conducting virulent written and spoken propaganda against the
Spanish Republic and the war, and that he used his position 'employed in a respon-
sible post by the Government' to lend authority to his statements.[51]

Mangan does not have much to say about Rubio; except that he was a
friend of Alvarez del Vayo's and that he went abroad often to Paris or
Geneva to plead the Republic's cause, in vain, at the League of Nations.
She then goes on to describe Constancia, who had quickly become second
only to Rubio in the office's hierarchy:

The second in command was Constancia de la Mora, an aristocratic, intelligent,
charming young woman, surprisingly tall. She had been married off very young
to a man she did not love – I think he was a Bolín[52] *and related to Franco's then*
publicity man. She had a daughter of eleven who had been sent to Russia. She
had had a divorce and was then married to Cisneros who was head of Republican
aviation. She was déclassé as a result of her divorce and had been running an art
and craft shop in Madrid before the war.[53]

Although Mangan is quite critical of just about everyone in the press
office in Spain, her impressions of Constancia, with whom she worked on
a daily basis, are consistently favorable. She mentions her temper, but not
in a derogatory way, and generally seemed to admire her a great deal. Her

memories are a valuable testimony because they represent one of the few surviving accounts of Constancia in the context of her work.

The press office, Mangan asserts, was a disaster under the reign of Rubio Hidalgo and Liston Oak. For example, the Spanish embassy in London had arranged for the poet W. H. Auden to go to Spain and prepare stories for the British public. When he arrived, he was "keen to arrange English broadcasts as well as cultural Spanish ones from Valencia."[54] Mangan "did her best to impress on everyone that Auden was a famous poet and they had better go out of their way to oblige him as he had a lot of influence in England."[55] But in those days the office only fussed over people of no importance, and the more Mangan talked about Auden, the more hostile Liston Oak became. Oak did not want a rival working in his office. Mangan contrasts the pettiness and shabbiness of the Oak/Rubio press office to the period when Constancia would take over:

> *At a later date, under the reign of Constancia who had a much more proper sense of things, he (Auden)[56] would have had either Coco[57] or me, full time, at his disposal. At the time Constancia had only just joined the staff. The place had only been going for about a month and was not properly organized*

It took a long time for the office to function efficiently. On February 8, 1937 Málaga fell to the Nationalists after days of heavy shelling from German and Italian ships. The consequences for the Republican population left behind, or trying to flee, were terrible. Those who weren't shot were imprisoned.[58] Mangan describes being in Valencia and learning about the fall of Málaga. She gives a detailed account of Constancia's reaction, which is one of the only vivid portraits of the press office at a critical moment in the war:

> *Suddenly it dawned on me; the town was in mourning for Málaga. I hurried back to the office. No one was there except Coco, who was in tears, and Constancia holding the fort in the inner office with a long, long face. "It's Málaga, isn't it?" I said, in my abrupt English way, so disconcerting to Spaniards. I took Coco by the arm, "It's gone isn't it?"*
>
> *Coco screwed up his face, a big boy ashamed of his tears, and nodded. I went into Constancia.*
>
> *"When did it go?" I asked, "I won't tell anyone though it is obvious the whole town knows."*
>
> *"Yesterday," she said, "it will be in the papers tomorrow."*
>
> *"Is it still going badly?" I asked . . . "How far have they got?"*
>
> *She gave a despairing gesture towards some Febus sheets on her desk and I picked them up. There was a confused, un-paragraphed account of thousands of refugees*

streaming out of Málaga, and of hordes of Italians and Boinas Rojas streaming in . . .

Constancia was crying too. She walked with me into the main sala where the big wall-map hung. On it, the line was marked with pins and small republican flags. The line in the south had been unrooted entirely and left unmarked.

"I think there", she said pointing to Motríl.

"But that is half-way to Almería!" I exclaimed, horrified.

"They may take Almería and keep straight up the coast for all I know," she said, "I don't know what is happening or who is going to stop them."

"I can't understand it," said poor bewildered Coco with a sob.

"But we musn't give way like this, " I said, "we must carry on as usual, the journalists will think the whole war is lost. We must pull ourselves together."

Constancia said nothing. She gave me the look out of her liquid brown eyes that seemed to put me in my place as a vulgar interloper. Too many foreigners were blind to such looks. The Spaniards were always subjected to cocksure interference in their business, treated as pawns in a game, and they are a proud people.[59]

What is interesting about this passage is the fact that after such a devastating loss, when everybody should have been in the press office working overtime to get the Republican story out, nobody was there except for Constancia and a young boy. The head of the office, Rubio Hidalgo, was nowhere to be seen, and neither was Oak. Constancia's reaction to the fall of Málaga, and to Mangan's coolness, shows a woman that is very close to the self-portrait of Constancia in *Place of Splendor*.

Mangan also recalls that she twice went to prisons full of Nationalist prisoners as an interpreter for American or English journalists. This should have been Constancia's responsibility, but she could not "bear to talk to Spaniards from the other side."[60] The visit to the women's prison, as described by Mangan, would have been especially excruciating for Constancia because it was filled with women of her own background, who may very well have known or recognized her from earlier days at social events in Madrid or summer resorts:

The inmates were all Spanish but very mixed socially. However, they all had their own cells. Some of them appeared to be prostitutes who had been taken up for spying, others were high born ladies. The latter were held as valuable exchange prisoners. Their relatives on the other side arranged to exchange them for aviators who had been obliged to bale out over enemy territory and who were very scarce and precious to us. There was Franco's niece with her baby in a cot covered with netting to keep off flies . . . There was Millán Astray's sister and a very ugly old lady in black who was some relation of the Duke of Alba but proved rather a bad investment as he did not seem anxious to ransom her. There were three lovely girls, titled sisters . . . These girls spoke good English as they had an English governess. They looked quite elegant. Someone from the British Embassy visited them every week and brought them reading matter. They had the 'Sketch' and the 'Tatler' and a novel by Anthony Trollope . . . They were cheeky. I was wearing a hair-band of twisted raffia, red and straw colour. "You are wearing our colours," they said, meaning red and gold . . . They said they were very bored but were annoyed with the prison governor, a lawyer, because he made them work . . . When I left they offered to shake hands with me. It was not long before they were exchanged.[61]

One cannot imagine these young ladies offering to shake hands with Constancia, nor she with them. The war was also a personal battle for Constancia, and the work at the press office must have been exhausting for her because she was so emotionally involved. The contrast between her passion and Mangan's coolness is also clear at the moment of censoring a story that described the office as being run by a communist bureaucracy:

. . . one of our visiting journalists had been watching funerals too. Constancia brought me a hand-written piece that she could not quite make out and asked me to type it as she doubted if it would pass the censor.

"There are many funerals," I read, "with masses of wreaths. These are sometimes shaped like a star, sometimes a hammer and sickle but never, never, the sign of a cross . . . I see here all the signs of a revolution including a formidable bureaucracy."

I laughed, "That means us, "I said to Constancia, "you must have wound him up in red tape and he is annoyed about it."

But she was on her dignity and very angry.

"He should have seen the bureaucracy in Spain before the war, when the government was in Madrid. We only have a shadow of that now. I shan't let it through."[62]

Constancia did not want to let this story through for the same reason she didn't want the American readers of *In Place of Splendor* to know she was a communist. She knew very well that the association of "hammer and sickle" with Republican Spain would preclude the hope of ever obtaining aid from the United States or Britain.

Arturo Barea[63] also worked as a censor in the press office, and some of his impressions coincide with Constancia's, including his feelings about Rubio Hidalgo and his seedy office. According to Barea, nobody liked Rubio Hidalgo but Alvarez del Vayo trusted him. However, in contrast to Constancia, Barea was not a communist, and his version of how things were run is that of an outsider. Barea says that he had been offered a job at the press office through a communist named Velilla who worked at the

1. Prime Minister Antonio Maura giving a speech, Bullring of Madrid, April 1917.
D-28 Fondo Gráfico Fundación Antonio Maura.

2. Prime Minister Antonio Maura and King Alfonso XIII, Calle Alcalá, Madrid, 1918.
C-86 Fondo Gráfico Fundación Antonio Maura.

3. Three of Antonio Maura's daughters: Margarita, Estefanía, and Constancia Maura (Constancia's mother), 1900. C-63 Fondo Gráfico Fundación Antonio Maura.

4. Portrait of Constancia in Paris, 1923. A-49 Fondo Gráfico Fundación Antonio Maura.

5. Portrait of Constancia, 1925. A-50 Fondo Gráfico Fundación Antonio Maura.

6. Portrait of Constancia and Luli, 1929. A-51 Fondo Gráfico Fundación Antonio Maura.

7. Ignacio Hidalgo de Cisneros, c. 1939. Comintern Archive (RGASPI), Moscow.

8. Ignacio Hidalgo de Cisneros (profile), c. 1939. Comintern Archive (RGASPI), Moscow.

9. Constancia and her cousins arriving at the trial of Miguel Maura, March 21, 1931. Courtesy of the Hemeroteca Municipal Madrid.

10. Jay Allen, *c*. 1939. Courtesy of Michael Allen.

11. Jay Allen (close-up), *c.* 1939. Courtesy of Michael Allen.

12. Constancia. Photo by John Condax, Philadelphia, Summer of 1939. Courtesy of Kate Delano Condax Decker.

Ministry of State. Barea was hired before Constancia, when the press office was still in Madrid, and it was Velilla who told him he would be working with communists:

> *"We don't trust him (Rubio Hidalgo). In this department there are two comrades and we should try to gain control of everything. Come see me as soon as you can. You'll have to join our cell. There are already eleven of us." He {Velilla} . . . had a mixture of simple good faith and muddled ideas. For him, the war would be over in a few weeks and Spain would become a Soviet republic. I thought the idea was completely absurd, but I liked the man and the idea of working with him appealed to me.*[64]

Barea, who became a censor for the radio, later went to the Valencia office where Constancia had been recently hired. He reports that "Rubio Hidalgo was gradually leaving everything in the hands of his new assistant, the communist Constancia de la Mora, who treated all our requests on behalf of the journalists with a consistent and bored disdain."[65]

These comments are surprising, because the last adjectives that come to mind in connection with Constancia are disdainful and bored. She portrays herself, as do many others, as full of enthusiasm. Did Barea see another side of her, or did she have a personal or political animosity towards him in particular? Here Barea gives a longer description of Constancia's first visit to the Madrid office:

> *I knew that she had virtually taken over the Valencia office and that she didn't like Rubio; that she was an efficient organizer, and very much the aristocrat who had joined the left of her own volition and who had greatly improved the relationship between the Valencia office and the press. I knew that the communist party backed her, and that she must have found it irritating that we in Madrid invariably worked as if we were independent of them, or of her. She was tall . . . with big dark eyes; she had the imperious manner of a matriarch, the simple mind of a convent school boarder, and the arrogance of being the granddaughter of Antonio Maura. It was inevitable that we would not see eye to eye.*[66]

Though Barea did not like Constancia, at this point he says he still trusted her. So when she suggested that he and his Austrian companion Ilsa, who also worked in the office as a translator, take a long well-deserved holiday, he thought her intentions were good. Ilsa, however, was suspicious. She was worried that because they were working independently, and were not a part of the communist bureaucracy that had taken over the press office, they had become undesirable.

According to Barea, Ilsa was right. The couple stopped in Valencia, on the way to the coastal village of Altea, and there a policeman who had once arrested the attractive Ilsa and who had not been able to forget her, warned them of what he had heard. Constancia and Rubio were not going to let Barea and Ilsa return to their jobs in Madrid. In fact, Constancia had already named their successor, a secretary from the *Liga de Intelectuales Antifascistas* that María Teresa León had recommended. The policeman warned that Constancia and María Teresa were ambitious and zealous communists: "these Spanish women hate seeing a foreign woman gain power. And, they are both new party members and full of enthusiasm."[67] Apparently, several complaints and accusations had already been filed against Barea and Ilsa. For example, Ilsa had approved an article for a Swedish Socialist newspaper that criticized the lack of socialist and anarchist union members in the government. This was seen as "proof" of her anti-communism, and together with other disloyalties they were both accused of, they were suddenly in a dangerous position. Feeling that they had nowhere to hide, they were desperate:

> *How could we fight against this accumulation of personal resentment and hatred, political intrigues, and the inflexible laws of the machinery of the State during a civil war? . . . We could only let a few friends in on the situation, those who were in high enough positions to actually do something should we disappear overnight.*[68]

Though Constancia claimed to be a neutral member of the foreign press office, Barea's portrait of her suggests otherwise. He saw her willfully crossing the frontier between necessary censorship and propaganda, and was convinced that her commitment to the communist party was total.

Not being able to draw the propaganda line would, in fact, almost cost her job. The following episode is, according to Louis Fischer, one of the most telling of her official career, and is not mentioned in her autobiography.[69] Fischer was one of the few people who both knew Constancia well and wrote about her, though by the time he wrote they were no longer on friendly terms. They had met socially in early 1936, through the del Vayos and the Araquistains. In early April she was assigned to be Fischer's interpreter during a meeting with Azaña. As we have already seen from Fischer's conversation with Uritsky, his first impressions of Constancia were favourable: " She was a handsome dark Spanish woman, in revolt against her aristocratic, Catholic upbringing . . . Constancia was an excellent translator because she spoke English perfectly and understood the political subject matter as well."[70] After Fischer had been in Moscow and seen Luli at Uritsky's in December 1936, he had eagerly brought news back to Ignacio and Constancia in Valencia.[71] Because of their friendship, he was concerned when one day in the early summer of 1937 he ran into a distressed Constancia in Valencia. He asked her what was wrong, to which she replied bitterly and abruptly "I've been discharged . . . Prieto did it."[72]

Before Ignacio and Constancia became communists, Indalecio Prieto had been a great friend of Ignacio's and was even a witness at their wedding; however, political differences had destroyed their friendship. Many years after the war, in 1962, Prieto wrote about his reasons for firing Constancia:

> *During the Civil War, our friendship came to an end, because they had both been drawn to Communism. Her partiality was so appalling that . . . I had Constancia transferred out of her post censoring telegraphic messages to the foreign press.*[73]

For Prieto the real problem was that the communist party was growing too quickly and becoming too powerful. It was because of the party's continued efforts to convert members of the armed forces that he issued a ministerial order on June 28, 1937 "forbidding all propaganda among the air, land, and naval forces aimed at encouraging officers and men to join a specific party or trade-union organization." The order stated "The proposal or mere suggestion by a superior to his inferior that he change his political or trade-union affiliation . . . will be regarded as a coercive act and will result in the demotion of the offender without prejudice to the criminal responsibility he might incur."[74] According to Burnett Bolloten,[75] Constancia had then "refused to allow foreign journalists to send information about Prieto's order abroad". In an interview with Bolloten in Mexico in 1940, Constancia explained the situation: "I had to suppress it . . . because it would have created a bad impression. Prieto forced me to resign."[76]

In her own memoir Mangan says, enigmatically, that in the summer of 1937 Constancia was "under a temporary political cloud herself." She makes no other reference to this "cloud" over Constancia, but she was surely referring to Constancia's censoring of the ministerial order and Prieto's reaction. There is no reference to any part of this episode in *In Place of Splendor*.

Fischer's version of the story fills in more details and suggests that, when forced to choose, Constancia's allegiance lay clearly with the communist party rather than with her own government.

> *Within the Loyalist Cabinet, Prieto and his friends had been engaged in a struggle with the communists to curtail the prerogative of the army's political commissars. Prieto had just succeeded in pushing through a decree to this effect. The press published the decree over his signature and on behalf of the entire cab-*

inet. But when the foreign newspapermen wanted to wire the news abroad, Constancia did not allow it. In other words, she was censoring her own government. She was putting her devotion to the communist party above her duty as a state official. Prieto lifted the telephone, talked with José Giral, and Giral dismissed her.[77]

However, Fischer claims to have been key in having Constancia reinstated. He spoke to Negrín, who said that Prieto had let her off lightly, and that *he* would have had her imprisoned. Fischer argued that though what she had done was unpardonable, she was irreplaceable and he immediately went to see Prieto to convince him to give her back her job. According to Fischer, Prieto said that though he had nothing against Constancia, he was wary of her, because "she is a Maura and like her famous grandfather Don Antonio Maura, Prime Minister of Spain, she is brusque and sometimes hysterical. She does things this way." He threw his arm swiftly from one side of the car to the other and shouted, "Bah, bah. Bah." Constancia may have had a temper, though surely not inherited, but it was her loyalty to the communist party Prieto could not abide. However, one must consider what was worse for the defense of Republic, Constancia's loyalty to the communists, or Prieto's anti-communism? Of his wartime offensive, Helen Graham writes: "Prieto's civil wartime anti-communism in some ways recalls that of his great rival and antagonist, Largo Caballero, in the UGT. Both were fuelled in part by bruised ego and personal political rancour, and both were politically myopic in that they undermined the Republic's ability to resist."[78]

Fischer did everything in his power to help Constancia get back to work in the press office. The journalists she worked with were all willing to sign a petition to have her reinstated, but Fischer worried that this might backfire, and interrupted the signing process because his "experience had been chiefly Russian, and in Moscow an official who had sinned would be endangered by the support of foreign journalists."[79] But after Negrín said that he thought the petition could not hurt her case, Fischer himself signed and got many other correspondents, including the big names such as Ernest Hemingway, to sign as well. A few days later Constancia was back at work. Within months the Minister of Foreign Affairs, José Giral, had promoted her to Bureau Chief.[80]

Ironically, the only detail concerning Fischer's involvement in her reinstatement that Constancia heard about was that he had refused to sign the petition. In fact, she thought that he was personally responsible for having her discharged in the first place. Fischer denied this and told her how he had campaigned to have her reinstated, and how he had signed the petition. Constancia finally said that she believed him, but their friendship was over:

> *Constancia's animosity had a deeper root than her ignorance of my efforts to have her restored to office. The Spanish communists resented my good relations with Negrín, Prieto, Azaña, and other loyalist leaders, and tried to interfere with them. Constancia told American visitors that my friendship with Negrín had been spoiled, and when in May, 1939, I arrived in New York on the Normandie with Negrín, thus giving the lie to such canards, she refused to speak to me. She has not spoken to me since. I had never done her any harm. In fact, despite her hostility towards me, I persuaded del Vayo to take her to Geneva as press aide in May, 1939, because I thought she would be effective there.*[81]

Fischer makes clear that the fact that he was not a communist made him *persona non grata* with Constancia. However, it is interesting to note how close he was to Del Vayo and Negrín.[82] It is possible that Fischer's contact with these leaders, with whom Constancia also worked, was a source of friction and tension. Perhaps she resented a non-party member, and an American, having so much power in Spain.

Burnett Bolloten remembered Constancia well from the press office, however his retrospective portrait of her was undoubtedly colored by his complete disillusionment with the PCE. After the war, he referred to Constancia simply as "the communist censor" and saw her actions as single-mindedly following the party line. He recalled that on one occasion, he had prepared a dispatch to the United Press in which he quoted a passage from a letter from the politburo to the PSOE that urged the fusion of the two parties "as a guarantee of military victory and as the essential prerequisite for the triumph and *consolidation of the popular revolution*." Constancia deleted the italicized phrase because, the Foreign Press Bureau, according to Bolloten, was communist controlled, and those who ran the office including Constancia, worried that the words "popular revolution" were "too radical for moderate opinion abroad."[83]

In another example, Bolloten highlights the power of the NKVD[84] in Valencia, and the significance of Constancia's collaboration with that organization. In June 1937 there was a coup against the POUM in which their headquarters in Barcelona were seized and their leaders, including party secretary Andreu Nin, were arrested. Immediately after these arrests, Bolloten, who at the time was sympathetic to the communist party (though not a member), was handed a communiqué from the director general of security by an NKVD agent. This document stated that the POUM had been involved in a vast conspiracy against the state, and that there was irrefutable evidence of the links between POUM leaders, specifically "N_____" (which Bolloten saw as a reference to Nin) and Franco. The conclusion was that the POUM, far from being a Republican ally, was an organization of spies for the enemy and that they kept Franco agents informed of future military operations.[85]

Bolloten, though doubtful of the document's veracity, saw the fact that it was being circulated as a "scoop" that should be published. He was frustrated, however, that the NKVD agent would not let him cite the director general of security as the source. Bolloten feared that if he did not cite the source, the story might be seen as propaganda and that his own credibility would be damaged. Eager to get the story, he finally agreed to suppress the source, but secretly decided to use it and typed up the story with the following opening line: "The director general of security has issued the following communiqué." He promptly delivered the story to Constancia, who immediately deleted his opening sentence, allowing him only to replace it with a vague "it is stated that . . . "[86]

Years later, Bolloten recounted how this episode revealed the influence the NKVD had on the Foreign Press Office and on Constancia:

> *In looking back at this incident with the benefit of subsequent knowledge, I have reached the following conclusions: (1) the NKVD was anxious to give the maximum publicity through a wire service to the alleged conspiracy . . . (2) the communiqué had not been issued by the director general, as I had been told, but originated in the offices of the NKVD in the Soviet embassy in Valencia, where the incriminating documents were fabricated (3) The Foreign Press Bureau, officially under the control of the ministry of foreign affairs – now occupied by José Giral, a left Republican and loyal friend of President Azaña – was actually controlled by the NKVD through the Spanish communists, who received their guidelines from the headquarters in Valencia . . . Giral . . . must certainly have known Constancia de la Mora's political sympathies when he made her chief of the Foreign Press Bureau a few months later.*[87]

Though suggestive, Bolloten's vision of the NKVD's role in the repression of the POUM may not be entirely accurate. Helen Graham points out that in the aftermath of the May days, the Comintern was more interested in pursuing foreign dissidents than Spaniards, and emphasizes that the order to arrest the POUM came from the police force, and did not originate in the cabinet. Graham also suggests that the violence that is often attributed to the Comintern may in fact have come from the unreformed Spanish police force, which included many army officers. When the POUM's Falangist activities were exposed, they did not hesitate to take apart what they saw as a treacherous, far left organization.[88]

Bolloten's memories of Constancia have much in common with those of

Fischer, Barea, and Prieto. They all give the impression that Constancia was too partisan, and that she was intransigent. So, was Constancia really willing to go to any lengths for the party, or was the image of her as some kind of fanatic simply a put down of the rich girl who was seen as trying to overcompensate for her privileged origins? Had she become a blind ideologue? If Constancia was protecting the communist image within the press office, does that mean that she was involved in other aspects of the party's operations? How far beyond censoring stories did her work go?

By February 1937, after the Republican defeat at Málaga, the position of Premier Francisco Largo Caballero (who had been in power since September 1936) was threatened, and he was eventually replaced by Juan Negrín. In Constancia's version:

> *the Prime Minister whom we had welcomed with such hope in September, 1936, had proved himself a hopelessly ineffective leader by February 9, 1937, the day of the fall of Málaga. Surrounded by the slippery generals of the old military caste who dazzled him with their superficial knowledge of maxim-book military rules, advised by corps of treacherous, boot-licking journalists, old Caballero had by this time succumbed entirely to his childish vanity.*[89]

Constancia had many reasons for disliking Largo Caballero. Ignacio had been involved during the May days in the dismantling of the POUM and FAI organizations. Largo Caballero had accused him of executing members of both groups and of other atrocities.[90] Though Ignacio denied responsibility for anyone's death, Largo Caballero insisted that he be tried. The communists in general were against Largo Caballero because he refused to support the dissolution of the POUM claiming that he was "above all, a worker and would not dissolve a brotherhood of fellow workers."[91] By May 1937, Negrín was made the new premier, and his cabinet included Alvarez del Vayo as Chief Political Commissar and Spanish Representative at Geneva. Constancia was thrilled by Negrín's appointment, which had been supported by the communist party though Negrín was not himself a communist.[92]

Her memoir is filled with praise and heroic anecdotes about Negrín:

> *The new premier believed in democracy – democracy in theory and democracy in methods of government. He came to power without the great popularity Caballero had enjoyed in his first weeks as Prime Minister. But Dr. Negrín had to wait only a few months before he became one of the best-loved men of Spain . . . he was one of the few men in high office in Spain who never for a moment doubted our victory, who trusted the people, who was ready to rely on their heroism – and who was always firm as a rock, calm in the face of disaster. He believed in Spain, we*

knew – for his two eldest sons were in the People's Army, one a pilot in the Air force. There were other Cabinet officials whose sons were conveniently far from the lines. Dr. Negrín, Prime Minister of Spain, asked no more for his sons than that they should have a chance to fight the invaders.[93]

From Constancia's point of view Negrín was an ideal balance. He supported the communists but was not a party member, which would have been both divisive within the Republican side, and damaged the campaign abroad for international aid and intervention. Helen Graham points out that Negrín was the best, perhaps the only, option and that President Azaña and Prieto "were in perfect agreement that the multi-lingual and cosmopolitan Negrín, with a good network of contacts in Europe, was the Republic's international politician *par excellence.*"[94]

Like Mangan, most of the foreigners who worked with Constancia came away with a favorable impression of her as an efficient and charming representative of the Republic. As she says in *In Place of Splendor*, Constancia not only censored articles but provided foreign visitors, when she could, with gasoline, cars, passes to the front, and anything else they might need to move around within Spain. In this regard, she was clearly an immense improvement over her predecessors Rubio and Liston Oak. When, in the midst of the war, the writer Langston Hughes was desperately trying to get from Valencia to Barcelona, he turned to de la Mora for help. His description underscores de la Mora's reputation as the person all foreigners turned to in Spain: "Even Constancia de la Mora, the charming aristocrat in charge of the Government Press Bureau, to whom members of the foreign press appealed for everything, could be of no immediate help to me."[95] Correspondent Philip Jordan wrote: "no one was so kind as Constancia, or took so much trouble to make life easy."[96]

Though almost everyone needed Constancia's permission to get around Spain, Kate Mangan recalls that there were some who simply had carte blanche to do as they pleased, and who did not need any passes, tickets or approval from Constancia. "There were a few visitors who slipped in and out without any visits to the Press Department, who went anywhere they wished and had cars and petrol. These were communists in good standing."[97]

Constancia also developed a longstanding friendship with the American communist Paul Patrick Rogers, a professor at Oberlin College and an observer of the war for an international commission. They met when she made arrangements for him to go to Valencia to a former Jesuit home, the Convento de la Pasionaria, that had become a prison for women.[98] On August 24, 1937 she arranged for a car and chauffer to take Rogers to the prison. Rogers wrote about it in his diary and noted that the "Director received me most kindly and while talking I noticed that the prison doors on the inside of the main building were open and prisoners allowed to receive visits. Among the women in this prison were the sister of Queipo de Llano, the sister of General Millán Astray (Carmen) . . . "[99] However, by the time Rogers left Valencia at the end of August, Constancia had evidently been quite rude to him, probably regarding America's non-intervention policy. Whatever his comments might have been, she lost her temper. Afterwards, she sent him the following brief apology, along with the ticket he had requested to Barcelona:

> *Dear Mr. Rogers: I enclose ticket to Barcelona. Comrade Vicens will give you a little envelope containing the fare from Barcelona to Toulouse as we were unable to get the ticket from here, as you were stopping at Barcelona. I want to excuse myself again for having been, perhaps too outspoken on the subject of some people not realizing the tragedy we are going through. You that realize it only too well, and like yourself many other comrades that have come to Spain will easily find an excuse for my feelings . . . and for having expressed them so abruptly. Hoping to see you back in our country, yours very cordially, Constancia.*[100]

Constancia came to trust Rogers, and in the postwar period, during her exile in Mexico, they would again work in the same circles.

Italian photographer Tina Modotti was another well-known communist woman and close friend of Constancia's, though one would never know this from *In Place of Splendor*. Like Rogers and other communist associates, she is not mentioned. During the Civil War, Modotti worked under an alias and was better known as the legendary "María" of International Red Aid (Socorro Rojo). Their friendship and the many parallels between their lives make them, comparatively, two of the most interesting female characters from the 1930s. Both women went to New York and then Mexico after the war, and their personal ties lasted until Tina's death in 1942.

At the time the war broke out, Tina was married to Vittorio Vidali. Under the pseudonyms of María del Carmen Ruíz Sánchez and Carlos Contreras, the couple worked for the communist party in Spain. "Comandante Carlos" as Vidali was known, had a fearsome reputation and

> *had gained notoriety as the Fifth regiment's political commissar . . . The commissars were no joke . . . serving as guardians of ideological correctness, their task being to stamp out pessimism and disloyalty. An "inspired organizer as well as a ruthless disciplinarian", Vidali was known to charge about with a pistol in each hand, haranguing the undisciplined militia recruits and ferreting out fascist sympathizers.*"[101]

According to then communist minister of education Jesús Hernández,

Vidali was "one of the main executers of the NKVD".[102] He was in charge of the *checkas* (interrogation squads) and his targets were fascists, spies, traitors, deserters, and leftists who weren't committed to Stalin.[103] During the war, Tina became the "virtual doyenne" of Socorro Rojo and, using pseudonyms, wrote articles for the publication *Ayuda*: "Some of these were straight reporting of events, such as solidarity visits by foreign delegations; others were to lay down the party line, such as the article urging parents to comply with an unpopular measure and send their children to Mexico and the Soviet Union."[104] In this respect, Tina's activities were very similar to the propaganda work Constancia was doing. As a letter from 1938 shows, Tina was also working closely with Alvarez del Vayo, Constancia's superior. She had commissioned him to write an article for a special issue she was preparing of the magazine *Nuestro ejercito*. The issue was to appear on July 15, in commemoration of the second anniversary of the start of the war. Most people, including Constancia, addressed Del Vayo formally (*Excelentísimo Sr. Ministro de Estado*) or corresponded with him via his personal secretary, Andrés Barbeito. It is worth noting that Tina began her letters to the minister with "Camarada" and signed simply "María".[105] Modotti's biographer, Margaret Hooks, concludes that though it is suspected that Tina was also a communist spy working in collaboration with Vidali, there is no evidence to support this.[106] In connection with his "more sinister activities, it is not clear whether as a disciplined party member, she simply tolerated them, covered them up or kept quiet about them out of fear."[107]

Constancia's administrative style in the press office was reflected in the weekly meetings she called for her staff. Mangan's account of these peculiar gatherings is important because it provides a description of the political atmosphere within the office itself, and shows how the ministry tried to keep up the staff's morale. It is also interesting to observe how they tried to run the meetings in a way that reflected the democratic and class free society they were trying to achieve:

The politically minded members of the staff {Constancia} used to have meetings once a week in conjunction with some from the propaganda ministry. We used to discuss our work, and suggestions were made for its improvement and various problems were raised. These meetings were held at lunchtime as it was impossible to assemble people who lived far away in the dark evenings. It was a duty to go, if one understood Spanish, though we achieved no positive results, at least everyone could have his say and they kept up our enthusiasm. One discussion was on the endeavour to unionise us all. This was a thorny subject as there were two rival unions, UGT and CNT. Those in favour of the moderate socialist union, UGT,

were in a majority but the CNT advocates were noisier and, at one meeting, one
of them brandished a revolver and we broke up in disorder. We were asked to go
into the fields and help the peasants on Sundays. We seldom had a whole Sunday
off and the local crop, rice, required expert handling . . . These were the strangest
meetings I have ever attended. There was complete equality between office boys and
heads of departments. We listened politely to whoever spoke.[108]

It was at once of these meetings in May 1937 that a thorny matter had
to be discussed. One of the office staff, who Mangan does not name, had
been arrested as a spy. The group was to decide whether or not to lobby for
his release. However, the discussion was cut short because, as usual,
"Constancia took charge of this." Ironically, Mangan's memoir makes clear
that the democratic running of the meetings had its limits, and that when
something important came up Constancia's power was deferred to.

Another tragic episode in Valencia in the spring of 1937 was the disappearance and execution of José Robles. What role Constancia and other
Republican officials had in these events is still a source of controversy that
has recently been revived by Ignacio Martínez de Pisón and in a novelesque
book by Stephen Koch.[109]

Though Spanish, Robles was a professor of literature at Johns Hopkins
University in Baltimore, Maryland. Every year he and his wife Márgara
and his children Coco and Miggie spent the long academic summer
holiday in Spain. In Madrid, he saw old friends including Valle-Inclán,
Ramón J. Sénder, and León Felipe,[110] and engaged in his cherished *tertu-*
lias or literary gatherings in cafés. It was during his summer visit to Spain
in 1936 that the Civil War broke out, and Robles immediately wrote to
Johns Hopkins asking for a leave of absence because he wanted to stay and
help defend the Republic. Robles became an interpreter, because he had
some knowledge of Russian (which he had studied in order to be able to
read Russian literature in the original) and translators were urgently
needed to help the Soviet officials in Spain communicate with Spanish
Republicans. His friends had advised him to return to America where he
could help the Republican cause without putting himself or his family in
danger, but he refused to leave Spain.[111] When the government moved to
Valencia, Robles and his family went along and there he continued to work
for the Soviet Embassy and the Ministry of War. Towards the end of 1936,
he was mysteriously arrested one night at his house by a group of unidentified men dressed in civilian clothes. He was taken to the Cárcel de
Extranjeros (the prison for foreigners), where his wife Márgara was assured
that it was all a mistake and that he would soon be cleared. But shortly
afterwards he disappeared and though his influential friends appealed to

both the Spanish and North American governments to find out his where-abouts and to secure his release, he was never heard of again. Robles's son Coco was working at the Foreign Press Bureau under Rubio Hidalgo and Constancia. Everyone was very fond of Coco Robles and Kate Mangan worked closely with him:

> *In the mornings we had to go through all the newspapers and magazines, Coco and I, and pick out bits suitable for translation. We had not the faintest idea what to pick but used to read things aloud in English to give Poppy an idea of what articles were about and she would seize on something and say "That would make a good story, translate that." We would do that and then she would edit it but soon she would let me write my own stories and she re-wrote Coco's. She did not know about politics only about news value but all our stuff was censored anyway. Later they trusted us and we sent out stuff almost without censorship and, occasionally, got into trouble afterwards . . . .we worked from ten to two and four to eight including Saturdays and Sundays, and sometimes longer . . . I often came back at three to work alone when I had a long speech or anything else to do. La Pasionaria, Uribe, Hernández, and Jose Díaz made a lot of fine, long speeches.*[112]

After his father's disappearance, Coco continued to work at the press office, and one day towards the end of February 1937 Rubio Hidalgo suddenly informed Coco that his father was dead.[113] Apparently, he had been accused of being a spy and a traitor to the Republic and had been executed.[114] But there was still no official word.

In April, the American writer John Dos Passos arrived in Valencia. He and Robles had been close friends ever since they met on a train in Spain in 1919. Dos Passos had always been an admirer of Spain, and when the war broke out he was, like Robles, a dedicated supporter of the Republic. He tried to rally the American government to intervene in Spain, and in April he arrived in Valencia to work on the documentary "The Spanish Earth" in collaboration with Hemingway and Joris Ivens. Dos Passos was anxious to see his old friend Robles and the news of his disappearance shocked and troubled him:

> *When I asked for him (Robles) in Valencia faces took on a strange embarrass-ment. Behind the embarrassment was fear. No one would tell me where he could be found. When at last I found his wife she told me. He had been arrested by some secret section or other and was being held for trial. I started on a new round of the officials. All right, if the man is being held for trial, what was he being accused of? . . . {I} knew that there was no possible doubt of his devotion to the cause of the Republic. How about arranging an interview with him so that I could help him with his defense? Again the runaround, the look of fear, fear for their*

own lives, in the faces of Republican officials. In the end I learned the truth. He had been shot. The higher-ups at Valencia tried to make me believe that he had been kidnapped and killed by anarchist "uncontrollables." It wasn't until I got to Madrid that I learned from the chief of the Republican counterespionage service that my friend had been executed by a "special section." He added that in his opinion the execution had been a mistake and that it was too bad. Spaniards closer to the communists I talked to said the man had been shot as an example because he had been overheard indiscreetly discussing military plans in a café. The impression I came away with was that the Russians had him put out of the way because he knew too much about the negotiations between the War ministry and the Kremlin and was not, from their point of view, politically reliable. [115]

Dos Passos portrays a Valencia that was dominated by communists and where people lived in fear. His efforts to get to the bottom of Robles' arrest and death were fruitless, for there seemed to be a tacit agreement that questions should not be asked:

Some of my associates in the documentary film project were disgusted with me for making all these inquiries. What's one man's life at a time like this? . . . I remembered Carlo Tresca's warning words, the communists were liquidating every man they couldn't dominate . . . By the time I left the country there was no doubt in my mind that my friend was no exception . . . [116]

Dos Passos tried repeatedly to appeal to Minister of Foreign Affairs Alvarez del Vayo to have Robles's disappearance investigated, but he claimed ignorance and dismissed the inquiries with vague promises of finding out the truth. By May 2, 1937, horrified by what he saw as the communist takeover of the Republic, Dos Passos had left Spain, taking a terrified Liston Oak with him. He also abandoned the "Spanish Earth" project, a decision that would end his friendship with Hemingway who saw Dos Passos as unfairly deserting the Republic.

In the meantime, Robles' son Coco was by now supporting his family by working with Constancia in the Foreign Press Office. His activities in the office did not include censorship, because he was very young, and according to Martínez de Pisón this task was given only to those whose communist allegiance was beyond doubt. [117] His mother Márgara also started to work in the office after Robles's disappearance. According to her memoir, Constancia was very fond of Márgara and her children and emphasized that they could have left Spain after José's disappearance, but that they stayed out of loyalty to the Spanish Republic, unlike others. *In Place of Splendor* makes only one reference to Coco and his father. Constancia had assigned Coco to accompany journalist Elliot Paul on a trip to Madrid, and

Paul later told her about the following conversation he had had with Coco:

> *One night Paul began to talk about a writer he knew – John Dos Passos. Dos Passos had visited Spain a few days before Elliot Paul came to my office. His time in Spain was very brief and he left suddenly. I felt that he had hardly stayed long enough to understand the war, but we could not do more than we did for him. "I don't know what has come over Dos Passos," Elliot Paul said to Coco one night. "I saw him in Paris and he won't even take an interest in Spain any more. He is full of some story about a friend of his being shot as a spy, some college professor from Johns Hopkins." Coco regarded Elliot Paul gravely, his great black eyes unwavering. "I hope that will not make Mr. Dos Passos lose his interest in the fight against fascism in Spain. The man he spoke of was my father."*[118]

Elliot Paul was impressed by the boy's bravery, and Constancia agreed praising his commitment to the cause and saying that "What John Dos Passos could not forgive the Spanish people, the man's wife and two children understood."[119] What exactly did Constancia mean by this? That the family understood there were some things one simply could not ask? Or that they felt that José's disappearance was justified in some way by the greater cause of the war effort? Kate Mangan also saw Coco's reaction to his father's death, and she presents quite a different image of his son's response:

> *After his father's death Coco was crushed and wretched, so ashamed he never spoke of it. He gave up his future at that point. He resigned from the communist Youth. He had been destined for the diplomatic service. He was very intelligent and was learning Russian with a view to going to Russia. During the time he remained in Valencia he devoted himself to being the man of the family and taking care of his mother and little sister . . . at sixteen (Coco) volunteered for the militia. He went to the front and disappeared forever.*[120]

It would be interesting to be able to compare Constancia's interpretation of Robles' disappearance with Dos Passos', but she says nothing more about the episode, an omission that is all the more notable because she worked closely on a daily basis with both Robles' widow and son. There were, of course, many "disappearances" but Robles was well known and connected to the group of foreigners Constancia worked with. The image of his wife and children wandering around Valencia searching for him haunted people's memories. It is most likely that Constancia did not casually omit this incident, but that she suppressed it because she knew more about it than she wanted to admit. Martínez de Pisón concludes that Coco and Márgara both *enjoyed the affectionate treatment they got from Constancia de la Mora and the protection of Alvarez del Vayo. The amount of attention he (del Vayo) lavished on the Robles is, to some degree, suspicious, and can only be explained as being the result of some kind of remorse or feelings of guilt. His inability to save the life of the head of their family must have still weighed on his conscience.*[121]

Though del Vayo often invited Márgara to his home, he never helped her obtain the one thing she needed: a death certificate for Robles. This would have enabled her to claim his life insurance and get the money to leave Spain with her children.[122]

According to one account cited by Martínez de Pisón, by June of 1937, "everyone in the press office knew that José Robles Pazos had been murdered by agents of the Soviet Secret Police."[123] Yet nobody in the office, with the exception of one American journalist identified only as "Poppy", even spoke out against the incident. Mangan recalled that:

Coco's father was working very closely with the Russians as an interpreter and was engaged in rather hush-hush work. What happened remained a mystery; it was inexplicable but it leaked out despite efforts to hush it up on the part of our communist friends. The only person who dared create a loud scene about it was Poppy. It was obvious that our Spanish colleagues {this would have included Constancia} were miserable and quite helpless to do anything about it. Robles was arrested as a spy by the secret police and, after a short time, executed.[124]

In her memoir of the Spanish Civil War, writer and then *New York Post* correspondent Josephine Herbst recalls how those around her were intent on hushing up the Robles case:

Hemingway . . . invited me to his room for a snifter of brandy. But what he really wanted was to urge me to talk to Dos Passos and to tell him to lay off making inquiries about Robles. It was going to throw suspicion on all of us and get us in trouble. (Luis) Quintanilla, the head of the Department of Justice, had assured Dos that Robles would get a fair trial . . . His request was terribly disturbing. I had known all along that Robles had been shot as a spy. I had been in Valencia before coming to Madrid and there had been told, in strictest confidence, and for the reason that Dos Passos was an old friend of mine, that the man was dead . . . The trouble was that I had sworn to keep this secret, just as my informant had been sworn by someone higher up. But the circumstances seemed to me more pressing than any promise.[125]

Was it Constancia who told Herbst that Robles had been killed? After Herbst revealed to Hemingway that Robles had been shot, they both went to give Dos Passos the bad news. Dos Passos wanted to know who had told

Herbst, but she would not tell him. She simply advised him to speak to Alvarez del Vayo when he returned to Valencia. Constancia liked and trusted Herbst, and saw her regularly. It is possible that she may have confided in her.[126] Alvarez del Vayo was Constancia's direct superior, and as Herbst's informant had been sworn to secrecy by someone higher up, it is logical that she would send Dos Passos to talk directly to Alvarez del Vayo so as not to jeopardize Constancia.

The full story of Robles's death was never completely clarified. According to Martínez de Pisón, some people (such as Joris Ivens) believed that Robles had been rightly punished for sending messages to the Franco side, while others thought he had simply been too free about the information he worked with and that he had unwittingly let something slip in one of his café *tertulias*.[127] One could also argue that there is no proof whatsoever that Robles was killed by communists. Martínez de Pisón concludes that Robles was a pawn in an internal NKVD power game and that his arrest and death were not punishments for anything he had actually done, but a warning. He may or may not have let information slip, but he had found himself in a vulnerable position. He was not a communist, and perhaps his work with Soviet officials meant that he had become "the man who knew too much." Martínez de Pisón agrees with Dos Passos that Robles's disappearance was used to enforce Soviet power in Valencia, and that it had "the desired effect of making people extremely careful when they spoke of the Russians."[128]

Did Del Vayo and Constancia, as Martínez de Pisón says, cover up his murder and then bend over backwards to keep Coco and Márgara and quiet? What, if anything, did Constancia know about Robles' disappearance and the following cover-up of his execution? Was she assigned by Del Vayo to mollify Márgara and Coco to divert suspicion? Did she think that Robles had been unjustly killed but felt impotent to do anything about it? Or did she consider that whatever the party did to one individual was a just mean to a collective end? Martínez de Pisón raises all of the above provocative questions, but he does not answer them with any evidence. In any case, as we will see later, Robles disappearance would come back to haunt Constancia in the summer of 1939 in New York.

Much better known than the Robles case was the other notorious episode that has become associated with Constancia and Ignacio's names: the assassination of Andreu Nin. In June 1937, in an anti-POUM coup, the party's political secretary Nin was kidnapped by a group said to be working under orders of Alexander Orlov, who ran the NKVD in Spain.[129]

Comintern agents imprisoned and sometimes assassinated dissident communists, most infamously in the case of the POUM leader Andreu Nin. The especially brutal treatment meted out to Nin was bound up with his dissidence being perceived as a betrayal from the inner circle. (Nin had lived in the Soviet Union throughout the 1920s and was an executive member of the Red International of Labor Unions. In 1926 he had joined the left opposition acting for a time as Trotsky's secretary.)[130]

Nin was arrested in Barcelona and eventually taken to a prison in Alcalá de Henares where he was not officially registered. From there he was taken to a house in the same town which had allegedly been the home of Ignacio and Constancia. It was here that Nin was tortured.[131] Wilebaldo Solano emphasizes the fact that this was the home of Constancia who, he says, was "closely linked to the Russian Secret Service."[132] Pierre Broué also implicates Constancia and Ignacio in Nin's murder, and refers to them as "those characters of Spanish high society, won over by Stalinism, who were the accomplices (of the Moscow agents) and the owners of the house where the assassination took place: Constancia de la Mora Maura and Hidalgo de Cisneros y López de Montenegro."[133]

As in the case of José Robles, although Constancia's name appears connected to Nin's kidnapping and torture, there is nothing to suggest that either she or Ignacio had any direct involvement in what befell him.[134] It is possible that because of the couple's prominent position in the communist party, the kidnappers had access to Ignacio's house in Alcalá. In their respective memoirs, neither Constancia nor Ignacio mentions Nin's name or his death. These are surely suspicious omissions, and the hostility Constancia expresses towards the POUM in her memoir seems to be implicitly a continuing attack on Nin, and perhaps even a veiled justification of his murder. Throughout her book, Constancia's attacks on those she saw as traitors are merciless, and she had no doubt in her mind that the POUM party was filled with Franco accomplices:

Franco's "Fifth Column" operated more powerfully in Catalonia than anywhere else in Spain. Disguised as ultra-revolutionaries, these fascist spies flocked into Barcelona, mouthing left phrases, talking of overthrowing capitalism, all the while they sapped the strength of the Republican rear-guard. The fight against fascism in Spain required three things from Catalonia: food, grown by the peasants; armaments, manufactured by the workers; and disciplined volunteers for the army. But the Trotskyites who acted as Franco agents, working through a political party called the POUM, wormed their way into high places.[135]

In October 1937 Republican headquarters were moved to Barcelona, and in November the press office was relocated. By the time it was operating in Barcelona, the office had been completely transformed and was a striking contrast to the amateur understaffed enterprise run by Rubio Hidalgo and Liston Oak at the beginning of the war. The government's decision to replace Rubio Hidalgo with Constancia may again have had something to do with Louis Fischer, who seems to have been a key behind the scenes advisor. On November 9, 1938 Fischer wrote to Negrín pointing out the urgent need to improve the relationship between the Republican side and the foreign press. Fischer saw clearly that the dry communiqués to the press that the government had relied on were never going to sway public opinion abroad, and that it was crucial that a massive international public relations campaign be launched on behalf of the Republic. The correspondents needed to be given access to the front, as well as much more information on a regular basis, including

> *A weekly survey of the military situation written by, say, Cruz Salido or some other good journalist. This is to be published in the Agence Espagne and simultaneously given to all foreign correspondents in Spain. It should deal not only with battles but with the question of our reserves, with the progress of war industries and with events behind Franco's lines. A comparison should be made with the past so that outsiders can see the progress and can view the whole situation in a perspective which is almost altogether lacking here.*[136]

An exceptional person needed to take charge of the foreign press department in Barcelona, someone who knew languages, had experience abroad, and who would be a liaison between the press and Negrín and Prieto. Most importantly perhaps, whoever was running the office had to be well liked by the correspondents. Though other candidates were considered, Constancia clearly fit the profile, and when chosen she took on her new post with zeal.

She later remembered how "The correspondents filled my office. My staff grew to include fifty-two people, mostly women . . . Everyone in the office worked with one thing in mind – to win the war."[137] The unlikelihood of a woman occupying such a high political rank is underlined by Constancia's letterhead. Her name is incongruous combined with the masculine title of "*El* Jefe de la Oficina de Prensa Extranjera de la Subsecretaría de Propaganda" and the embossed greeting is also designed for a male signer, and reads "Constancia de la Mora aprovecha gusto*o* esta ocasión para expresarle el testimonio de su consideración más distinguida."[138] The few surviving examples of her correspondence as "Jefe" show that throughout the fall of 1938 she continued to work closely with Alvarez del Vayo, and with his secretary Andrés Barbeito on propaganda matters. For example, when K. Scott Watson,[139] the correspondent of the *Daily Herald* in Spain, wrote directly to Alvarez del Vayo to ask for the "facilities given to a correspondent here" including "a personal interview with" the Minister of State himself, Alvarez del Vayo simply scrawled an initialed note in the margin saying "For Constancia de la Mora".[140] Her time was largely devoted to matters such as these, fielding all interview requests and having journalists vetted before giving them accreditation. She was also a press liaison between the ministry and the Spanish embassies abroad. For instance, when Father Leocadio Lobo, who was one of the few clergymen to side with the Republic and was active in *America* Magazine's Spanish Relief Organization, prepared a letter to the *Times* to set the story straight on the role of the church in the war in Spain, it was first sent to Constancia. She then sent it to Alvarez del Vayo for approval, after which it was returned to the Press Office, signed by Lobo, and finally sent to the Spanish Embassy via diplomatic pouch and from there to the *Times*.[141]

Though Ignacio was of a famously cool temperament, the pressures of the war had taken their toll on his health. Shortly after the move to Barcelona, he had a stroke. Sleepless nights, chain-smoking, and worrying about the fall of Republican strongholds, the lack of military supplies, and traitors in the army and air force had worn him down. His doctor recommended a change of climate and Ignacio and Constancia decided to go to the Soviet Union because, Constancia said, "No other country in Europe could cure Ignacio, I knew"![142] Every aspect of their Soviet experience is described in *In Place of Splendor* in the most positive light, and the trip allowed Constancia to see Luli for the first time in a year and a half. She was delighted to discover that her daughter was speaking Russian, German and Italian and praised the conditions in which she and the other Spanish children lived and how well looked after they were.

Once Ignacio had recovered, they returned to Barcelona in February 1938. That spring was an especially tragic period for the Republic and Constancia was overwhelmed by the massive bombings going on directly outside her office, and the news of Nationalist victories all over Spain:

> *Day after day I had to sit behind my desk, looking calm and cheerful for my visitors. I could not be less heroic than the Spanish people. It would have been a pleasure to scream . . . Correspondents drifted into my office, wanting news from the front, or just nothing in particular . . . I was more afraid of flying glass than a bomb. The glass would blind you; after the bomb, there would be nothing at all to worry about.*[143]

Though the Nationalists seemed to be advancing from every direction, and many were giving the Republic up for lost, Negrín continued to rally Republican Spain to resist.

In May 1938, Alvarez del Vayo gave Constancia a new assignment. She was going to accompany him to Geneva when Spain made its appeal to the League of Nations. First, they wanted to show the world that Republican Spain was still standing and functional, and they also hoped to have the arms embargo overturned. Del Vayo called on the League of Nations to end the British led "Non-Intervention" committee, which, from his point of view, only served "as a convenient mask for the invasion of Spain by Italy and Germany".[144] Constancia saw that while nobody questioned Del Vayo's stand, neither did anyone rally to support him:

> *Of course Spain was being invaded by Germany and Italy. Of course. And what rude, uncouth fellows we were to even bring the unfortunate matter up. And the Halifax steam-roller worked. The vote on the resolution was four to two: England, France, Poland, and Roumania voted "no"; Spain and the Soviet Union voted "yes". Nine members of the Council abstained. Immediately afterwards the American government, following in the wake of England, refused to lift the embargo on arms to Spain.*[145]

Towards the end of 1938, she and Ignacio made a second trip to the Soviet Union. This is another significant episode that Ignacio recounts in his memoir, but that Constancia makes no reference to in *In Place of Splendor*. In December 1938, Negrín sent Ignacio on an urgent mission to Moscow to secure armaments, accompanied by Constancia and air force Colonel Manuel Arnal. Ignacio gives a detailed account of the couple's evening at the Kremlin, including the unforgettable expression on Constancia's face when Stalin, Molotov, and Vorochilov rose to greet her in the Kremlin dining room. He was also impressed by how much Stalin knew about one of his ancestors, the last viceroy of Argentina, and how the Soviet leader patiently taught Constancia to debone the fish they were served. From Ignacio's account, one is struck by the intimacy and relative informality with which Stalin received them. It is easy to see why this evening would have been left out of a book written to curry American favors in 1939.

Ignacio himself admits he was surprised that he had been chosen for this assigment. The quantities of armaments Negrín demanded seemed preposterous to him: two hundred and fifty planes, two hundred tanks, four thousand machine guns, and so forth. Daniel Kowalsky highlights the strange nature of this diplomatic mission, and the fact that it should not have fallen to Ignacio:

At no time was the embassy's low status and almost complete emasculation more painfully evident than during Ignacio Hidalgo de Cisneros' December 1938 emergency visit to Moscow. The Republican government had dispatched its air force chief to the Soviet capital in a desperate attempt to secure fresh military hardware from the Russians. It need hardly be underlined that the purpose of this mission might have easily been executed by a competent and operational embassy. Indeed, Cisneros' task was identical to that with which Pascua had earlier been charged.[146]

Negrín had given Ignacio personal letters of introduction to Stalin, Kalinin, and Vorochilov, authorizing him to make any decision he saw fit in the name of the Spanish government. It was clear that if the arms were not sent to Spain, the consequences would be disastrous. According to Ignacio, he simply presented the long list of arms the Republic wanted in his meeting at the Kremlin. To his surprise, the Soviets agreed and told Ignacio he was to speak to the Soviet Commerce Minister, Mikoyan, the next day to work out the details, even though the total bill ran to $103 million and in the Spanish Republic's gold reserves in Moscow there was less than $100,000 left.

The Soviet government agreed to ship the armaments on credit, and the only guarantee they asked for was Ignacio's signature.[147] Ignacio was moved by the trust of the Soviets and their commitment to help, and because of this his views of the Soviets never changed. Even in the mid 1960s, he remained loyal and concluded that:

Between then and now, all the complexity of Stalin's personality has come to light . . . Nevertheless, I want to reiterate here my conviction that the Soviet Union's position vis-à-vis *the Spanish Republic during the Civil War was one of complete solidarity and support . . . The Soviet leaders received me with the same affection that the Soviet people everywhere showed to the Spanish people and their cause.*[148]

Helen Graham points out that in his memoir Ignacio exaggerates "the significance of his trip"; that "we certainly cannot assume the accuracy of Hidalgo de Cisneros' claim that a one hundred million dollar loan was agreed, virtually over dinner"; and that" As Marcelino Pascua, Republican ambassador in Moscow, indicated, previous Soviet credits had always been negotiated by Negrín personally through formal diplomatic channels, and there is no reason to suppose that it was any different in the last months of 1938." Ignacio's trip may have been important, but according to Graham, only for the following reasons: as a "way of underlining the urgency of Negrín's – independent – request . . . as a kind of 'diplomatic semaphore' to Britain and France that the Republic intended to continue resisting", or to "stay the PCE's diminishing belief in Negrín's own commitment to resistance."

Back in Barcelona, while waiting for the Soviet shipments to arrive, on January 3, 1939 Constancia had received orders from the undersecretary of her department that she was to pack the office up and leave for France. She says she did her best to make sure her staff would get out of Barcelona safely.

The Republican exodus to France was one of the most harrowing and chaotic experiences of the war. That Constancia kept her staff working up until the very last minute is corroborated by Irene Falcón who recalls that on the same day they planned to leave Barcelona, her sister Kety, who worked in the press office, had been sent by Constancia to the Vorochilov barracks in Barcelona on an agitprop mission. By the time she got back to the office, the section chiefs were busy getting their passports in order to cross the border. Kety panicked as she tried to get herself and her mother out of the city. The car that was supposed to pick them up – which she says belonged to Ignacio's friend Sánchez Arcas – never showed up. Apparently, the chauffeur had disappeared. Negrin's secretary, Benigno Rodriguez, came to the rescue with his own chauffeured car, but by the time they set out the roads had been closed off. Kety's mother's only option was to go back to Madrid, where another daughter, Carmen, lived. Soon afterwards, Carmen was arrested for working for Negrín, and Kety's mother, left alone, became gravely ill and died.[149] This is the story Irene Falcón recounts in her memoir, but Kety remembered another version, one that involves Constancia.

Kety told Dolores Ibárruri that Constancia instructed her to wait at home, with her mother, until Constancia came to pick them up to take them across the border. They were not to leave, under any circumstances, until Constancia's arrival. They waited and waited for her, but she never showed up. Whether Constancia simply could not get there or make arrangements for someone else to do so, she failed to send Kety a message telling her to find an alternate means of leaving Spain. Because she and her mother followed Constancia's instructions and relied on her, they attempted to leave Barcelona too late. There are many possible reasons why Constancia might not have been able to go to her friends or communicate with them, but in Kety's mind, her mother's death would always be linked to Constancia's negligence.[150]

Constancia and Ignacio got to a house near the border and waited to cross into France. According to Ignacio, though the Soviet arms had been loaded onto seven supply ships headed towards French ports, the French put up all kinds of delays and they did not arrive in Spain in time.[151] In hindsight, Ignacio blamed the French for the delays, but at the time Constancia had other theories. Enrique Castro Delgado, the founder and first commander of the Fifth regiment and one of the leaders of the Spanish communist party remembers meeting Constancia and Ignacio (and an unnamed Soviet advisor) at the house where they stayed en route to Perpignan in February, 1939. Castro was alone with Constancia with whom he had the following conversation about the end of the war:

> Constancia: *"Is it bad?" she asked.*
> Castro: *"It's the end of a stage, Constanza (sic)."*
> Constancia: *"Why"*
> Castro: *"They are stronger than we are."*
> Constancia: *"Better?"*
> Castro: *"No, just stronger."*
> *And there was a long pause, and when she broke the silence, Castro learned something that he had suspected many times, but that he had never been able to confirm:*
> Constancia: *"Why didn't Stalin send us what he promised the general?"*
> Castro: *"Promised what general, Constanza (sic)?"*
> Constancia: *"Hidalgo de Cisneros . . . Yes, we were in Moscow by orders of Negrín . . . And the General spoke to Stalin. And Vorochilov and Molotov were there."*
> Castro: *"And? . . . "*
> Constancia: *"Hidalgo complained that the Russian comrades that work with us were accusing us of waging a very expensive war."*
> Castro: *"And what did Comrade Stalin reply to that?"*
> Constancia: *"First he smiled. Then he looked at Vorochilov, who also smiled . . . Then he answered in his style: to the point, and said: 'Your war is a very inexpensive war . . . Very inexpensive! . . . So inexpensive and so important that we will continue to send you everything you need. Whatever you need! Our advisors are wrong . . . . What do they know about what's expensive or not? General, tell president Negrín that our help will be enough for you to win the war . . . .'* Why hasn't he kept his promise? Could he have tricked us, Castro?"
> Castro: *"Stalin never tricks anyone, at least not communists."*[152]

Though it is impossible to know how much of this remembered dialogue is true or not, it is easy to imagine that Constancia would have felt extremely anxious at this point. She had spent two and a half years fruitlessly campaigning to engage the allies in the Republican defense. The Soviet shipments of arms were the last hope Spain had.

At the same time that Constancia and the rest of Republican Spain were frantically waiting for the ships to arrive, Prime Minister Negrín was pressing the Soviets for explanations. They, in turn, were planning their diplomatic response, as shown by the following memorandum, dated February 16, 1939 from Voroshilov to Stalin:

> *Negrín through Pascua*[153] *is trying to get an answer to his additional request for the delivery of arms for the Republican army. I would suppose that it is necessary to give directives to our people that in case Pascua or other people turn to them about aid with weapons it is necessary to answer, for example, the following:*
> *1. The USSR has always treated the needs of the Spanish government with benevolence and met, as far as possible, their requests for aid with weapons and other fighting resources in a timely fashion.*
> *2. The latest request of the Spanish government for the sale of arms, which was announced through Cisneros, was, to a significant degree, met by us and if the Spanish government could not agree with the French government about the timely transfer of these arms to Spain than we can only deplore that.*
> *3. To demand new deliveries of arms for Spain at the present time, when the weapons already supplied by us in enormous quantities are in the territory of France and risk falling into the hands of the French fascists as trophies, is, at the very least, inopportune.*[154]

All was lost for the Republic by this point. Gerald Howson mentions that that there is a scribble by Stalin in the margin of the memo: "This question is no longer important."[155] Howson also points out that a mere eleven days later the British and French legally recognized the Franco regime. In the meantime, however, a desperate Negrín continued to urge the Spanish people to hold out for the delivery of the Soviet armaments.

It has since been established that though the vast majority of the material never arrived to Republican hands, it had in fact been shipped as promised:

> *Archival documents indicate that the Soviets quickly dispatched to the Republic a shipment of weapons valued at $55,359,660. These arms included 40 T-26 tanks, 134 aircraft of various types, 15 torpedo boats with 30 torpedoes, 359 artillery guns with 1,382,540 shells, 3,000 machine guns, 40,000 rifles with 100 million cartridges, and 1,350 tons of gunpowder. M. S. Shumilov, a Soviet advisor who oversaw the reception of the arms in France, confirms Cisneros' claim that the transfer was carried out by seven ships, and that all of these sailed from Murmansk via the North Sea to French ports.*[156]

Just before the fall of Cataluña, Ignacio and the rest of the air force officials crossed the border into France, under government orders. The conditions of the makeshift camps the Spaniards were assigned to were abominable. Constancia was horrified by the way the French government treated the Spanish refugees, an issue that would continue to concern her in the postwar period. She used her power to help those that she could, including war hero General Enrique Líster (famous for his role in the Battle of Guadalajara) and his family. During the evacuation, Líster had been separated from his wife and daughter who had just missed being interned at the women's camp at Le Bolou. Líster credited Constancia for arranging their reunion and for directing them to go to the Hotel Regina in Toulouse where the Spanish Politburo was meeting.[157]

Constancia set up a press office in Perpignan, and during her final press conference in France, she tried to defend the Republic against the rumors that they were ready to surrender. When asked by a correspondent if President Azaña, himself already in France, would be returning to Madrid, Constancia panicked as she imagined headlines reading "Azaña deserts Republican cause". Though she was furious with Azaña for not returning to Spain, she defended him by saying that he was carrying on absolutely necessary talks with the French and British Governments and that it was essential that he remain in France.[158]

A year and a half before the exodus to France, Constancia had helped her English colleague Kate Mangan and her wounded lover Jan Kurzke leave Spain. In her memoir, Mangan looks back with sadness at the work she had done, and their hope that they could change the minds of the non-intervening countries:

> *I did not feel too bad about quitting just then. I was still naïve enough to believe that propaganda was effective and that my job was useful to the cause. I now know that issues of war and peace and commerce are manipulated by a very few people without regard for public opinion and very little for governments. War is made first and patriotism whipped up afterwards. Decisions are made, then a publicity campaign to reconcile the public to them. Now I am cynical enough to see the futility of protest. However, I thought our work was important then.*[159]

But Constancia had not given up, even in the early spring of 1939. She was asked by Negrín to go to the United States to make a last effort to convince America to send more food and, more importantly, to finally lift the embargo and send arms to Spain. The only official description of her mission to New York is in the Comintern archive and says that before the fall of Catalonia she was sent to the United States to work for the benefit of the Spanish Popular Front.[160] On February 20, 1939, she and Ignacio split up. As his Douglas transport plane took off to fly in the dark over rebel territory back to Madrid, Constancia set off to Paris and then Le Havre to take the boat to New York. As she left, she did not yet know when or how she would see Ignacio or Luli again. She certainly had no idea that what she had planned as a brief diplomatic trip would be the beginning of a permanent exile, and that she would never set foot in her country again.

III
Mission to New York
Propaganda and Diplomacy

---

*The Government decided to make a last effort to convince
America to send more food – and arms, arms! – to help the
Spanish people. We had to tell our friends in America that the fight
was not over, the central zone could be defended. Spain still lived.
I was chosen to take this message and this appeal to the United States.*[1]

In Place of Splendor

In February 1939, Constancia de la Mora was chosen to go to New York on
a diplomatic mission representing the Negrín government. Hidalgo de
Cisneros stayed behind in France. Though she had never been to America
before, she was welcomed by the Communist elite and was hailed as the
"darling of the New York progressives."[2] She soon became well connected
amongst society leftists and liberals through the many American journalists and cultural figures she had met in Spain. The relationships she forged
would have a dramatic impact on her life. It is important to understand the
atmosphere in which she moved in New York, because *In Place of Splendor*
was in important ways a product of the context in which she found herself
in the spring and summer of 1939.

Constancia's reputation had preceded her and many New Yorkers were
eager to meet the model for the bust that sculptor Jo Davidson had shown
in the exhibit "Spanish Portraits" at the Arden Gallery on Park Avenue on
November 19, 1938. Since the 1920s, the prolific Davidson had been
famous for his portraits of the powerful and talented, including his figures
of Franklin D. Roosevelt, Mahatma Gandhi, and Albert Einstein; and in the
summer of 1938, Davidson had done a series of Spanish Republican figures
(including Manuel Azaña, Alvarez del Vayo, General José Miaja, and an
"unnamed peasant refugee from Old Castille") in order to show in the
United States. Constancia and *Pasionaria* were the only women in this
series.[3]

Davidson had insisted on using Constancia as a model, and yet the bust
he made of her is surprisingly unflattering. She looks a number of years older

than she was and her face is grim and austere. In fact, she looks remarkably like the famously severe and plain female farmer figure in Grant Wood's "American Gothic". She herself noted that "I must have looked very tired to Davidson, whose beautifully modeled head of me makes me seem an ascetic."[4] One reviewer wrote that "Davidson's head of this handsome woman is not a fortunate piece of work. Of colored terracotta, it has something of the feeling of an Egyptian ceramic, but the mask like appearance of the face is not pleasing."[5] After closing at the Arden Gallery, the show was moved in January 1939 to the Whyte Gallery in Washington, D.C. In both cities the show was held as a benefit for the Spanish Children's Milk Fund, chaired by Dorothy Parker. The exhibit had been reviewed in the *The New York Times* and *The Washington Post* and was effective in bringing attention to the Republican cause. In Parker's words, from the exhibit's catalogue:

Many things can happen in a few years. There was Spain about which no one thought much until the Spanish people had to fight, not in a civil war but against an invasion; not for lands and revenues and power; not to abolish anybody's God, but for their lives – and more than their lives: for the right to live those lives in decency.[6]

The show was also successful in promoting Constancia, largely because of the extremely complimentary piece Elliot Paul wrote about her in the catalogue. This is also one of the only published descriptions of Constancia's role in the war and was effective publicity for the Republican cause and *In Place of Splendor*. Paul's piece was key in paving the way for her arrival in New York, and the later success of her book.

"Constancia will attend to that." In Madrid, Valencia or Barcelona, wherever the Spanish Government has made its headquarters since the war began, that phrase has been a watchword. Think of Constancia as a young wife and mother whose husband is almost constantly flying in combat, whose child is in a foreign country far distant from her so that she may be wholly free to do this job, whose friends are working feverishly or dying nobly, whose country is in peril. Think of her working calmly night and day in the midst of the most barbarous bombardments, supplying what her country and her ideals need most desperately, a steady patience and efficiency. I knew Constancia in Madrid in the early days of the Republic. To her, the Republic was what it should have been to all of Spain. For Constancia – she was Connie then to us all – was by birth of the Old Spain . . . Constancia had never been susceptible to their reactionary ideas and she had seen clearly through the muddled thinking of the others who were balanced between two irreconcilable schools of thought. But life was not easy for her in that cobwebby world. It was, in fact, very hard. Then came the Republic

and release . . . I think of Constancia then, of her incredible beauty and of her dignity that is a part of all Spanish beauty . . . This piece is about Constancia and her own legend . . . She was one who was prepared, like few others, to face the present war, for she knew too well the selfishness and fanaticism of the former ruling class and cast her lot with the people long before the firing began . . . One hears more about Pasionaria because Dolores' work keeps her constantly in the public eye. The opposite is true of Constancia and the work she does. Outside of Spain it has seldom been mentioned. Even when the whole heroic story of the fight for democracy can be told, much of Constancia's contribution will be overlooked.[7]

In New York, Constancia at first stayed at the home of Martha Dodd Stern and her husband, the wealthy Albert Kaufman Stern. Martha's father had been US ambassador to Germany from 1933 to 1938. In Hitler's Germany, Martha had learned, albeit rather slowly, something about European politics. Though she began by admiring Hitler and his ideas, she eventually saw the magnitude of the Nazi threat and became attracted to communism. By the time Constancia arrived in New York, Martha Dodd and her husband had strong left-wing sympathies and were happy to give shelter to Spanish Republicans.

Although perhaps neither woman would have appreciated the comparison, there were certain parallels between the lives of Constancia and Martha Dodd. They were roughly the same age (Martha was born in 1908), from wealthy powerful families, and had become Communist sympathizers through the men in their lives. Though Martha had married Stern, the most important man in her life had been the Soviet diplomat Boris Vinogradov. What Dodd did not know was that Vinogradov had been used by the NKVD to "draw Martha into our work."[8] As women who were well educated as well as socially and politically connected, Constancia and Martha were considered ideal assets to the left.

Dodd became a "talent spotter" for the Russians, identifying potential agents from her large group of international friends. The benefits of Dodd to the party were counterbalanced by the risks she posed. As a society girl, she lacked the discipline of other party members, and required close watching over, as this NKVD cable reveals:

A gifted, clever and educated woman, she requires constant control over her behavior . . . It is necessary to continue activating her activities as a successful journalist. She should also be guided to approach the President's wife, Eleanor, through different social organizations, committees and societies . . .[9]

Constancia herself would soon form a friendship with Eleanor Roosevelt.

Was she also "guided to approach" the First Lady? Would she also, in time, come to be considered unpredictable and risky because of her headstrong independence?

Through the Dodd Sterns, Jay Allen, Ernest Hemingway, Martha Gellhorn, and other influential friends and contacts, Constancia was able to contact and impress many powerful people in her effort to seek American aid for Spanish exiles. Jay Allen got in touch with every branch of the government in Washington to discuss the refugee crisis and Franco's Law of Political Responsibilities. The assistant to the Secretary of Agriculture wrote that he and Secretary Henry A. Wallace (soon to be Roosevelt's second-term Vice-President) agreed entirely with Allen and Constancia's point of view on Spain, and that they "found Constanzia (sic) de la Mora most interesting and were glad to have the opportunity to talk with her."[10] Allen also sent a letter of his own, along with one from Constancia describing the situation in Spain to the National Labor Relations Board in Washington. The reply he received was sympathetic, though discouraging because it clearly reveals the United States government's position on the war:

> *I am showing your letter together with the one from Señora de la Mora to friends here. Her letter gives a disheartening picture, but what is even more disheartening is the realization of how few of her suggestions can be carried out. Things are going to the abyss so swiftly that by the time suggestions can reach here from Spain another great section of the scene there has crumbled. The attitude in Washington is all too common now, that "Spain is no longer a special case, just an incident subordinate to much more menacing problems." That sort of thing is simply the latest rationalization of "friendly" government people excusing their inability to do anything. The news from Spain is now too tragic almost even to read. One can see too much between the few lines that there are.[11]*

Constancia, from February onwards, lived in New York without Ignacio. He would not join her until September 1939.[12] This was the first time since she had studied in England that Constancia was abroad and alone, far from her family, her daughter, and husband. She and Ignacio were both still working directly under Prime Minister Juan Negrín. On September 4, Ignacio listed Negrín as a reference in his application for a visa to enter the United States, and he is again mentioned in a telegram sent from Connecticut by Constancia to her friend Soledad Sancha (who would become the Cultural Attaché of the Spanish Embassy in Moscow). In this message, which is approximately from May 1939 when Negrín was with Constancia in New York,[13] Constancia wrote that she and Ignacio had been given "permission" by Negrín to meet and work together in the United States:

Ignacio Paris (sic) approved our reunion. Don Juan[14] considers America the best work for both of us . Wants reports on the outcome of the negotiations there. He'll leave for Paris on the twelfth. If Ignacio could come I wish he could bring Luli. Countless schools here . . . Friends will understand that insistence is not personal convenience but interest in work.[15]

In July, she again wrote to Moscow asking for permission to at least visit Luli.[16]

Unfortunately, the "friends" Constancia referred to did not understand, and she would have to wait several years to be reunited with Luli. Why was Luli kept in the Soviet Union in a children's home when her mother had the desire and the means to bring her to the United States?

While she waited for Ignacio and also possibly for Luli, who she had not seen for three years, to join her in New York, she was accompanied at the Dodd-Sterns' home by her friends Tina Modotti and Irene Falcón. The latter describes the first period of exile as fascinating and encouraging because everyone in New York seemed to want to meet and help them. Falcón remembers that Stern announced that his solidarity with the Spanish Republicans was a way of paying for the capitalist "sins" of his father. Despite his explanations, she was shocked to see how politically committed so many wealthy New Yorkers were. Though they had luxurious lifestyles and tastes, to Falcón they seemed as militant as any miner or worker she had met. She describes her friendship with Constancia, who she knew during the war from their work within *Mujeres Antifascistas*, as "very close":

Constancia was adamant that we be as unobtrusive as possible. So we picked up after ourselves, ate out to not make a mess, and slept in the living room . . . I remember the two black maids that they had looking at us in surprise because we refused to let them serve us. Soon afterwards I heard them say in the kitchen: "They aren't ladies", since they couldn't imagine us not wanting to be served. This made me laugh . . . Every day we had a get together at the house of an American, generally someone from the intellectual world, but we even went to the houses of wealthy property owners, like the couple who we stayed with. In these houses twenty-five people would get together for lunch or dinner, while we told them our story. There was an enormous enthusiasm; especially because we had just arrived from Spain and this lent credibility to our information, because they distrusted what they were reading in the press which they didn't believe. They said, "It's all lies, but we believe you because you've lived through it". There were also meetings in clubs and union locales; after a presentation by an American and a talk by an exiled Spaniard, they would pass around a hat and collect money for the Aid Fund for the Antifascist Spanish Resistance (Fondo de Ayuda a la Resistencia Antifascista Espanola).[17]

Irene Falcón's description of the New York that welcomed her and Constancia shows that they were still hopeful that the United States would do something to aid Republican Spain. Furthermore, her account shows how ideally positioned they were to lobby on behalf of the Republic in New York. They received attention as well as financial and moral support. Constancia hoped to galvanize this into fully-fledged cooperation at the national level. There seemed to be an unending stream of events organized so that Martha Dodd, Jay Allen, and Constancia could speak to a wider public about Spain. In May and June alone the places where she spoke included the Manhattan Center of the Greater New York Committee for Spanish Relief, the luncheon of the metropolitan Panhellenic groups, the symposium of the American League for Peace and Democracy (where she appeared along with Mrs. Alvarez del Vayo), and the Spanish Refugee Relief Campaign's symposium on "Spain's Culture in Exile" (where she spoke with Luis Aragón).[18]

In Place of Splendor

Shortly after Constancia's arrival in New York, it was suggested to her by her correspondent friend Jay Allen[19] that she start thinking about the project that would become *In Place of Splendor*. Allen had known Constancia since the early 1930s when he and his wife had rented her apartment in Madrid, and he also continued to work for Negrín after the end of the war. Allen was to play a tremendously important role in promoting the Republican cause in the United States. Another prominent Republican woman, Isabel de Palencia, wrote the following about Allen in her memoir *Smouldering Freedom*:

> *If I were asked who I thought was the best-informed North American on the Spanish conflict, I would unhesitatingly say, "Jay Allen". Spain has many other friends of distinction in the United States who are also personal friends . . . Freda Kirchwey, Vincent Sheean, Elliot Paul . . . But no one has compiled the history of the Spanish war or had the patience to build up the files that Jay Allen has.*[20]

The idea was that Constancia should create a platform by writing a book which would reach the maximum number of sympathetic Americans and plead the cause of the Spanish Republic. As an eyewitness to the events, everything was fresh in her memory and it was important that her story be told before the United States forgot Spain. Essentially, she would continue the propaganda efforts she had been in charge of in Spain, but instead of working behind the scenes she would now go before the public and use her own life story as the thread on which to hang her appeal. The fact that she was Spanish, highly educated, a wife and mother, and that she furthermore came from a privileged background made for a dramatic personal narrative.

Constancia soon moved into Jay Allen's house on Washington Square, and it was there that Vittorio Vidali found her when he arrived in New York in March. Vidali rushed over to see her to discuss their work in the Spanish refugee relief situation. During his visit, she told him that she was writing a book. Vidali claimed to have read the completed manuscript in March of 1939, and said that the book came out in July of the same year, but in reality *In Place of Splendor* was not published until November 1939.[21] Vidali had his dates wrong, and timing is relevant to understanding just when and how the book was written.

In fact, the manuscript was not finished until July 1939. Surprisingly, the fact that Constancia was neither a native English speaker nor a writer did not seem to raise the suspicions of any readers or reviewers of *In Place of Splendor*. Nobody, at least not publicly, suggested that she might have needed a great deal of assistance writing "her book". Furthermore, it was her first and, in the end her, only book. It does seem rather incongruous that she could have written a beautifully constructed narrative in English that is clear, engaging and fast-paced. Not to mention the fact that the 426 pages were written at an impressive speed in just a few months.

There are two conflicting hypotheses about how the book really came about. The first is that she had a great deal of help from a number of friends and collaborators who helped her give the book its shape. The second is that an experienced writer wrote the book more or less single-handedly under Constancia's name.

The first theory is supported by Vidali and Manuel Fernández Colino (an exiled Cuban who had also been in Spain working with the Communists). Fernández Colino remembered that he and photographer Tina Modotti (who had worked under the alias of "María" for *Socorro Rojo* in Spain during the war) had been enlisted to help Constancia edit the manuscript in the spring of 1939:

> *I had arrived – via France – to the United States where I was working on behalf of the Spanish refugees. One day, walking down the street I bumped into Constancia de la Mora who asked me if I had time to help Tina Modotti with some work. As I knew who Tina Modotti was, I accepted the job with enthusiasm because I had long been eager to meet Mella's companion.[22] Can you imagine my surprise when I found out that she was none other than "María" of Socorro Rojo fame? Constancia had written her book* In Place of Splendor *in English, and Tina and I were supposed improve the style a bit and make corrections. So, for*

four or five weeks we worked together . . . She was living at Martha Dodd's house at the time . . . [23]

There is no reason to think that Fernández Colino's recollection is not sincere, however it was too early for the manuscript he refers to (the same one mentioned by Vidali) to be the book we now know as *In Place of Splendor*.

The second theory is more disconcerting: Constancia did not write the book at all, but merely told her story to a professional writer who created *In Place of Splendor*. There happened to be one person in her immediate circle of friends who had the talent, experience, and political sympathies to embark on such a task: Ruth McKenney. McKenney was a left-wing author who had also managed to conquer mainstream America. On the one hand, she had written the acclaimed 1939 *Industrial Valley*, a classic example of American proletarian literature, and on the other, she was popular as a journalist for the *New Yorker*, *Women's Day*, and *Publisher's Weekly*. Furthermore, her collected articles were the basis of a bestselling book that would later become a famous Broadway show, *My Sister Eileen*. The stories were based on autobiographical essays about the McKenney girls' adventures, from their childhood in Ohio of the 1910s to their escapades in 1930s Greenwich Village. The sisters were a famous pair in New York and each had her distinct appeal. According to Ruth, she was the smart one and Eileen was the beauty.[24] The book had come out in 1939, but Ruth McKenney never saw the 1940 Broadway play based on it. Just before it opened, Eileen and her husband, the author Nathaniel West, were killed in a car accident, and McKenney couldn't bear to see the comedy celebrating her late sister's beauty and wit. The Broadway show was only the beginning of *Eileen's* trajectory in the entertainment world. After eight hundred and forty-two performances, writers Jerome Chodorov and Joseph Fields transformed the story into a screenplay in 1942. The film version starred Rosalind Russell. In 1953 a musical for the stage, also featuring Russell, was written by Chodorov and Fields. The score was by Leonard Bernstein, and the lyrics by Betty Comden and Adolph Green. The musical won a Tony award and in 1955 MGM produced a film version starring Betty Garrett, Jack Lemmon, and Bob Fosse.[25]

The book of *My Sister Eileen* had been published in 1938 by Harcourt, Brace, & Co., the same publisher that would publish *In Place of Splendor*. Thus McKenney, who knew the editor at the publishing house very well, would have been in a very good position to help Constancia. So, did McKenney write Constancia's book for her? It is certain that she was involved in the writing of *In Place of Splendor* to some extent because Constancia says so in a letter to Jay Allen. While revising the manuscript,

Constancia was with her. She decided at the last minute, following McKenney's suggestion, to include her personal views of the newspapermen she had worked with in Spain and she sent Allen this new "insert" that "we" (she and McKenney) had written and asked for his immediate feedback:

> *I enclose an insert that we have written[26] for the book about the newspapermen. I was reluctant to put anything about them, but Ruth insists that I should do so. Now I think she is right. But I would like you to go over it carefully. First to see if it is the kind of thing that is alright or the kind of stuff that sounds stupidly personal – like Martha Dodd [27] or something like that, which I would hate. Secondly if you think it is correct and accurate. Thirdly if we have left out someone important who should be mentioned. And lastly I would like you to change and rewrite anything you like and in the way you like. But please do it SOON . . . send all three copies to me quickly, for we must see in which part we are going to make the insertion . . . Thank you very much and please do all this as soon as you can, for we are very short of time.[28]*

McKenney was indeed tailor-made to write *In Place of Splendor*. She was an experienced journalist who was used to writing quickly and meeting deadlines. She herself had already written a best-selling autobiography just the year before, and she and her husband were members of the Communist party.[29] Her husband Richard Bransten, who was the heir to the large MJB Coffee Company, had been a correspondent in Spain for *The New Masses* in which he published under his party name, Bruce Minton. Though McKenney had not covered Spain herself, she knew enough about the war to speak about it in public. On February 25, 1939 she and Colonel George Watt (third in command of the Abraham Lincoln Brigade) had addressed hundreds of New York University students at a rally held to protest the United States' embargo on Spain. There were fifteen other such demonstrations held in New York that day, and the slogan was "America's fate depends on Spain".[30]

There is another piece of evidence that makes it seem more likely that McKenney did much more than house her Spanish friend and edit her work. In 1959, Ruth McKenney gave her daughter, who she had named Eileen, after her sister, a collection of all the books she had written. Included in the set, along with *My Sister Eileen*, *Industrial Valley*, and *Eileen*'s sequel *The McKenney's Carry On* was *In Place of Splendor*. The title page of *In Place of Splendor* is inscribed with the following dedication dated May 28, 1959 and signed in Cleveland, Ohio:

> *This is a complete set of my books of which this is Volume Four. Written at Westport, Conn. (sic) the summer of 1939 for Constancia de la Mora and*

published under her name, 1939. To my daughter Eileen Bransten . . . With Love and Pride . . . Mother.[31]

It is worth emphasizing that she says the book was written "for" Constancia, and not "with" her. It seems highly improbable that McKenney would have lied to her daughter about writing the book, and Eileen Bransten recalls that her mother, who died in 1972, was always bothered by the fact that Constancia had taken sole credit for *In Place of Splendor*.[32] This is not surprising, since the book sold extremely well, was translated into several languages and made Constancia famous. The venture must have seemed quite unjust to McKenney, for *In Place of Splendor* was the only book she did not sign, but was by far the most successful, even more so than *My Sister Eileen*.

In Place of Splendor was published without a preface, epilogue, or introduction of any kind. The only words added to the manuscript were in the dedication, "For Ignacio and Luli". There are no acknowledgements. Though it may never be known exactly how much of the book McKenney wrote, its shape, language, tone and structure bear the mark of an experienced writer, and of an American writer. We must consider that Constancia had learned English at a convent school in England, and no matter how many American journalists she had met during the Spanish Civil War, it is impossible to believe that the following (among many other examples) could have been written by a foreigner on their first visit to the United States:

> *none of the good correspondents suffered from Richard Harding Davis overtones. Now and then some new agency man – sent, as is the wont of news agencies; direct from the police beat in Hoboken, fancied himself a Knight of the Typewriter.*[33]

This is not Constancia de la Mora writing, nor are these her words polished by an editor at Harcourt, Brace & Co. These are the words of a tough talking New Yorker, such as Ruth McKenney. What did Constancia know about Harding Davis (a popular journalist and former editor of *Harper's Weekly*) who died over twenty years before she arrived in New York? And the "police beat in Hoboken" seems rather colloquial for someone who, as far as we know, had never set foot in New Jersey. She may have heard this kind of language in Spain, but that she would have managed to make it her own and work it seamlessly into her narrative is implausible.

Curiously, as if to justify the fluent English throughout the book, there is a mechanism of self-defense built into the second chapter, "Spanish Awakening". Here, Constancia recounts her first meeting with her tenants,

Jay Allen and his wife and son, and how their "American" transformed her English:

> *Three days later an English friend told me that I had an American accent –*
> *horrors! It wasn't really true then but as soon as I began to know Americans I*
> *did indeed speak American. I had been brought up on Irish brogue and Oxford*
> *English, but the vivid and colorful language my American friends spoke blotted*
> *out my foreign accent. English had always seemed a rather distant tongue, not*
> *like the warm and graceful Spanish of my own country. But American seemed*
> *quite different, a living, sharp, precise, and staccato speech. I took to it like a*
> *duck to water and a few months later an Englishman told me he was sure I learned*
> *English in Kansas.*[34]

Undoubtedly, the American reader of *In Place of Splendor* eagerly believed that this educated Spaniard admired their language and spoke it like a native.

Constancia's correspondence supports McKenney's claim that the book was written at her house in Westport, in the summer of 1939. Constancia and McKenney were clearly together when she wrote the previously cited letter to Jay Allen.[35] Furthermore, Constancia's letters to Eleanor Roosevelt from the summer of 1939 show that she was living at Ruth McKenney's house at 258 Kings Highway in Westport,[36] Connecticut at least from July 17 to August 16, and most probably stayed with McKenney for most of the summer.

If *In Place of Splendor* was indeed written, as seems likely, by McKenney, it should be examined as a complex artifact of the political period. Constancia offered the story of her private life, her political activity, and her name while McKenney contributed her narrative and rhetorical skills anonymously as a means to an end: a rousing appeal to wake the American public from apathy and isolationism. This was an audience to which McKenney knew how to appeal. It seems that only Jay Allen was aware of the full extent of the partnership between the two women. Neither Constancia nor Ruth McKenney ever made their collaboration a matter of public record.

However, the collaborative nature of the project does not seem to have been a closely guarded secret. Clara Sancha,[37] who taught at one of the *colonias* for Spanish children in Moscow and was a prominent member of the exiled community remembers that when she first heard about *In Place of Splendor*, she knew that Constancia had written the book with the "help" of "una americana". Sancha says that she had no special knowledge, that everyone knew Constancia hadn't written the book alone. Sancha must have heard about the book while it was being written or when it came out, either in the summer or fall of 1939. By this point, she was in Russia so "everyone" is everyone in Moscow. This is significant because from evidence in the United States and Mexico there is no hint that Constancia had not written the book singlehandedly. Her whole identity abroad was based on being the author of *In Place of Splendor*. No doubt, by disguising McKenney's participation, she was not only more highly esteemed personally, but the message of her book was more effective by being perceived as authentic. Today, when asked whether Constancia was a heroic figure, Sancha is surprised by the qualifier: "Heroic? Why? Her husband, the aviator Ignacio Hidalgo de Cisneros was a hero. Constancia was very cultivated and kind, but she was not heroic, she just worked in the Ministry of Foreign Affairs."[38] To Sancha, who knew and worked with Constancia during the war, she was quite a different person than the extraordinary personality she was to the readers of *In Place of Splendor*.

The aim of establishing McKenney's crucial contribution now is not to discredit Constancia. The facts of her life, and her willingness to use her personal story as a means to reach the American public, make her an exceptional defender of the Republic. However, *In Place of Splendor* is a dramatization of Constancia's story, and it seems fair that McKenney, who was an important figure on the American left in her own right, should receive credit for her central part in its creation. *In Place of Splendor* should simply be reconsidered in the larger context of the political aim to awaken American sympathy for the Spanish Republic. It was certainly not the first such project. Joris Ivens, Ernest Hemingway, and John Dos Passos had made it to the White House and Hollywood with their 1937 film that championed the Republican cause – "The Spanish Earth". However, *In Place of Splendor* came at a different moment, was a much more finely tuned example of propaganda, and would reach a vastly larger audience. The villains of its narrative were not only Fascist Germany and Italy, but the isolationist United States. The most heroic participants in the Spanish war were the nearly sixty thousand members of the International Brigades, who had defied the non-intervention pact and gone to Spain as volunteers to defend the Republic: "Governments betrayed and abandoned us but men from all over the world came to die in our country – that democracy might live . . . History had no greater story to tell than the record of the International Brigades."[39] The veterans of the American Abraham Lincoln Brigade had been given the derogatory label of "premature antifascists" by the American military, and *In Place of Splendor* gave a new image of these volunteers to the American people. The gratitude and praise of a Spanish aristocrat who had seen their bravery in Spain highlighted their disinterested heroism.

Much of the summer of 1939 was spent worrying about John Dos Passos.

To Constancia's dismay, in June the subject of the disappearance in Spain of Dos Passos' friend José Robles was resuscitated in the pages of *The New Republic*. In 1937 Robles had been mysteriously arrested and executed in Valencia and Dos Passos still suspected Constancia's superior, Alvarez del Vayo, and perhaps even Constancia herself of taking a part in the cover up. Journalist Kate Mangan, who worked with Constancia in Spain, described the suppression of Robles's disappearance in the press office. According to Mangan's own memoir, only "Poppy", the one American working in the office, dared bring the matter up:

> *What happened remained a mystery; it was inexplicable but it leaked out despite efforts to hush it up on the part of our communist friends. The only person who dared create a loud scene about it was Poppy. It was obvious that our Spanish colleagues were miserable and quite helpless to do anything about it.*[40]

Now, two years later, Malcolm Cowley was unimpressed by John Dos Passos' new novel *Adventures of a Young Man*, and his review sparked an exchange of letters on the subject of Robles. Cowley said many things that Dos Passos may have been tempted to respond to, but the only point he was angered enough by was this reference to Robles:

> *In the spring of 1937, John Dos Passos went to Spain with his friend Ernest Hemingway. He has described the trip vividly in the last few chapters of "Journeys Between Wars." But in that book he gave only oblique hints of one episode, the key to much that followed. Dos Passos' Spanish translator, a young man whom almost everybody knew and liked, was arrested as a Fascist spy. People who ought to know tell me that the evidence against him was absolutely damning. Hemingway, who interceded for him with the highest officials of the Spanish government, became convinced of his guilt. Dos Passos continued to believe he was innocent, even after learning that he had been convicted and shot.*[41]

Dos Passos promptly wrote to the *New Republic* to discredit these charges. The editors immediately sent the galley proofs of his letter to Constancia, who was in Westport with Ruth McKenney. She sent her response, which McKenney surely "helped" her write, to Jay Allen for approval:

> *I enclose two things to which I beg you to give attention. First is a reply to Dos Passos (sic) letter to the New Republic. The New Republic sent me the galley proofs of his letter – which reached me with great delay, and asked me if I wanted to reply. You read my reply carefully and if you approve of it as it is, PLEASE . . . send it to them post-haste. IF YOU WOULD LIKE TO CHANGE SOMETHING I AM QUITE WILLING TO DO SO, BUT PLEASE (sic) call me up and tell me, and if you think for any reason at all*

that I should not answer it and someone else should sign the reply it is perfectly ok with me. But let me know whatever you decide.[42]

Constancia was agitated by Dos Passos' letter. In it, he claimed to offer for the first time the facts leading up to Robles' death. He described how Robles, who spoke Russian, had been hired by the Ministry of War and had come into close contact with Russian advisers and experts. Through his work at the ministry, Robles became more important, and more vulnerable:

In the fall of 1936 friends warned him that he had made powerful enemies and had better leave the country . . . He was arrested soon after in Valencia and held by the extra-legal police under conditions of great secrecy and executed in February or March 1937. It must have been about the time of his death that I arrived in Spain . . . His wife, whom I saw in Valencia, asked me to make inquiries to relieve her terrible uncertainty.[43]

Dos Passos received contradictory information about what had happened to Robles. When he appealed to the Minister of Foreign Affairs Alvarez del Vayo, he was promised that the facts would be looked into. He was also assured that wherever Robles was he certainly was not in any danger. However, on the same day journalist Liston Oak, who worked in the propaganda department with Constancia and also reported to Alvarez del Vayo, told Robles's seventeen-year-old son Coco (who also worked with Constancia) that his father had been killed.

Those that admitted that Robles might have been killed attributed the arrest and murder to Anarchists:

Mr. Del Vayo, then Foreign Minister, professed ignorance and chagrin when I talked to him about the case, and promised to find out the details. The general impression that the higher-ups in Valencia tried to give was that if Robles were dead he had been kidnapped and shot by anarchist "uncontrollables".[44]

Dos Passos did not believe this version of events. He had more faith in the story he heard later in Madrid from the chief of the Republican counterespionage service "that Robles had been executed by a 'special section' (which I gathered was under control of the Communist Party) . . . Spaniards I talked to closer to the Communist Party took the attitude that Robles had been shot as an example . . . because he had been overheard indiscreetly discussing military plans in a café."[45] Furthermore, since Robles had met with his Nationalist brother, who was in prison in Madrid, to convince him to join the Loyalists, he had put himself in more danger of being suspected as an anti-communist agent. Dos Passos concluded that Robles had simply become the "man who knew too much" about relations between the Spanish war ministry and the Kremlin, and that Russian secret agents had decided he was unreliable. Alvarez del Vayo had never helped Robles' widow obtain the death certificate that would have enabled her to claim his life insurance, as he had promised to do.

Though Dos Passos had held onto these ideas since the spring of 1937, he had now stated them publicly to the same audience that Constancia wanted to impress with her book. Her response, which she sent to Jay Allen, was lost. Nothing was ever published in *The New Republic* under Constancia's name. However, a related letter was published by Milly Bennett. Constancia had told Jay Allen that she would be happy to have someone else sign her letter: perhaps that was Bennett? It is not implausible because Bennett had worked with Constancia in the Foreign Press Office[46] and her husband, Hans Amlie, had been a commander in the Lincoln-Washington Battalion. The letter seems to express what Constancia would have said to rebut Dos Passos' indictment of the Communist Party, Alvarez del Vayo, and the Foreign Press Office.

> *The very day that Dos Passos walked into the Press office at Valencia, March, 1937, and Francisco (Coco) ran to greet him, was just about twenty-four hours after the Robles family had been informed that the Colonel had been executed. Dos Passos raced around frantically for several days in March . . . attempting to establish the innocence of the dead Colonel Robles. Naturally, as there was a war going on, he was not able to find out very much. Dos Passos . . . unable to get "satisfaction" anywhere, dashed out of Spain, his companion on the trip being Liston Oak, who had previously been the editor of the Press Bulletin. Oak was "unhappy," as he put it, about Spain.[47]*

Bennett's letter concludes by claiming that Robles had openly criticized the Anarchists and that they had "framed him". The Anarchists and Syndicalists being "less vigilant in accepting members than any other organization, and their ranks must have included many real Fascist spies and agitators."[48] This, Bennett claimed, was what Robles' family believed to have led to his death. Furthermore, she said that Robles' son and daughter continued to support the Loyalist cause after his death. Francisco continued working for the press office until he joined the loyalist army and his younger sister Miggie was sent to the United States in 1938 as a delegate to the Youth Congress. Coco would not have remained in the press office if he had suspected that its staff had anything to do with the cover-up of his father's murder. The point of this letter was to clear the communists of murder, and the press office staff of having any inside knowledge.

Did Constancia write or contribute to the substance of this letter? There are some clues that she may have. We know that she had written a letter to

Allen in which she expresses the intent of responding to Dos Passos in the *New Republic* herself, or having a letter published in this issue under her own name or that of a third party. Some of the language makes it seem as if the text had been rapidly translated from Spanish (for example, *"the family of Robles* believed . . . "*) and Milly Bennett was, of course, not Spanish. Most importantly, Constancia would also have blamed the anarchists for Robles' murder, thereby protecting the reputation of the Communist Party and of the Press Office. As for Robles' family, the uncomfortable role she and Alvarez del Vayo took in looking after them as well as protecting them from the truth while making sure they did not suspect anything should not be forgotten. In any event, Dos Passos' suspicions had come back to haunt Constancia, and the last thing she wanted was to be implicated in this unsavoury incident prior to the publication of *In Place of Splendor.*

She need not have worried, for when released *In Place of Splendor* was given a massive publicity campaign by Harcourt and Brace and the reviews were enthusiastic. Constancia became a celebrity and many were genuinely sympathetic to her story. Though Franco had been in power for several months by the time the book came out, Constancia hoped that her version of events would discredit his legitimacy by showing how he had come to power thanks to Hitler and Mussolini. In her account, the war had not really ended in a Nationalist victory over a defeated Republic. What had really happened, she said, was that the important Republicans Julian Besteiro and Colonel Segismundo Casado (Commander of the Central Army) had undermined the authority of the Negrín government and staged a coup against him which ended in a surrender negotiated directly with Franco. According to the book, by the time Negrín's government found out about the coup, Casado's men had occupied the central zone and agreed to hand Negrín and all the members of his government over to Franco. Constancia was in New York during the final stages of the war, but her husband was an eyewitness to these events and it is his account that appears in the book. Ignacio had pretended to play along with Casado and Besteiro, who trusted him as a former military officer of the Monarchy. But he had really been spying for Negrín, and as soon as the deal had been made with Franco he rushed to tell Negrín that they all had to leave Spain immediately because the traitors had Franco's promise that they would be spared in exchange for the key members of Negrín's government. Aside from the fact that leaving was tantamount to defeat, what worried Ignacio and the others most was that Franco had just proclaimed his law of "political responsibilities" which gave the new regime the right to sentence every Spaniard over the age of fourteen who hadn't actively been on the Nationalist side to the death penalty and/or decades long prison sentences. Today it is known that the law was

applied mercilessly and extensively. *In Place of Splendor* claims that in their
negotiations with Franco Casado and Besteiro did not secure mercy for the
Republicans. This was the crucial issue at the end of the war. Negrín had
demanded a guarantee of non-retaliation, and because it had not been
achieved he initially refused to leave. But he soon saw that if his government stayed, they would simply be killed, and said: "If there is no other
way out . . . I feel that we should adjourn and meet again in a foreign country
to carry on our fight, which we will never give up for a free and democratic
Spain."[49] Constancia omits the Communist presence in this crucial moment
of her story. In these last moments of the war with Negrín, leading party
members, including La Pasionaria, were also present. La Pasionaria and
other Communist leaders were evacuated in the same group of small planes
and at the same time as Negrín, his secretary, and Alvarez del Vayo.[50] Their
evacuation to France had been arranged by Ignacio, who would leave Spain
on the last plane. The end of the war, is summed up as: "A group of Spanish
cowards and traitors delivered Madrid – and after Madrid the rest of
Republican Spain – tied hand and feet to Franco, Hitler, and Mussolini."[51]

Because the end of the war came while Constancia was in the United
States, her mission to get America to obtain American food and arms for
the defense of Madrid became obsolete. Her new objective was to discredit
any perception of the legitimacy of Franco's "victory" and, most urgently,
to bring attention to the plight of hundreds of thousands of Republican
refugees. Her book's conclusion conveyed a message designed to provoke
and rally Americans into action. The following often quoted lines, so
poignant in retrospect, expressed hope for the near future in 1939:

> *The fascists cannot make Spain fascist. We are a democratic people. We shall
> always be a democratic people. I know that Spain will soon again be free. Nothing
> can prevent it for the united people of Spain will make a democracy with their
> blood and courage. ¡Viva la República!"*[52]

Constancia sincerely believed that Franco would not remain in power for
long, and that the United States would be instrumental in removing him
with her encouragement. Indeed, until 1945, she was certain that the
Republic would be reinstated, and hoped to play an important role in her
country's future at that time. These beliefs were alive during the first years
of the post-war period. Her disappointment that they were not fulfilled
would become a source of bitterness in the late 1940s.

Once the manuscript had gone to press, Constancia left Ruth
McKenney's house in Connecticut and went back to New York City, this
time to stay with Martha Dodd (instead of Jay Allen). While she was there,
Nan Golden of The League of American Writers requested that she donate

the original copy of her manuscript to them. She responded in agreement, in a modest tone, and making no mention that anyone else had been involved in the writing of the book.

> *I have asked Miss Pindyck to send you my manuscript to be sold for the aid to Exile Writers. I hope that is what you wanted – or rather what I was supposed to do according to a letter I have received bearing several signatures. It seems very unlikely to me that anyone will be willing to pay anything at all for my m.s. (sic) at present, but it is up to the League, and they surely know best what to do. Of course, to call these typewritten sheets a m.s. is only a manner of speaking, but this is all I have and some of it has been cut out for publication, for no other reason but because the book was too long.*[53]

Before the manuscript was sent out, Constancia added a personal, hand-written note to the first page. Though this note, or a similar version, could have perfectly well been added to the published version of the book, it wasn't. The following words of Constancia's exist only on the original manuscript donated to the League of American Writers:

> *I am not a writer. I do not pretend to be a writer. But I wanted to tell, through my own experiences, the story of my country in these last years. The heroism of the Spanish people did not need anymore than the plain story told. That was all I could attempt to do, and if it helps in any way to make my people better known to the world, it shall be my best reward.*[54]

Her claims that she "is not a writer" can be read as a modest writerly pose, but they may also represent a veiled confession that reveals how *In Place of Splendor* came to be. She told her experiences, but did not write them. The confessional aspect is tempered, however, by a perhaps unconscious defensiveness in the line "I do not pretend to be a writer". In fact Constancia did "pretend to be a writer", and she kept the pretense up until her death. She may not have wanted to, and the situation for her must have been awkward and fraught, but she never revealed McKenney's role.

By December 1939, Constancia was in Mexico with Ignacio. Their plan was to spend several weeks there before returning, together, to the United States. From Mexico, Constancia read the reviews of *In Place of Splendor* in the US press. Most were positive and suggested that her story had success-fully created a Spanish Republican heroine and figurehead. In the *New York Times*, Rose Feld wrote:

> *It is quite possible that after reading this book one will agree with Miss de la Mora when she writes "By now nobody in the world can doubt what we said over and over during the two and a half years of the war: the Spanish war was*

*not a civil war but the invasion of a peaceful democracy by Hitler and
Mussolini."*[55]

In the *Los Angeles Times*, Mildred Barrish praised her "persevering
loyalty" in the face of the "Fascist holocaust" and described her appeal:

*the indignation which arises from every page of this autobiography is the more
striking in that Constancia de la Mora was never herself a member of the multitude who loved the Republic because it offered their first taste of social justice. On
the contrary, she was born into Madrid aristocracy . . . She had, however, one
attribute not always concomitant with noble birth: the quality of nobility.*[56]

As a so-called aristocrat who sided with the people, Constancia seemed
the image of heroic idealism. This is what undoubtedly captivated the
American public. In her book, she was intelligent, glamorous, righteous,
romantic, tough and idealistic. This was a woman who could tell the United
States that Franco, Hitler, and Mussolini had destroyed Spain. She could
indict the US government's policy, and she could tell them that they had
responsibility for the consequences of "non-intervention". There was no
mention of Communism. Hardly anyone in *In Place of Splendor*, not even the
Soviets, is described as Communist. The only predicates she attached to her
side in the war are Republican and democratic.

For the book jacket, her friend Ernest Hemingway wrote "She was a
legend, and this book shows why" and Leland Stowe said "She is one of the
noblest women I've ever met." Nobody could have imagined what an enormous success the book would be. It was on the *New York Times* recommended
"Christmas Books" list, and de la Mora received more invitations to speak
than she could accept. By 1940, it was in its fifth printing. In 1941, Edward
Chodorov (brother of the playwright Jerome Chodorov who had written the
stage and film versions of *My Sister Eileen*) began adapting the memoir[57] for
the stage, and screenwriter Richard Collins wanted to turn Constancia's
story into a film. Neither of these projects came to fruition, but they demonstrate the impact *In Place of Splendor* had. They also reveal how Americans
affiliated with the Communist party, like the Chodorov brothers and
Collins, rallied to Constancia and the cause of Republican Spain.

In Place of Splendor also had its detractors from the left as well as the right.
Her family, of course, considered it all lies. Her father, who somehow
managed to get a copy in Spain, filled its pages with furious comments.[58]
Hollywood actor Errol Flynn, who Constancia had accused of pretending to
be wounded on the Madrid front as a publicity stunt, filed a two million
dollar suit against the author, the publisher, and the printer.[59]

In *The Nation* Constancia was accused by Leigh White, who had been an ambulance driver in Spain in 1937, of writing thinly disguised Communist propaganda.

> *The last half of her autobiography is devoted to the war years, 1936–1939, and this should have been the better portion of the book. Unfortunately it is not. For despite a good running account of the war, seen from her position as propagandist, wife, and mother, Señorita de la Mora betrays the stoppage of her growth as an individual and her subjection to a party line . . . Señorita de la Mora lays it on so thick in the last half of her book that one can predict her every opinion in advance. Everything Prieto does in the war is wrong; everything Negrín does is right; and this seems to me not only debatable but mathematically impossible. Prieto is condemned for using his position to send his daughter out to France to escape the rigors of the war;*[60] *yet Señorita de la Mora sees nothing wrong in the fact that she later sent her own daughter out to Russia, or that Dolores Ibárruri had a grown son there all through the war . . . This sort of sectarian distortion extends even to the reporting of events. Of the rearguard clash of May, 1937 . . . . Señorita de la Mora naively writes: "The P.O.U.M. militiamen, the Trotskyite heroes who had played football with the fascists . . . started for Barcelona, this time in dead earnest about the fighting. They intended to slaughter the people of Barcelona on the street – as they had never slaughtered fascists." Nonsense, there were fascists in the P.O.U.M., certainly, but there were fascists in the P.S.U.C. (the Communist Party) too – in every party. The P.O.U.M. had no monopoly on spies and ogres any more than the P.S.U.C. has a monopoly on heroes and saints.*[61]

In Mexico, Constancia was furious about the review. She expressed her anger in a letter to Jay Allen in which the language and tone stand in marked contrast to those of *In Place of Splendor*.

> *I can see that the offensive against me is already starting. I have not seen Leigh White's review in the Nation, but your friend Frida Kerchway*[62] *(sic) should better know what a low class Trotskyte (sic), in the pay of the catalan Poum (sic) she has for a book reviewer. It is not personal spite but just the knowledge that Leigh white (sic) was ready to "lamer el culo" (sic) of all the agencies or newspapermen and at the same time of the most extremist parties all the time. He dislikes me personally as a reaction to my dislike for anything as slimy as him . . .* [63]

On January 1, 1940, *The Nation* published a letter by Mildred Adams responding to White's review.[64] Adams knew Spain well, and had reported on the Spanish Civil War. She defended Constancia's portrayal of the war. Most significant to Constancia was Adams' rebuttal of White's claim that *In Place of Splendor* was Communist propaganda.

In claiming that Miss de la Mora follows the Communist line when she relates what came under her personal observation and what she heard, is Mr. White quite sure that he is not following the line of another and competing party? . . . As any number of us who knew Spain long before 1936 have tried to explain, the line which the Communist Party adopted there was in many respects similar to that which intelligent Spanish liberals have been advocating for years. Constancia de la Mora was first of all a Spaniard and a liberal. Whatever her later party affiliations may have been, they never weakened the force of those primary allegiances . . . What he seems in some strange way estopped (sic) from understanding is that Miss de la Mora's book, in picturing with such warmth and spirit the life of a girl growing up in the ruling circles of Spain, is making comprehensible that main struggle to hundreds of Americans who have never understood it, and is winning such friends for the defeated Spanish Republic as might have changed the whole American attitude toward the conflict had it been published in 1936.[65]

The letter was possibly another volley in Constancia's public relations campaign, and not the spontaneous expression of Mildred Adams. Constancia turned to Jay Allen whenever something went wrong, and it was probably Allen who behind the scenes was organizing Constancia's defense in the American press.

Leigh White was not the only American journalist to criticize in *In Place of Splendor*. The *New York Times* journalist William Carney, who had been in Spain during the war, wanted to sue Constancia because of how her book had portrayed him. She said that he had numerous fascist friends,[66] and that he used his reporting to communicate strategic information to the Nationalists:

Spanish hospitality cost the Republic dearly. Mr. William Carney, the correspondent for the New York Times in Madrid, was allowed to travel about freely, for instance, though he was known to have fascist sympathies and fascist friends. Mr. Carney's curiosity took him to strange places and when he left Madrid for Paris, he wrote a series of articles giving the exact details of gun emplacements around Madrid, and so on. I myself have seen a pamphlet reprinting these damaging articles. How many hundreds of Spaniards fell by reason of his "uncensored" articles we can never know. Mr. Carney received later a fine fascist uniform . . . Mr. Carney's "impartiality" was further revealed long afterwards, when he signed a letter to the Primate of Spain congratulating the facsists on "their glorious victory".[67]

Carney denied her accusations and sued for libel.[68] She once again appealed to Jay Allen asking him to act on her behalf in New York:

I received yesterday a letter signed by Mr. Donald Brace, partner of Mr. Alfred

Harcourt giving me the tidings that our friend Mr. Carney is ready to start a libel suit against me!! The letter from the lawyer (A. David Schenker, 141 Broadway) to the publishers says as follows: "I have read the book and agree with him that he has been the victim of malicious libel and this should be immediately deleted from the book. The authoress claims that Mr. Carney is a fascist and that for distorting the facts he received a fine fascist uniform. Mr. Carney informed me that he is not a fascist, never owned any uniform of a fascist, and certainly never wore one. The authoress further claims that he signed a letter addressed to the primate of Spain congratulating the fascists on a glorious victory. The truth is that the letter that he signed was signed by English speaking catholics (sic) congratulating the Primate on the fact that the end of the war had not seen the disappearance of religion from Spain . . . " I thought you would be interested to know about this incident and also that I would ask you whether you would not do me a great favour. Read again the paragraph . . . find the original references . . . AND write one of your CAUSTIC letters in my name to Mr. Donald Brace . . . I am certainly not going to let Mr. Carney get away with this, and I am quite helpless to do anything from here . . . WOULD YOU DO IT, JAY?[69]

It seems that Constancia could not write important letters on her own and always needed Allen's help, another element that supports the hypothesis that Ruth McKenney wrote *In Place of Splendor*. Anyone capable of putting her point of view across in a stirring autobiography would surely have been able to write a short letter defending her book.

Errol Flynn, William Carney, and Leigh White were the first antagonists that Constancia would encounter, but their attacks didn't amount to much. Constancia's reputation in the United States would collapse soon enough, but not because of her critics.

IV
Refugee Crisis
From the White House to the Blacklist

Promoting *In Place of Splendor* was only one of the projects with which Constancia had been occupied since leaving Spain. There was a vast network in place in New York to support the Spanish Republic. The Medical Bureau and the North American Committee to Aid Spanish Democracy, for example, were two leading organizations that had close to a hundred well-known speakers at their disposal. Jay Allen regularly gave talks on behalf of the Republic. During the war, speakers were trained to tell "the truth about Spain's fight for freedom". They addressed why Americans should be interested in Spain, how and why the war began, the role of Hitler and Mussolini, and the question of neutrality. They also countered Nationalist propaganda that the Republic was a Communist government, that it was anti-religious, and that the heinous atrocities of the war had been committed by Republicans.[1] After the end of the war, the efforts of these organizations turned to the tragedy of the Spaniards in exile. From the day Constancia arrived she was trying to raise funds for the refugees and Republicans in Spanish prisons. Hundreds of thousands of Spanish refugees were living in terrible conditions in French camps and it was urgent that they be relocated. More important was that they should not be sent back to Spain. While staying with Jay Allen in Washington Square, they worked together on the refugee problem, and to publicize the political reprisals taking place in Spain.

Allen, who was on the board of New York based North American Committee for Spanish Refugee Relief, which had been organized to provide emergency aid in France and to facilitate emigration to Latin America, got in touch with many prominent figures in New York and Washington. But among the many polite, sympathetic replies they received Constancia and Allen were never offered concrete support. A typical, luke-warm response from the Political Advisor of the Department of State (to a letter from Allen and Constancia about the refugees in March, 1939) concludes "I, myself, can only hope for the best."[2] With the outbreak of World War II, America's concern for Spanish exiles only diminished more.

Also representative was the response of Stanley M. Isaacs, President of the Borough of Manhattan: "The Spanish Refugees seem to be forgotten in this overwhelming holocaust – it is fine that some people still have them in mind. I do appreciate hearing from you and your willingness to keep me informed."[3] When in June 1940 Allen wrote to the Assistant to the Secretary of Agriculture J. D. LeCron asking for help to get Negrín out of France, LeCron suggested that he turn to Great Britain instead.[4]

However, an avenue that held out real hope was to open up, at least for a short period. Constancia had only been in New York a few weeks when the journalist Martha Gellhorn, who was married to Hemingway, introduced her to Eleanor Roosevelt. Gellhorn's brief note of introduction read: "Dear Mrs. Roosevelt; Constanzia (sic) de la Mora, about whom I wrote to you, will send this note to you . . . I hope you will have time to see her, as she is one of the finest people I ever knew anywhere."[5] The First Lady had been a supporter of the Republic since the beginning of the war, and had repeatedly urged her husband to lift the embargo to Spain. She often listened to the 'Six Songs of the International Brigade,' and distanced herself from her husband's isolationist policy with lines that could have come from *In Place of Splendor*: "I am not neutral . . . I believe in Democracy and the right of a people to choose their own government without having it imposed on them by Hitler and Mussolini."[6]

A few days later, Constancia wrote to Mrs. Roosevelt, who had already agreed to see her informally at the White House: "I have heard from my friend Martha Gellhorn that you would be so kind as to receive me. I fully realize that in the present situation of my unhappy country, my visit would be a strictly private affair."[7] It had taken Constancia just a matter of weeks to meet the Roosevelts. She formed a friendship with Eleanor Roosevelt which lasted for nearly two years, and which gave her and the Republican cause entrée to the White House. She had become, in effect, the unofficial ambassador for the Negrín government to the United States.

The correspondence between Constancia and Eleanor Roosevelt between 1939 and 1940 reveals an unknown chapter in Constancia's life. It also gives a closer view of the United States' policy towards the Spanish Refugee situation. One gets a clear impression of the intimate relationship that developed between Constancia and the First Lady.

Mrs Roosevelt sent a personal invitation to Constancia: "We want so very much to see you. Can you come to Washington for the night of May fourth?"[8] From Constancia's thank you letter, it seems that their first meeting was a success:

> *I am writing to tell you how much I appreciated your hospitality and your very great kindness to me. We who have been forced to leave our countries find a great*

*comfort in such understanding and are reaffirmed in our faith that national bar-
riers between human spirits do not exist. I was very honored to meet the President
and wish to thank you for your kindness and his in giving me the opportunity.*[9]

During her visit to the White House, Constancia asked Mrs. Roosevelt
to try and arrange a meeting between the President and Negrín, who was
coming from France. On April 17, Negrín had written to Claude Bowers,
the US ambassador to Republican Spain, at the embassy in St. Jean de Luz.
In his letter, which Louis Fischer edited, he addresses the status of the
Spanish Republican government in exile, and rues the fact that Roosevelt
did not decide to fight Germany and Italy in Spain:

> *Although my government is no longer recognized by yours as the government of
> Spain I nevertheless take the liberty of conveying to you my views on the message
> which President Roosevelt addressed several days ago to Hitler and Mussolini.*[10]
> *I trust that I require no excuse for expressing my opinion on this matter. For nearly
> three years of war my government and yours maintained the friendliest relations
> which transcended the formal and were based on a kinship of democratic ideas.
> Spain, moreover, has been one of the victims of the totalitarian aggression which
> the Presidents seeks to stop. And notwithstanding the apparent and provisional
> success of this aggression, we remain the constitutional and therefore the legal
> Spanish government . . . All this is the justification, if justification is necessary,
> for sending you this letter. Needless to say, I approve of the President's initiative
> and my only regret is that it was not taken earlier when it might have saved the
> Spanish democratic republic. Europe, it seems, is already paying for the fascist
> military victory in Spain. We always felt, and I said publicly on several occa-
> sions, that we were fighting for Europe, and recent events – the recent naval
> activity in and around Spain – have proven that we were right.*[11]

Negrín also informs Bowers of his plans to make a "private" visit to the
United States the following week. A few days later, Constancia reminded
Mrs. Roosevelt of her request for a meeting for the exiled Republican
Premier. The President's calendar was full, and he cannot have been eager
to meet with the Republican leader, so Negrín and Constancia met Mrs.
Roosevelt.[12]

In the meantime Bowers had responded to Negrín to help him prepare
for his visit to the White House. On April 20, 1939 Bowers wrote a candid
and admiring letter to Negrín giving him a detailed list of the politicians
and other figures in Washington and New York who were known supporters
of the Republic. He also advised the Prime Minister not to show any bitterness or aggression towards the American government, and to show
gratitude for the sympathy and contributions (money and food to feed

Republican children). However, Bowers encouraged Negrín to make a few points very clearly. First, that the fight for democracy in Spain was the fight for freedom everywhere, and that Spain was the only democracy that had fought fascism. Second, that they had lost the fight because the "non-intervention" pact had deprived the Spanish government of its legal right to buy arms, while Italy and Germany freely equipped Franco with what he needed to win the war. A final piece of advice was that Negrín not let "extreme elements to push in too conspicuously upon you, thereby giving your enemies the kind of stuff they use in their propaganda." Bowers concludes by asking Negrín to destroy the letter.[13]

There is no indication as to whether Negrín followed these guidelines or not when he met with Eleanor Roosevelt, but the agenda coincides closely with the overall arguments of *In Place of Splendor* indicating a coherent approach to presenting the war in the United States.

Constancia continued to raise the Spanish refugee problem in her letters to the First Lady throughout the spring and summer of 1939:

> *I hope we did not overburden you. But I was very anxious that Dr. Negrín should have another opportunity to see you before he sailed for France . . . Do you think there is some possibility of the President's Advisory Committee on Refugees taking up the question of the Spanish exiles, or of another similar committee being formed to deal only with the Spanish question? Please, forgive me for putting this question so bluntly, but I am sure that some constructive plan could be worked out with the help of such a committee; a plan both to raise money and to use the Spaniards arriving in the new world to foster the democratic policies of the United States in Latin and South America. We should not forget that many of our exiles are men of the greatest prestige in the Spanish speaking countries. Their words and writings carry great weight; but they must be given the opportunity to establish themselves in their new surroundings. It will surely interest you to know that our Catholic writer José Bergamin[14] (now in Mexico City, heading a group of Spanish intellectual exiles who plan to start a publishing house) has already started giving a series of lectures on the great Spanish literary figures: Unamuno, García Lorca, Machado, etc. The first lecture was only attended by anti-Fascist intellectuals, but the last one was sold out. Everyone in the cultural world of Mexico, reactionary or liberal, was present. To me, this is a most significant thing, and very indicative of the way we can use our people, both to counteract the Nazi and Fascist penetration, disguised in Spanish "Imperial" language – the kind of language the Phalangists (sic) have now copied from Mussolini – and to keep the real tradition of Spanish culture alive. For the tradition of our culture is essentially democratic! . . .*[15]

Mrs. Roosevelt responded that, unfortunately, the "question of the Spanish exiles cannot be brought up probably until the September meeting." The First Lady seemed genuinely to like Constancia. From Hyde Park, the President's New York summer residence,she extended another informal invitation to Constancia and Ignacio: "I hope you will let me know if you want to stop by here and also that you will surely bring your husband to meet me."[16]

Further proof of Constancia's diplomatic skill was that Mrs. Roosevelt immediately responded to her request to have the President's Advisory Committee discuss the issue of the Spanish Refugees. In fact, she promptly forwarded Constancia's letter to Sumner Welles, the Under Secretary of State. He answered:

> I have read with a great deal of interest the letter to you from Constancia de la Mora . . . I have the utmost sympathy with the work that she is doing, and I fully share the belief expressed in her letter that many of the Spanish refugees can find appropriate and worth-while (sic) openings in the New World if they are given a chance. As you know, the President's basic idea in suggesting the creation of the Intergovernmental Committee on Refugees was to provide a practical form of international cooperation through which, over a term of years, there might be worked out a way of solving the problem of the resettlement of refugees in an orderly manner. It would seem to me entirely suitable and completely in line with the fundamental ideas which we hold that some thought be given at the meeting to be held this autumn between the President and the members of the Executive Committee of the Intergovernmental Committee on Refugees to the question of the Spanish refugees. I have, therefore, recommended that the agenda to be submitted to the President include the resettlement of Spanish refugees.[17]

Mrs. Roosevelt passed on to Constancia the news that the refugee crisis would be on the presidential agenda. Thus her dialogue with Eleanor Roosevelt, and by extension with the United States government, could not have started more promisingly. There was support in the State Department for the Spanish refugees, and the issue was now going to be on the presidential agenda for discussion.

On August 5, 1939, a letter about the terrible conditions for refugees in French camps was published in *The Nation*. Written by Madeleine Braun, General Secretary of the International Committee for Coordination and Information to Republican Spanish Aid,[18] the letter contradicted a May 13 article published by Francis G. Smith on the Spanish exiles in France. Smith's article had given an optimistic portrait of conditions in the camps. Braun wanted to set the story straight and she described the disease ridden refugees, and the lack of shelter, food, water, and clothes. In addition, the refugees were denied the right to mail, and to receive money sent by family and friends. Braun concluded that "It is only by recording the facts as they are that international opinion will be made to understand that the lot of hundreds of thousands of unfortunate Spanish refugees is still far from being regulated in a manner either human or satisfactory."[19] Constancia sent a copy of this letter to Mrs. Roosevelt, writing that it described "in very sober terms the present conditions of the Refugee Camps in France."[20]

On November 8, 1939 Constancia had asked her publisher to send Mrs. Roosevelt an advance copy of *In Place of Splendor*. Mrs. Roosevelt wrote to her in early December that it was one of the three books she had enjoyed the most in the past year.[21]

At the same time as Constancia was making progress in the United States, there were developments in France that would tarnish the reputation of the Servicio de Evacuación de Refugiados Españoles (SERE), which was the official Spanish relief organization in charge of transporting and looking after the Spanish refugees in France. Their offices were raided by the French authorities and closed. The raid had been ordered by then Foreign Minister Georges Bonnet, a Nazi sympathizer. The closing of SERE put those involved in the refugee relief efforts into a panic and Constancia wired Mrs. Roosevelt who in turn contacted Secretary of State Cordell Hull to see what could be done. The conflict between the French authorities and the SERE would ultimately lead to the polarization of the groups supporting the Spanish Refugees. Constancia placed herself on the opposite side of the issue *vis-à-vis* most Americans. As a result, she would lose her credibility, which would soon lead to an irrevocable break with most of her important friends and allies in the US.

One of Constancia's main collaborators in New York, Herman F. Reissig, who was the Executive Secretary of the Spanish Refugee Relief Campaign (SRRC) in New York, had sent a telegram to the Department of State pleading for an official protest to be lodged with the French government by the United States. Interestingly, Adolf A. Berle Jr., the Assistant Secretary of State, prepared an "official" response to Reissig, and a private one that was sent to the First Lady. In them, he explains   in contrasting ways – why the United States could not intervene to have the SERE reopened. These documents signal the continuation of the wartime "non-intervention" policy of the United States towards the problems of Spanish refugees in the post-war period. Berle responded to Reissig in a letter that lays out the official line of argument under the heading of national interest. Berle acknowledged that the French authorities may have raided the Paris offices of the SERE, and that Reissig's concerns were humanitarian, but maintained that the United States could not make representations to the French Government on behalf of Spaniards:

13. Constancia with Laura Condax (with her back to the camera) and friends, Philadelphia, Summer of 1939. Courtesy of Kate Delano Condax Decker.

14. Luli (back row, sixth from left) with Dolores Ibarruri's daughter Amaya (back row, eight from left) and other children at a summer camp in the Soviet Union. Date not known. Archive of Dolores Ibarruri.

15. Luli and friend in the Soviet Union, *c.* 1943. Archive of Dolores Ibarruri.

16. Constancia, Anna Seghers, and Ludwig Renn, *c.* 1944. Archivo Teresa Miranda. Photo by Hans Gutmann.

17. Constancia in Mexico with the First Secretary of the Soviet Embassy, *c.* 1943.

18. Portrait of Constancia in Mexico. Courtesy of Eladia de los Rios.

18. *Mexico is Theirs* advertisement from the Modern Age catalogue.
Courtesy of Kate Delano Condax Decker.

20. Luli, *c.* 1945. Comintern Archive (RGASPI), Moscow.

21. Constancia and Lini de Vries. Constancia's house, Cuernavaca, December 1949.
Courtesy of Constancia Moreno.

22. Ignacio in exile in Zakopane, Poland, undated. Courtesy of Maria Sanchez and Juan Haro.

23. Ignacio at the home of Manuel
Sánchez Arcas in Warsaw, 1947.
Standing (left to right): Hidalgo de
Cisneros, Maria Cruz-López, delia
Neruda, Maria Sánchez Cruz-López,
Delia Neruda, Maria Sánchez Cruz-
López, Rafael Alberti, Wenceslao Roces.
Seated (from left to right): Hdalgo de
Cisneros, Maria Cruz-López, Pablo
Neruda, Ilya Ehrenburg y Uribe. Undated.
Courtesy of Maria Sanchez and Juan
Haro.

24. Ignacio and Pablo Neruda in
Poland, 1947. Courtesy of Maria
Sanchez and Juan Haro.

*You will appreciate, I feel sure, that this Government must confine its represen-
tations to a foreign government to matters which directly affect American
citizens or American interests. Any deviation from this policy, particularly
under the circumstances now prevailing, could not be other than prejudicial to
our efforts to extend the fullest possible protection to legitimate American interests abroad . . .* [22]

Constancia received a similar letter.[23] However a different story was
given to Mrs. Roosevelt in an internal memorandum that discloses that
"non-intervention" was just a cover for the real reason the Department of
State wanted nothing to do with the SERE The truth was that Berle and
his colleagues thought that the French had rightfully raided the SERE
offices and that it was a communist organization. He admits to Mrs.
Roosevelt that Constancia had been given the "official position" based on
"the settled practice of not monkeying with other people's politics". But he
adds that the SERE was suspected of doing much more than relief work and
that it was closely linked to Spanish Communist organizations. Berle did
not have any evidence against the SERE, but he had heard rumors linking
the communists to the SERE and to Negrín, and was more sympathetic to
the French than to the Spaniards in exile:

*I can't, therefore, say that the French, who were in their view fighting a war to
defend their very existence,*[24] *were wholly without reason in wanting to assure
themselves of what was going on in any of these Spanish groups. It is impossible
to be clear in a welter of accusations and cross-examinations, and I am only sure
of one thing, which is that we have not got the full story from either side – by a
long shot.*[25]

The French authorities did not find evidence to close the offices permanently. The SERE did not need to rely on foreign intervention, and was
functioning again soon after the raid.

The news that the SERE and Negrín allegedly had known Communist
connections did not seem to affect the First Lady's opinion of Spanish
refugee relief efforts, or of Constancia. A few days after Berle's internal
memo, Mrs. Roosevelt wrote to Constancia to say that she had done what
she could, which was not much, about the situation in France and that she
was glad to hear that the SERE was functioning again.[26] She did not yet
associate communism with Constancia, who she invited to visit her with
Ignacio, in February.

Mexico

Constancia and Ignacio had been in Mexico since December 1939, but planned to return to the United States in February 1940.[27] They had arranged to spend Christmas in Cuernavaca and Constancia wrote to Eleanor Roosevelt's secretary Malvina Thompson that she was "having a rest in this quiet and beautiful spot" and that they were "both thoroughly enjoying the warm sun and the wonderful climate." She also said: "I hope to be allowed to return to the U.S.A. in February when I have a lecture engagement for two months."[28] This last line underscores the fact that although a celebrity, Constancia had no diplomatic privileges, and was a refugee like other Spanish Republicans who depended on the goodwill of the United States government to be allowed into the US.

From Mexico, Constancia continued to appeal persistently to Mrs. Roosevelt, asking her for help in solving the refugee crisis. She also worked on a Spanish translation of *In Place of Splendor*. Herman Reissig of the SRRC was anxious for her return to the United States, so she could embark on the lecture tour he had organized. However, Constancia seemed strangely reluctant to leave Mexico. From December onwards, her relationship with the SRRC seems to have become strained as she dodged her original commitments and postponed her return to New York. The relationship became a tug of war and the more she resisted leaving Mexico, the more Reissig and his associates pushed for her scheduled return. Her letters to the committee members grew progressively ruder as she chided them for their inefficiency and laid out her conditions:

> *I received your letter and two more . . . all dealing with the same unpleasant subject: speaking. I am going to try, once for (sic) all to make the situation as clear as possible so that we can understand ourselves . . . I certainly did not intend to have every other day of the week tied up to speak in New York. THE MAIN REASON why I went to a lecture bureau was to avoid receiving letters (about three a day) asking me to speak for different Committees or organizations and from three or four different persons . . . who never seem to know what the other people in the same Committee are planning or have previously arranged . . . Now, there is no question of my taking any fee for speaking on the refugees, for the simple reason that a fee would entail speaking for an hour at least, and you simply cannot speak an hour or even half an hour on the subject of the Spanish refugees WHICH IS THE ONLY SUBJECT on which I am willing and ready to speak . . . and it will simply do no good to continue writing me letters here in Mexico . . . taking a lot of time and preventing me from having the very slight peace in search of which I have been forced to come thus far . . . [29]*

But there was no way of convincing Constancia to do anything she had made up her mind not to do and she had decided to stay in Mexico. She gave a number of reasons for canceling her early 1940 lecture tour. First, she was concerned about obtaining her Mexican citizenship:

> *if, as it seems, the Mexican government grants all the Spanish refugees the Mexican citizenship, as it now seems quite likely, AND we have to live in Mexico for at least three months before we get it, I may be delayed one or two more months . . . This is only an IF until the present and I cannot tell until the President signs the decree whether this will happen or not . . .* [30]

The second reason was that she was busy translating *In Place of Splendor* into Spanish, and simply seemed to be quite happy in the warm climate of Mexico:

> *I will remain here until I finish my book and perhaps a little longer to do some travel pieces on Mexico. I love this country and we would gladly remain here until the end of March or April. Also, the cost of life is about one third and this is always an interesting item for us to keep in mind!* [31]

Constancia's arguments did not satisfy Reissig who thought that she was squandering crucial opportunities to help the refugees. He replied:

> *We were rather floored by the news that you are remaining in Mexico, since we had counted so much on your being here for the functions indicated to you previously. Of course, you know best what you can and cannot do, but something has come up which I think merits your special consideration . . . Mrs. Vincent Sheean has contact with a few very wealthy women who have been extremely impressed with you and your book and who are consequently very eager to meet you. She feels that now is the time to take advantage of this feeling to make these new contacts and to raise very large sums of money for our campaign, which she thinks very possible . . . she is writing to you . . . suggesting that you try to come back here for a week or two . . . How about it?* [32]

Constancia refused to return even for a week and her unwillingness to cooperate seems to have put an irrevocable distance between her and the Americans involved in helping the Spanish refugees. In this case it is easy to see Reissig's point of view. In early 1940, Constancia was perhaps the best prepared, most appealing and best-known Spaniard who could convincingly speak to Americans about the refugee situation. A great deal of work had gone into making her such a figure. It must have been intensely frustrating to see her cancel and postpone speaking engagements that would have brought large groups of Americans, many of them wealthy and powerful, together in support of the refugees. Even if Constancia had important things to do in Mexico, which she perhaps did not share with Reissig, her refusal to return to the US for any length of time seems to indicate a serious loss of interest in the SRRC.

Apart from the reasons she gives in her letters there is little evidence about why she turned her back on these important opportunities to employ her celebrity for the refugee cause in the United States. It is clear, though, that she was happy to be reunited with Ignacio and other Spanish Republicans. From Mexico, she continued to work on behalf of the refugees and hoped that many of them would be relocated there and/or to other Latin American countries. Furthermore, she now had more freedom. Reissig and others were no doubt surprised that she was not the conscientious personality of *In Place of Splendor*, and she had avoided being at the beck and call of the SRRC. In a private letter to Jay Allen she wrote:

> *We intend to remain here where we can live for less than $100 a month, very well. Which means that we can live for quite a while without worrying. We would both like to return to the States with something worthwhile, otherwise we do not know what we will do. I have slipped out of the lectures with great glee, because I really dreaded them. We feel that unless Ignacio learns some English before we return I would have to be his slave to translate all the time or he would be unable to get around and this place is ideal to work in, quiet and warm . . . We hope to be able to return to the USA without difficulty with a year's visa . . . after we have our resident Mexican cards, but of course, anything can happen. Anyway now I am hard at work on my book.[33] I already have a definite offer from South America and also from England.[34]*

What she did not mention to Reissig or Allen was that PCE and Comintern leaders had made Mexico the central base of operations for communication with the communists in Spain.[35] Her activities in Mexico show that she continued to be a mouthpiece for the PCE, though it is unclear whether she chose to stay and collaborate or whether she was under orders. In any case, Constancia thought that her return to the United States could simply wait and she was sure that she would resume her lecture schedule sooner or later. She was uniquely useful to the Comintern as a figure beloved by powerful and wealthy Americans. Unfortunately, she would soon lose her prestigious position. Tensions grew within the SRRC that would ultimately ostracize her from the organization and she would be refused reentry to the United States.

But in early 1940 she still had considerable influence in the United States and in Mexico, and one of the events she participated in was the Pan-American Conference in Mexico City. She sent Mrs. Roosevelt a two-page "report" afterwards:

Because I will always remember the great interest you have shown towards the Spanish people, I would like to tell you about the Pan-American Conference to help Spanish refugees just held in Mexico City . . . The latest reports from France tell us in detail of the horrible conditions under which our people are now living and of the increased need to bring them to new homes in this hemisphere. For the first time we now see a real possibility of achieving this, now that so many Latin-American countries have indicated their willingness to accept the Spanish refugees. One of the few remaining problems is that of securing the adequate financial assistance necessary for their transportation and resettlement. It is perhaps not too much to hope that the great people and the government of the United States will take a share in solving this difficulty . . . After more than a year in the concentration camps preceded by two and a half years of struggle against fascism surely the democratic countries of the world will want to show their sympathy for our people in a practical manner . . . [36]

Constancia also mentioned that she was hopeful because the (Quaker) American Friends Service Committee had applied to the United States government for funds to transport and resettle the refugees. She clearly hoped that she could pressure Mrs. Roosevelt to have the Committee's request approved. Mrs. Roosevelt's reply was brief and, as usual, promised little: " I have heard how successful the Pan-American Conference was and I am so glad. The Quakers are usually successful in obtaining what they set out for, but, of course, I have no way of knowing definitely what they will be able to accomplish." [37]

There is a coolness to this note that contrasts to the warmer tone of earlier months. Was Mrs. Roosevelt simply busy and distracted, or was she getting tired of the Spanish refugee situation and of her persistent friend? Whatever her feelings were in late January, this reply does seem to portend the demise of their friendship which was in fact only a few months away.

On March 11, Constancia wired the First Lady with news of the political reprisals and executions taking place in Spain. She was particularly concerned because of an official French order to send thousands of refugees from France back to Spain. This was a subject she had already written about in the January 1940 issue of *Volunteer for Liberty*, the publication of the Veterans of the Abraham Lincoln Brigade. [38] In her article, she stressed the urgent need for international help to evacuate the refugees from France.

You know how the women and children are being treated in France – how they are being forced back to Spain. We have almost come to accept as a normal thing that the women and children should return . . . But we must see that those people who are in danger of being killed when they are forced back to Spain must be saved. There are about 20,000 of these people still in France. Of the 200,000 refugees, we should concentrate at least on the 20,000 who we know face certain death. We know how much it costs to get them to South America . . . Today, the United States is the one country which can help us financially. We can also ask President Roosevelt to urge the South American countries to accept Spanish refugees. We can charter ships – if not American ships, then Belgian, Dutch or Greek ships and transport the refugees to the Americas. Today, the British and French are trying to appease Franco by turning over those refugees who are the greatest danger to Franco and the best assurance of a rebirth of freedom in Spain. These are the people General Franco wants. These are therefore the very people we must save – those who will rebuild a democratic Spain.[39]

Seeking advice about how to reply to Constancia concerning the policy of the United States towards the refugees, Mrs. Roosevelt forwarded this telegram directly to the Department of State. On March 25, the Assistant Secretary of State, Adolf A. Berle, Jr. gave her a copy of his response to Constancia, which echoed his stance regarding the raid of the SERE offices in Paris:

In reply to a number of communications of this kind which have been received from time to time during the past year, the Department has been obliged to point out that this Government is not in a position to make representations to the government of another country regarding the treatment accorded persons within its jurisdiction, unless, of course, the persons in question are citizens or nationals of the United States entitled to the protection of this Government. I may add, with reference to the reported order for the expulsion of Spanish refugees from France, that the French Ambassador upon his own initiative has informed the department that he has been officially advised by his Government that this purported order is a forgery which has been widely circulated as the basis for a campaign against France. P.S. I have also checked personally. There never was any such order.[40]

But the truth was that the situation in France had become desperate for the refugees. General Jean Ménard, Superintendent of Camps, had worked efficiently since February to empty the camps and by April there were only 6,000 Spanish refugees left.[41] Just a few weeks later, Constancia wrote to Mrs. Roosevelt's secretary, Melvina Thompson:

Since I sent a telegram to Mrs. Franklin D. Roosevelt on March 11th, telling her of the sad plight of the Spanish refugees in France in danger of being forced back to Spain, I have received further evidence in the form of numberless letters from women refugees from the different camps in France. I take the liberty of sending you excerpts from these letters translated in to English, with the hope that they will dispel any doubt as to how well-founded was my concern when I

telegraphed Mrs. Roosevelt. I hope I am not inconveniencing her too much with
my persistence in asking for her support every time that I feel she can do something
for my compatriots; and I beg you to express to her again my very sincere grati-
tude for all her kindnesses.[42]

Mrs. Roosevelt's reply was "I am always more than glad to do what I can
for your people, but the State Department insists that people are not being
forced back. However, the letters which you enclosed will go to the
Department at once."[43]

The situation of the Spanish refugees only became worse when the
Germans invaded France. On June 18, 1940, Constancia implored Mrs.
Roosevelt to arrange for ships to evacuate the now even more vulnerable
refugees.

> *Once again I appeal to your kindness on behalf of the Spanish refugees in France.*
> *We have just managed to escape the German onslaught in the provinces invaded*
> *by the Nazis are massed at the harbor of Bordeaux. They anxiously await some*
> *means of leaving France to escape being turned over to Franco as soon as they fall*
> *into the hands of the Germans. The horrors of the harbor of Alicante where over*
> *15,000 Spaniards waited helplessly for boats that would allow them to escape*
> *the reprisals of Franco, in March 1939, are being repeated once again in the*
> *harbor of Bordeaux . . . Surely, something can be still be done and ships can be*
> *sent under the Red Cross or other flags, to take these brave men and women from*
> *sure death and carry them to their destination in the New World.*[44]

By the time Mrs. Roosevelt replied with a discouragingly brief note
saying that everything possible was being done for the refugees but that
ships could not be guaranteed – France had capitulated to Germany.[45]

In September, the tone of their correspondence became tense. Constancia
wrote criticizing a statement that Elliot Roosevelt (the president's son) had
made to the press claiming that Spanish military officers exiled in Mexico
were joining the Mexican army and militia. His claim made Constancia
furious and though her letter was polite, she did not mince words:

> *I was astonished to see your son Elliot's statement on Mexico to the press. I am*
> *afraid he is seriously misinformed on the subject . . . For not one single Spaniard*
> *has been incorporated either to the Mexican Army or the unarmed C.T.M. militia*
> *. . . I cannot help feeling afraid that misinformed statements on the activities of*
> *the Spanish refugees . . . will only make their lot more difficult in the new world*
> *. . . I trust you will forgive this rather passionate cry from the depth of my heart,*
> *but I see very closely the hardships of the majority of my compatriots . . . And if*
> *it is not asking too much, I would beg you to find a way or means of conveying*
> *the truth on this question to the American public.*[46]

In her terse reply, Mrs. Roosevelt said that she had been very busy over the summer and had no knowledge of her son's statement, but that she would forward Constancia's letter to him. When President Roosevelt was reelected in November 1940, Constancia sent the First Lady a congratulatory note, which was answered with an impersonal acknowledgement. A month later, their friendship and dialogue would come to an abrupt end.

In December 1940 Constancia decided to finally return to the United States to continue her work on behalf of the Spanish refugees. The American Rescue Ship Mission, whose sponsors included Helen Keller, Princess Helga Lowenstein and her husband, André Maurois, had invited her back to the States. As she prepared her trip, she applied for her visa, and to her surprise her application was denied. Again, she appealed to the First Lady:

> *Due, I am sure, to some misunderstanding, I was refused a visa, and the Consul here informs me that it was because of the State Department. I hate to trouble you on a personal matter, but as it was felt that my presence in the States might be of considerable assistance to the campaign, which of course means so much to the Spanish people, I am approaching you in this matter. If you should think fit, perhaps you could use your influence to find out just where the misunderstanding arose.*[47]

Evidently, Constancia thought this was just a bureaucratic glitch, but she was wrong. The finality of the response she received from Mrs. Roosevelt must have been very disconcerting:

> *I have forgotten the circumstances, but I seem to remember reading in the papers some mention of the trouble in the Spanish Refugee Committee with which you were connected here in the matter of affiliation with communists. This may be the cause of the State Department's decision. I think it is understood that you sympathize with Russia and since the Nazi pact and the war with Finland and the taking over of other countries in that area, there is more suspicion here than ever of Russia. I understand your feeling, but also see the point of the feeling here.*[48]

There can be no doubt that this letter was upsetting to Constancia. She was given no opportunity to defend or explain herself, nor was there any prospect that she would ever be welcome again in the United States. This was the final communication between Constancia and Eleanor Roosevelt, and explains why she came to settle permanently in Mexico.

Why had Constancia suddenly been blacklisted and what was "the trouble with the Spanish Committee" which the First Lady referred to? Were her activities and views in fact so different from those non-Communists working to help the Spanish refugees? Why didn't her other prominent American friends such as Jay Allen or Ernest Hemingway come to her defense? To understand the position Constancia found herself in, the impact of the Hitler–Stalin[49] pact on Spanish Refugee Relief must be taken into account. Constancia's life had again been dramatically affected by political events, and between June and August 1940 Germany's occupation of France and the Hitler–Stalin non-aggression pact caused the SRRC to change its approach. The changes, outlined below, were vehemently opposed by Constancia, who found herself in the minority. The following is an excerpt from an SRRC circular:

> *The North American Committee was an alliance of supporting organizations. Among these, the Socialist Party and the Communist Party were represented on its board. The new Spanish Refugee Relief Campaign was an entire break from this setup. Party representatives were asked to drop out of the board, new members were added, drawn from wider reaches of public interest . . . The outbreak of the European war not only hampered the national money-raising drive planned by the Spanish refugee Relief Campaign last fall, it was to change the climate in which it operated . . . As in a number of other organizations, the change in climate manifested itself after the Nazi–Soviet pact and the Russian invasion of Finland. The suppression of the Communist Party in France by the war government affected even more directly the fortunes of Spanish relief, provoking Communist retaliation here and abroad.*[50]

Jay Allen and the majority members[51] of the committee were wary of what they saw as the communist ideology of the minority members.[52] They saw the latter as putting their political interests before their commitment to helping the refugees. In early 1940, there was a sharp split in the governing board of the SRRC over three major issues. First, the majority members of the North American Committee (which included Jay Allen) wanted the relief funds in France to be distributed by the Quakers, who had "free elbow room in getting relief through in France, at a time when war tensions were handicapping other bodies."[53] The minority members opposed this resolution, but it was passed. As Jay Allen wrote: "it was I who cast the deciding vote one day in Constancia's absence that cut off the distribution of funds thru the old channels and turned them over to the Quakers."[54]

Secondly, during an aid conference in February in Mexico City, the minority members of the committee wanted to issue a resolution condemning the French government's treatment of the refugees. Their proposed statement talked about "the terrifying situation which has developed among the refugees in the concentration camps after one year of misery and despair due to the conduct of the French government." The support for this resolution was led by a "Communist member of the Spanish Cortes who was in attendance."[55] The majority members of the committee, and in addition Republican political leaders such as Negrín, and Foreign Minister Alvarez del Vayo, opposed the resolution because they thought that to criticize France harshly and publicly would make them seem like blind supporters of the Communist line. The Relief Campaign wanted to pass a resolution that they thought was both fairer and more diplomatic. It would criticize the French treatment of the refugees, but also acknowledge the fact that the arrival of 500,000 Spanish refugees presented the French government with a serious challenge, and that France had spent millions of francs to help the Spaniards.

Finally, there was the famous "Ménard Order". This was the much-disputed order that had allegedly been issued by General Jean Ménard to deport thousands of refugees back to Franco Spain that Constancia had urgently wired Eleanor Roosevelt about in early March. The Refugee Relief Campaign's report received a copy of the order on March 8, 1940:

> *we received a mimeographed copy of an order attributed to General Ménard calling for the repatriation to Spain by March 15th of all Spanish refugees with exception of those who were soldiering or working in France, had relatives in the French army or at work, or who could "produce weighty evidence for not going back to Spain." This order, if authentic, knocked French claims of observing the right of asylum into a cocked hat. It would play into Franco's hands and jeopardize the lives and liberties of hundreds of exiles. It reached us from the International Coordinating Committee at Paris, an agency for centralizing aid, first to Loyalist Spain and, later, to Spanish refugees. It was only a mimeographed copy and it was freighted with such an overwhelming indictment of French policy that as a responsible organization it was up to us to check its authenticity before raising a hue-and-cry.*[56]

With only a week to go before the order was to take effect, the board of the SRRC sent a copy of the order to the French embassy in Washington, and Herman Reissig made it clear to the embassy that if any steps were taken by the French government to implement the order there would be vigorous public American protests against France.

French Premier Daladier sent a statement to the SRRC through the embassy claiming that the order had been fabricated: "General Ménard confirms to the French Minister of Foreign Affairs that the Circular you referred to is a fake. The suppression of Spanish refugee centers was never decided nor thought of. No isolated individual of Spanish nationality and, furthermore, no group of refugees was forced to go against his will to Spain. No change has occurred in the disposition of the French Government which was defined at the end of 1939". Reissig released this statement along with a comment in which he said that "We heartily welcome the information contained in this cable and hope that the French Government will cooperate in every way possible with international efforts to emigrate Spanish refugees to American countries."[57] The internal report of the committee concluded that "The French denials . . . might be construed . . . as diplomatic evasions; but true or not, once made, and part of the record, they made impossible any categorical assertion on our part that such an order was being put into effect."[58]

The majority members of the committee, including Reissig and Allen, seemed willing to take the French denials at face value. In essence, they worried that a confrontation with France would harm the refugees more than it would help them: "American protests carry obligations with them. It is for us to help make existence more possible for the refugees who remain. It is up to Americans not to leave the whole burden on French shoulders."[59]

The minority committee members, who had held an unauthorized meeting and picketed the French consulate in New York, were voted out, and anyone who thought differently on any of the three issues related to France – distribution of funds by the Quakers, the resolution passed in Mexico City, and the Ménard order – was thought to have partisan political motivations. Allen wrote to Amaro del Rosal Díaz, a former Socialist and UGT militant, in exile in Mexico to explain the controversy, and said that in the end "It is interesting to note that the only supporters the Spanish Refugee Relief Campaign (SRRC) lost were those with definitive sympathies for a political group."[60] In the context, "political group" must be understood to mean Communist.

Amongst the supporters the campaign lost was Constancia. She wrote an "open letter" to Allen on April 9, 1940 that caused the definitive break-up of their friendship. Allen was furious: "I have been attacked by my good friend Constancia de la Mora in an open letter! I enclose a copy. Her facts aren't terribly good. They split the organization when they tried to use it for their own purposes. I have written to Constancia to tell her that there are at least two ways in betraying the refugees: one is to abandon them to the French authorities and the other is to hoist them over the hammer and swastickle. We have refused to do either. I am proud of the fact that we got through this crisis with no 'red baiting,' the only baiting has been done by them."[61] Over twenty years later, Allen was still angry about this letter and wrote to Louis Fischer: "It's all ancient history now but do you happen to remember when Allen came in . . . for excoriation by the Faithful, open letter from Constancia,"[62] and that

> *I did indeed express myself . . . about what I considered to be the harshness of the French towards the Spanish refugees but also about the ghastly unwisdom of the*

Lincoln Brigade boys[63] picketing the French consulate in New York. On this subject I had several times spoken my piece in public. (Incidentally, I find a letter from Ernest Hemingway at that time saying that while the French were bastards any other nation would have simply called out the cavalry and driven our people back to Franco.)[64]

Constancia's letter to the committee also ended, indirectly, her relationship with Eleanor Roosevelt. It shows the fundamental schism between her view of the predicament of the refugees in France and that of her former American friends. Constancia was a Communist, but her views and her impolitic anger at France had more to do with the need of the refugees than with ideology. For all her weaknesses, and she was surely hot-headed and impulsive as her personal attack on Allen demonstrates, Constancia perceived the American stand on the refugees as yet another form of non-intervention. From Mexico, she was in contact with many of the exiles as well as with the aid organizations in Paris, and undoubtedly thought that she knew how to help them most efficiently. She was particularly upset by Allen's belief that the Ménard order was a fake:

I cannot now comprehend what has come over you . . . This order was to the effect that before March 15th tens of thousands of Spanish refugees would be forced to return to Spain. Four days later, representatives of the French Government in the United States denied the authenticity of the order. Without further investigation, you, a newspaperman always keen to prove your assertions with facts, accepted this "official denial". You thereby condemned wholesale those whose courageous protests have done more than anything else to prevent the refugees from being shipped back to a certain death in fascist Spain. I have seen and read extracts from over fifty letters written from different camps in France by Spanish women like myself . . . They write in tragic tones of desperation . . . Do you know that in Douarnenez (Finistere), Plouneze (Cote du Nord) and other camps forced repatriation actually began as early as March 2nd? . . . Besides the Ménard order, I have in my possession a copy of a circular order dated February 13th, 1940 and issued by departmental prefects to the Mayors of towns and villages where there are Spanish refugees. This order states that women, children, orphans, and invalids who lack natural means of support will be forced to return to Spain. The only exceptions are those who find work before March 15th. But do you know that these letters I mentioned above repeat again and again that none is allowed to leave the camps in search of work?"[65]

She enclosed excerpts from the letters and goes on to say how merciless the French were. For example, while those refugees who could prove by documents that they would suffer reprisals in Spain wouldn't be sent back, everyone knew that no refugee had such a document. After describing in detail the impossible situation faced by the exiles in the French camps, she defended the source of her information, the International Coordinating Committee in Paris. Made up of "distinguished French men and women", this committee was to be trusted and admired because they saw what was happening on their own soil and had the courage to speak out. The Americans, on the other hand, were unwilling to see the facts:

I feel that you and others have thus abandoned the Spanish refugees in this their hour of greatest need. You still live in a beautiful and peaceful country ruled by democracy . . . If those French men and women who are so much nearer the actual scene than you risk everything to make the truth . . . known to the world, we have the right to expect the same from our friends in more distant countries. Otherwise we will be forced to believe that in the present era of competitive journalism it has become impossible to make a comfortable living and still have the courage to tell the truth.[66]

An editorial in *The Nation* at the end of March about the demonstration at the French Consulate, entitled "The Fifth Avenue Riot", claimed that the police action at the protest had been like Mussolini's victory over Albania: five hundred police were in place hours before the picketing was scheduled to start. When the a few dozen pickets appeared, many of them women, they were violently "pounced upon". The pretext given "for the demonstration was an order supposed to have been issued by General Ménard at Daladier's behest, calling for the immediate expulsion from France of all Spanish refugees who refuse to enlist in the French army or accept military labor service. The French government declares that the report of the order was "faked' by Communists for political purposes."[67] However, the article also points out that while the refugees had not been "forced" back into Spain, "tens of thousands have returned under pressure."

As it turns out, Ménard had indeed issued a January 15 order to close down all the camps and refugee centers for Spanish Republicans. On 7 February, Spaniards in the following four categories of refugees were ordered to leave France and to return to Spain if they had no other option: children with parents in Spain, orphans, women and children with no established means of financial support, and the sick and invalid who had left Spain to avoid the war.[68] This order was signed by the Minister of the Interior, not by Ménard, but Constancia's concerns were justified. The only exceptions made were for those who could quickly find a job and prove that they could support themselves. Finding well-paid employment quickly was a highly unlikely scenario for orphans and invalids. Most had nowhere to go and their only option was to return to Spain. As historian David Pike points out: "Real danger awaited all of the refugees who returned to Spain, despite the guarantees offered by Franco. As late as 1949 French authorities reported that Spanish officials were still opening fire on Spaniards as they crossed the border into Spain."[69]

There was nothing Constancia could do to prove to her American friends that the order to send Republican refugees back to Franco Spain was true, and not communist propaganda. Convinced that she was a fanatic communist and more interested in ideology than in the refugees, Allen, Hemingway, and Eleanor Roosevelt no longer supported her.

By 1940, her former champion Ernest Hemingway wrote, in a letter to Jay Allen:"Connie gives me a pain in what remains of my ass. Can't anybody ever write anything that is true?"[70] In another letter to the Spanish exiled painter Luis Quintanilla, he continued to rant against Constancia (and La Pasionaria, and Alvarez del Vayo) in crude Spanish that is vaguely intelligible.[71] Allen himself, who had been one of her closest friends and supporters for years, refused to lift a finger when she asked for help to return to the United States: " I sent her a message by a mutual friend to the effect that I worshipped her memory and hated her guts. And this was fairly accurate."[72]

The dynamics and divisions of the Spanish Civil War had spilled over into the immediate post-war. Constancia was once again trying desperately to get "the truth" out to the world about the injustices faced by Spanish Republicans in exile and felt betrayed, as she had during the war, by the Americans she had thought were true allies of Republican Spain. She saw the SRRC position as an extension of the Unites States' non-intervention policy during the war. The consequences of the schism were that she had no option but to remain in Mexico. The years she spent there would be the second and definitive period of her life in exile.

V
Mexico, 1940–1950
Exile

"We hope to be able to return to the USA without difficulty with a year's visa ... but, of course, anything can happen."[1]

Mexico became a haven for Spanish Republican exiles. The Soviet Union and Mexico had been the only countries to provide arms for Republican Spain, and the policies of President Lázaro Cárdenas towards refugees made it the most welcoming country in the world. Starting in 1937 when Cárdenas' wife, Amalia, had brought five hundred Spanish Republican children to Morelia, Mexico was the best option for thousands of Spaniards who had nowhere else to go.[2] As early as 1938, when the Republican defeat seemed inevitable, Cardenas said he would let up to sixty thousand Spanish refugees into Mexico, though the costs of transporting and housing them were up to the Republican authorities.[3]

> *Cárdenas's motives for receiving the Spaniards displaced by the Civil War were in great part, but not solely, humanitarian. Since the Revolution (1910–1920) Mexico had prided itself on being a haven for political refugees ... Aiding the Republican refugees also seemed to follow naturally from Mexico's previous support for the Republic, which in turn had been motivated by its anti-imperialist stance and its strong belief in national self-determination.*[4]

The years that Constancia de la Mora spent in Mexico represent a complex and challenging period. Yet the numerous studies of Spanish exiles in Mexico hardly mention that she lived and worked in Mexico City and Cuernavaca for the rest of her life. Though she continued to collaborate actively in anti-fascist efforts and to work for the Spanish Communist Party (PCE) and the Soviet Government, in both political and personal terms her situation would become increasingly difficult throughout the 1940s.

■ ■ ■ ■ ■ ■ ▩

In early January 1940 it seemed impossible that Franco could stay in power for long, and Constancia was happy and relieved to be reunited with Ignacio in Cuernavaca. She adapted easily to Mexico, and returned to her role as a spokesperson for the Republic with enthusiasm, still believing firmly that the United States would intervene on behalf of the exiled government once they saw clearly how Franco was oppressing Spain. She and Ignacio had surrounded themselves with Spanish friends and spent the new year with journalist Burnett Bolloten who was interviewing them for his book on the Spanish Civil War. Constancia was impressed with his work and wrote to Jay Allen to ask him to help Bolloten find a publisher:

> *These last three days we have (sic) Bolloten here with us. He has brought me seven chapters of his book, which will be really THE (sic) historical documentary study of the war. I wish you could see some of it! It is simply marvellous . . . ALL from our side; but it is a most fascinating political as well as historical and military study of the war, with details and data that no one – I am sure – has or can ever get . . . the thing now is to find some kind of a foundation or society . . . or university to give him a sum or an advance that will enable him to live at the rate of $20 a week! Have you any suggestions as to whom he could write? Obviously we have thought of Negrín or other sources, but all these he very justly rejects, for immediately the book would be branded as propaganda etc. and would lose all its value.*[5]

Was Bolloten still sympathetic to the PCE and to Ignacio and Constancia, or was he simply a convincing interviewer? In any case, Constancia clearly believed that he was an ally.

In the meantime, the news from Spain was terrible. She and Ignacio had just received a letter from Negrín's secretary, Benigno, who was in Paris. He reported that conditions within Spain were horrific and that the Republicans left behind were no longer considered a political threat, they were simply treated as a nuisance to the public order and a matter for the police to deal with. She promised Jay that she would obtain a copy of a list of death sentences from Spain to send him. Despite the tragedy of the situation faced by her fellow Spaniards, there is a certain optimism in Constancia's tone. She and Ignacio were together, she was working, and she still held the belief that it was just a matter of time before they would return to a Republican Spain. This hope would fuel her efforts for the next several years.

Another exiled Republican, Aurora Arnáiz, recalls meeting Ignacio and Constancia at their house in Mexico City and the atmosphere in which they lived:

> *Vercaruz, 56 was a small building . . . How can we imagine . . . the incred-*

ible people who lived there? The ingenuous and kind Vicens, the Rodriguez Mata brothers, the Mantecóns (Ignacio and Conchita), and Ernesto all lived in apartment number 2; and Connie and Ignacio – the soul of the building – in their splendid, cozy, and welcoming apartment number 1. Though the building and its historical neighborhood were interesting in and of themselves, they were nothing compared to the unforgettable characters who lived there. Today they have all vanished . . . As have the visitors who stopped by regularly: Buñuel . . . Bergamín, the the Nerudas . . . Whenever former Lincoln Brigade members came through Mexico they stopped by to see Connie. It was so moving to listen to their memories, their love for the cause . . . They always had trouble saying goodbye to Connie. They didn't want to leave her because for them she was like a living piece of Spain . . . [6]

Until she met Constancia, Arnáiz had been staying at the house of Communist leader Pedro Checa. After Trotsky's assassination on August 2, 1940, all of the Spanish Communists fell under suspicion and Checa and his wife, Angelita, thought it would be safer for Arnáiz to stay with someone else. Constancia and Ignacio, who she had never met, agreed to have her to stay with them:

Connie came to pick me up and I was very impressed by her. She was overflowing with energy. She had dark skin and she was dressed up like an Indian, her hair was parted down the middle and she had two braids, she wore a gathered skirt, a shawl, and huaraches. With her restrained mannerisms and steady gaze she was quite an imposing figure. Her second last name {Maura} seemed to weigh her down. There was a severity to her features and expression. She never smiled and treated people distantly, without getting too involved. She was reflective, not very spontaneous and not sentimental at all.[7]

Arnáiz was taken to the apartment at Veracruz 56 and slept in an unused servant's room. She met Ignacio who was quite a contrast to Constancia:

His rapid chatter . . . hid a cold, reflective person, who had managed (at least apparently) to take life with all its challenges as a sport . . . I never knew to what point his apparent frivolity hid a mature person . . . (he) was the prototypical aristocrat, cheerful and always ready to see the best in everyone. In contrast to Constancia's rigidity, Ignacio always seemed to take things as they came . . . [8]

The difference between Ignacio and Constancia was also evident in their clothes. Ignacio, despite the hardships of exile, remained a European dandy:

Ignacio was extraordinarily attractive . . . He never changed his style . . . wherever he went, along went his white shirts, his gray heather tweeds, his brown suede shoes, and his ever-present white socks.[9]

Arnáiz remembers their apartment fondly. It was filled with flowers and decorated with indigenous objects and furniture. Constancia quickly figured out where the most beautiful and authentic indigenous crafts were made and she traveled far to augment her collection. Thanks to learning about handicrafts before the war, when she worked with Zenobia Camprubí in her Arte Popular shop in Madrid, she had a knack for finding the best local markets. Many American women who admired her because of *In Place of Splendor* came to meet Constancia in 1940. She took many of them on shopping trips to villages where she had bought objects from local craftsmen.[10] Arnáiz says that to this day she has never met anybody who loved Mexico more than Constancia.[11]

> *She was perhaps the one who best knew how to capture the strange magic of Chiapas, Morelia, Zacatecas, and who best knew how to relate to the inditos and inditas . . . She was always down to earth and treated everyone equally. She never mentioned her aristocratic background, and simple people always felt at home with her.*[12]

Mexican culture and her friendships combined to make the first period of her exile relatively easy. Her letters to Jay Allen and Eleanor Roosevelt show she planned on returning to the Unites States soon, and like so many other Republicans she was convinced that if Germany lost World War II, Franco would be removed from power. In 1940 she saw Mexico as an appealing place to bide her time temporarily, until she could return to Spain definitively.

Because of her book's success, Constancia was in a much better position financially than most exiles. She was able to live well and to support Ignacio, who was not interested in working. Yet soon after they were reunited, their relationship changed dramatically. Constancia and Ignacio divorced, by mutual consent, in Mexico in 1941.[13]

Their friend, aviator Hernández Franch, who was also in exile in Mexico, remembers that Ignacio was not contributing much to the couple's finances. His fondness for women, drinking, and his dislike of work caused tension. Pablo Neruda had found Ignacio a job representing the Domecq wine company in Mexico, but instead of making a profit, they drank most of the wine themselves. Hernández Franch's remembers:

> *There were parties . . . every week. Buñuel, Neruda, Mantecón, we'd all get together there . . . All the wine Neruda received that he was supposed to sell, they drank it all there. At Veracruz 56. . . . Ignacio didn't quite go back to his old ways, because he didn't have money like he used to, but he didn't lift a finger. He did nothing. He lived off Constancia's memoir, that's the truth.*

*When he was offered another job, selling books door to door, he turned it down
so I took it.*[14]

Like Aurora Arnaíz, Hernández Franch emphasizes Constancia's
generosity both in Mexico City and in Acapaztingo, Cuernavaca where she
later built a house.

*When I got to Veracruz (56) I could only get a job making bricks . . . We didn't
have a cent so Constancia said we could come and live with her in her first house
in Acapatzingo, and we did. Later she sold that house and built a new one, also
in Acapantzingo, and we also lived in that one. Because she would always let us
stay in her house whenever she was in Mexico City.*[15]

Hernández Franch was puzzled by their decision to end their marriage:
"Nobody knows why they separated, I don't even think they themselves
knew. They split up, but in a way they stayed together."[16] Though Ignacio
was a well-known ladies' man (his nickname was "Casanova") some people
heard that Ignacio had left Constancia because she had an affair with
someone in Mexico.[17] However, Fredericka Martin wrote to Alvah Bessie
that Ignacio had met a Polish woman who worked for one of the aid
committees in Paris: "Ignacio came to Mexico and didn't like it. Then went
to Poland – and I suspect was drawn there by the Polish secretary we knew
about in New York . . . He was here briefly and left a heartsick Constancia
behind him."[18] Another version of the break-up is that Ignacio had an affair
in Mexico with an American girl.[19] Whatever the motive, and although she
did later have at least one companion in Mexico, Constancia would never
get over Ignacio. They remained in touch for several years after the
divorce.[20]

Despite the end of her marriage, Constancia's great energy was still in
evidence. She devoted her time to numerous activities, often simultane-
ously. She worked for the Soviet Embassy in Mexico City under the famous
ambassador Constantin Oumansky, translated *In Place of Splendor* into
Spanish and arranged for it's publication in other languages,[21] collaborated
with other exiled women in refugee relief and anti-fascist committees,
bought and sold Mexican crafts and antiques, and also gave tours of Mexico
and Guatemala to wealthy Americans.

New Book Projects

In Mexico Constancia reunited with the Italian photographer and activist
Tina Modotti, who had been the famous "María" of *Socorro Rojo*. Because of

her political activity, she continued to go under this pseudonym in Mexico, and her husband Vittorio Vidali was still known as Carlos Contreras. Constancia and Modotti saw each other frequently at regular gatherings at Neruda's house. Though Tina had stopped taking photographs, Constancia wanted to write a book on Mexico and Tina had agreed to collaborate though she would not take the photographs herself. The book was to be called *Mexico is Theirs*, and with it Constancia wanted to "tell the story of how reformist president Lázaro Cárdenas had breathed new life into Mexico's revolutionary agenda."[22] Constancia had planned the book earlier in New York with a young American couple, John and Laura Condax. She invited the Condaxes down to Mexico to stay with her, and they used her apartment as a base as they they made trips around Mexico with Modotti. Constancia herself was too busy at the time to accompany them.

The Condaxes became close friends of Constancia's and, according to their daughter, they had an exceptional affection and admiration for her. John Condax was a well-known photographer, and thought that the combination of his images and Constancia's text would be a great success. Condax admired *In Place of Splendor*, and he was shocked when he saw her first attempt to write something about Mexico, in English, for their project. What she had typed up was so badly written it was comical and he realized immediately that she could not have written *In Place of Splendor*. Constancia confessed to the couple that Ruth Mckenney had in fact written her memoir.[23] It was a shame that she could not write well, because she had the opportunity to capitalize on her fame as an author, and she did have a great deal to say about Mexico. It was decided that she could perhaps write the text with help from others.

In the meantime, Constancia herself seems to have become temporarily swept up by her fame and believed the hype that she was a writer. She had tried to write a fictionalized account, in English, of the lives of the Spanish refugees in Mexico, a sort of sequel to *In Place of Splendor*. She had been encouraged in August 1940 by Chester Kerr, of the Atlantic Monthly Press, to embark on this project who had written to her saying:

> *I have been turning over in my mind . . . the notion of your doing a book about the Spanish refugees in Mexico. If ever there is to be a logical sequel to In Place of Splendor, this is it. It seems to me that the story of the Spaniards who are trying to make new lives for themselves on this continent has tremendous dramatic possibilities – and I know of no one better equipped to write it than yourself.*[24]

On the basis of what he considered her first book, Kerr thought Constancia was a strong commercial prospect. She was enthusiastic about writing on the Spanish refugees in Mexico, and was confident that she could tackle the project, in English, by herself. By the early summer of 1941 she had completed a draft which she sent to Modern Age, a publishing house in Boston where she and her friends had contacts. Her manuscript was rejected. Although Ruth Mckenney's talent had made *In Place of Splendor* a success, Constancia thought she could at least write a decent book on the refugees. But she had underestimated how difficult writing was, especially with no prior experience and in a second language. She had also sent the draft to Mckenney, and asked for advice. Mckenney agreed with Modern Age that Constancia's effort was simply not good enough. The rejection did not surprise her, but must have been discouraging, despite her denials. She wrote to the Condaxes and implored them to find someone else to write *Mexico is Theirs*:

> *I did not feel in the least discouraged or hurt or crestfallen. I just got the satisfying feeling that I was right after all. Since my arrival in Mexico I had the intimate conviction that I was no writer, that my first book was a sheer "casualidad" (chance) with the help of an interesting subject and Ruth, and that never again would I attempt to write anything else . . . I would rather do anything else than write. The truth is that I have nothing very definite to do at the present moment, but that does not mean that I must write, either. In fact, I loathe the idea of writing more than anything else in the world. Yes, this is the truth, the pure and simple truth. And since I have acquired the conviction that I can't write I am much happier, for there is no reason why I should do something which I can't do and which I dislike doing . . . Add to this the fact that I simply cannot concentrate on the subject of Mexico. It seems horribly far away and unimportant and stupid and impersonal to me.[25] I couldn't even sit down and do a schoolgirl's task about it . . . Your photographs are swell and somebody should do something about them, somebody who can write and will do them justice . . . Please forgive me.[26]*

Constancia and Modotti had made a trip for *Mexico is Theirs* at least once, to Tehuantepéc, however it was Modotti and the Condaxes who spent months traveling around together. They were already back in the United States when the news broke that on January 5, 1942, Tina had died unexpectedly in Mexico City.

Her death immediately raised suspicion. She had been at a party at the house of Bauhaus architect Hannes Meyer, when she suddenly said she did not feel well. A friend, Nacho Aguirre, walked her to a taxi. She gave the driver her address, but by the time the taxi stopped in front of her house, she was dead.[27] Her husband, Vittorio Vidali, was apparently unable to cope with her sudden death and hid out at Constancia's house for days, since he was either upset, or perhaps "still lucid enough to realize the Mexican press would try to muddy her name and insinuate foul play."[28] His "disappearance" only added fuel to newspaper stories saying that Tina's death had the mark of a Communist purge. The headlines read "Mysterious Disappearance of Tina Modotti's Lover, Carlos Jiménez Contreras" and "Tina Modotti's Death Follows Pattern of Communist Purges".[29] Vidali did not even attend the burial. A few months later, Constancia wrote to the Condaxes about the death. She claims that Vidali had gone to Ignacio's house to recover:

About María, I guess it's too soon to talk or write about it. You know how fond I was of her and the news was something awful to stand (sic). I read it in the paper! I rushed to phone Ignacio and he had just heard it. Poor Carlos was in a terrible state. Ignacio took him to live with him and there he remained four or five days. Now he is much better, still I think he will never be able to forget María. And to think that no one of us knew she had this illness. She never, never spoke about herself and I suppose we just got used to it.[30]

It is strange that Constancia took so long, over four months, to write to the Condaxes about "María's" death. Her letter also seems disingenuous. It is hard to believe that she found about the death from the newspapers, that she thought Modotti had a "secret illness" or that Vidali went to Ignacio merely for emotional support. Her friend Eladia de los Ríos clearly remembers Vidali hiding out at Constancia's house, not Ignacio's. Later Vidali's enemies, including the famous anarchist Carlo Tresca, would accuse him of murdering Modotti.[31]

The suspicions eventually died down, but they were never really cleared up. There are several studies of Tina Moddotti's life, but none clarify the circumstances of her death. John Condax was convinced that Tina had been murdered. He and his wife had only recently traveled extensively with her, and remembered her as a "strapping girl" in fine health.[32] They thought it absolutely implausible that her health could have deteriorated so radically in such a short period of time. Tina was buried with full Communist honors and everyone praised her kindness, her abnegation and her devotion to the cause. In a commemorative booklet edited by her friends, Constancia wrote about her comrade "María":

María was a hardworking, understanding, loyal, modest comrade; a beloved, sweet, and kind-hearted friend; a firm, honest, and humane woman. For those of us lucky enough to have known her well, and to have shared her affection, her memory gives us strength and provides a haven – in the midst of so much wretchedness – for our thoughts.[33]

What Constancia, of course, could not know in 1942, was that in retrospect the suddenness of Tina's death in strange circumstances, the party's glorification of her memory, and Pablo Neruda's eulogy in many ways antic-ipated Constancia's own funeral.

Decades later, Vittorio Vidali would say, mistakenly, that the text for *Mexico is Theirs* was never written, and that the photographs taken had been lost.[34] Constancia did complete the text, with the help of many American friends, and the book with text she signed and Condax's photographs was set to be published in early 1942. It appeared in the Modern Age catalogue of forthcoming books: "Constancia de la Mora and John Condax have merged two notable talents, in writing and in photography, to give this vivid picture of the Mexico of today. Constancia de la Mora, who won instant literary recognition two years ago when her autobiography, *In Place of Splendor*, was published, is a brilliant young Spanish writer . . . "[35]

However, *Mexico is Theirs* was never released. At that time, a photog-raphy book was a costly enterprise with very uncertain returns, and with the United States now in World War II, Modern Age cancelled the book at the last minute.[36]

Articles: Propaganda

Unable to write a successful book, over the years Constancia managed to publish a few short articles under her name, mostly propagandistic. One of the few articles that she wrote on a non-political subject was a short piece of cultural reporting she did for the *New York Times* in 1941 on "fete of Guadalupe" in Mexico City.[37] Even in this piece, though she describes in detail how the festival was organized and what people wore and ate during the celebrations, she infuses the folklore with a political tone. She described the indigenous Mexicans, who traveled barefoot or by donkey to come to the shrine of their virgin, and who honored the Virgin of Guadalupe because she was the friend "of the poor Indian". The parallel between the virgin and Constancia is implicit, she was also the friend of the people. She goes on to explain that during the Mexican war of independence Miguel Hidalgo carried a banner with the Virgin of Guadalupe (while the Spaniards carried an image of the Virgin of Los Remedios). Throughout the piece, her ideal-ization of the poor and humble, of the "people" (el pueblo) comes through strongly.

In 1942 Constancia published an article in *Soviet Russia Today* entitled "Young Spain in the USSR."[38] The article's headline reads: "A glowing account of the tender care the Soviet people have lavished on 3,000 Spanish children, by the mother of one of them." Her account is indeed glowing. She begins by claiming that those Spanish parents in Mexico and South

America whose children were in the Soviet Union felt lucky to have their children there. She writes that their faces actually lit up when asked where their children were:

> *They know that in the USSR these Spanish children have everything their parents could give them and something else besides – they are growing up to be women and men such as Spain will need when we can go back to our country. And few are the Spanish refugees who do not think morning, noon or night of that day.*[39]

She goes on to recycle passages from *In Place of Splendor* and recounts how she sent Luli to the Soviet Union in 1936 and the first time she visited her in 1937, and then tells the story of the children of the Air Force officers who were evacuated to the Soviet Union from Barcelona early in 1938. Constancia writes that she followed the lives of these children closely and that the treatment they had received had been consistently excellent – although of course conditions were a bit "sterner" since the German attack:

> *Until the Nazi attack on the Soviet land there was no country in the world where the children were happier. And our children had more than their share. Sometimes I thought they were even a little spoiled, for nothing was too good or too much for them.*[40]

Not only did the children have everything they could possible need, but their education was absolutely Spanish. According to Constancia:

> *Only the Russian language, Russian history and geography, where Spanish teachers were not available, are taught in Russian. The children sign and dance as many Spanish songs and dances as their teachers know. And on every big feast the Spanish republican flag – red, purple and yellow – floats over the Spanish Children's Homes, all the way from Leningrad to Odessa.*[41]

This article is a transparent example of propaganda. According to her, the Soviets were full of tenderness and generosity, but were by no means trying to transform the Spanish children into Soviets. Having her daughter in the Soviet Union gave Constancia peace of mind for, as she argues, she was well looked after and safe, and any hardships would simply prepare her better for the struggle that lay ahead in Spain:

> *We Spaniards know that to fulfill our desire of returning to our country we will have to undergo many hardships. The doors of Franco Spain will not be flung open nor trumpets sound to welcome us. We know that the greatest, if not the worst part of the struggle, is still ahead of us. And, I for one, do not regret that my daughter be now steeled for that struggle.*[42]

Her account of how the children were educated and treated seems idealized, and shows how committed she still was to defending Communism. Because of the propagandistic nature of her writing, it is difficult to ascertain whether she had any reservations about the Soviet system. Her outlook may also have been influenced by the fact that Luli was in Russia, and that her well-being was surely contingent on her mother's politics. After all, three years had passed since she had sent a message to Moscow via Soledad Sancha to have Luli rejoin her in New York. She had clearly wanted, to no avail, her daughter to leave the Soviet Union and live with her. Her request had been denied.[43] In reality, the education of the Spanish refugee children in the Soviet Union was not what Constancia described in her article. The Politburo had a free hand in training the children in Communist ideology. In fact, the children were indoctrinated relentlessly, both in school and in their "free" time. One Soviet Director of a Spanish Children's Home defined their mission as ensuring the childrens' loyalty to Marx, Engels and Lenin, and their love for the Spanish Communist Party and the Soviet Bolshevik Party.[44]

Luli was given special consideration in Moscow because of who her parents were. Almost all the documents in her Comintern file list her father as Ignacio (instead of Bolín),[45] and she was thus treated as the daughter of the former Commander in Chief of the Republican Airforce. There is little information about Constancia on file. She does not have her own dossier in the Comintern Archive, though she is included in Ignacio and Luli's files. One certificate from Luli's file describes Constancia as a writer, a member of the Spanish Communist party, and states that she worked for the party in Spain during the war.[46]

Like most of the refugee children in the Soviet Union during World War II, Luli's life was peripatetic. From 1937 to 1940 she was in Moscow School 39; from 1940 to 1941 she lived in the Spanish Children's Home 5, also in Moscow; and in 1941 she went to the Spanish Children's Home 5 in the Saratov region where she stayed until 1942. From 1942 to 1943 she lived in Kushnarenkovo, and from then onwards she seems to have stayed in a residence in the Rostokino district of Moscow. From 1943 to1944, Luli studied at the Moscow Institute of Energy, but she dropped out before completing her first year because the courses were too difficult. She then began to work in Research Institute 205 as a "librarian" on a trial contract. Her references for this position were given by Dolores Ibárruri and she was paid the quite generous salary of 350 rubles a month.[47]

Luli's personal and political progress in the Soviet Union were watched carefully. This August 1943 report is typical:

Luli Hidalgo de Cisneros. Born 26–II–1927. Father is a military officer of the Communist Party. Mother is an intellectual in the Communist Party. In the USSR since December 1936. Konsomol since 1942. Has completed 7 classes. In the school of the Communist Party since October 1942. Is constant in her desire to become politically developed. Her achievements, nonetheless, in her studies have been weak. Throughout the year she has had serious difficulties in keeping up with her comrades. Today, her political level is low and because of her young age and her complete lack of knowledge of the life of the worker youth, she finds great difficulties in combining her political studies with our fight. She has a flair for writing. She has great affection for the Konsomol and the Party. She has trouble facing any given problem. Her physical condition is not good.[48]

María Sánchez lived with Luli in one of the Moscow homes and remembers how often she could be found writing stories in her notebook, perhaps inspired by the idea that her mother was a great writer. In 1942 Luli, along with Wenceslao Roces' daughter, was in very poor health and needed medical attention in, and in 1943 she still had not recovered. Though there is no diagnosis in her file, she may have had tuberculosis, which was quite common in the children's colonies.

In Luli's case, the fact that her mother was well known and considered to have powerful connections to the press in the United States ensured that she was handled with exceptional care. During World War II, when the children were moved frequently, a "top secret" message from Comrade Belov (of the personnel department of the Executive Committee of the Communist International) from March 19, 1942 gave special instructions for Luli's move to a new home: "Luli Hidalgo de Cisneros is arriving to Ufa [Tatarstan]. Her mother will probably come to the USSR as a correspondent for American newspapers quite soon. We request you to provide Luli with everything necessary."[49] Another "secret" internal party memorandum from Comrade Belov dated June 10, 1942 requested medical attention for Luli, who was then at a children's home in the Saratov region, implies that she should be well looked after because both parents were loyal party members.[50] It identified her mother as Constancia de la Mora, a writer who planned on coming to the USSR to work as a correspondent for very well-known North American newspapers. However, there is no evidence that Constancia ever traveled to the Soviet Union from Mexico, and the only English language periodical in which Constancia wrote about the Soviet Union was *Soviet Russia Today*, which was certainly not a mainstream publication. In another secret communication Constancia was described as "a famous Spanish journalist and a public figure."[51] Belov also pointed out that Luli's parents were respected and popular amongst journalists and government officials, and that they had been in the USSR in 1938 and 1939 and had met with Stalin and Voroshilov.

On November 15, 1945 Luli at last left the Soviet Union, "as her parents requested" to meet her mother in Mexico.[52] She arrived in Cuernavaca sometime in early 1946. She moved in with Constancia, but did not stay long for she soon fell in love and married Severiano Caraballo. He was an attractive young man, and Luli, who had by then spent most of her life in the Soviet Union, was eager to marry him despite the fact that he was a poor cowhand. Constancia was appalled at Luli's choice of a husband, and complained about him to her friends.[53] Ironically, Constancia seemed to perpetuate the same bourgeois dynamic that had created tensions between herself and her own parents. Severiano was the illegitimate son of a wealthy landowner and a laundress, and when his father died, he inherited a great deal of money. Severiano bought a herd of cattle, land, planted lemon groves, and a ranch in Colima. He would become a very successful farmer.[54]

In Mexico, Constancia became good friends with the German Jewish writer Anna Seghers who was just a few years older than Constancia. She had been a member of the Communist Party since 1928, and had also been in Spain during the Spanish Civil War. She arrived in Mexico in 1941. Though Seghers was a real intellectual, they had a great deal in common. Seghers had written a best-selling anti-Fascist novel *The Seventh Cross* which had been published in the United States in 1942, the same year she learned her mother had died in a concentration camp.

The anti-fascist movement thrived in Mexico. In April 1942 a full-page advertisement was taken in *El Popular* to announce the formation of the Anti-Nazi-Fascist Federation of Foreign Residents in Mexico.[55] Together, Constancia and Seghers were active in the organization *Alemania Libre* (Free Germany) as well as in the Joint Anti-Fascist Refugee Committee.[56] The Committee had its headquarters in New York City and chapters in nine major American cities. Among its supporters were well-known Jewish and Christian religious leaders, professors, writers, union leaders and celebrities including Paul Robeson, Princess Helga Zu Loewenstein, Heinrich Mann, and the famous screenwriter Dalton Trumbo.

In the summer of 1944 Constancia and Seghers collaborated on a pamphlet entitled "Anna Seghers and Constancia de la Mora Tell the Story of the Joint Anti-Fascist Refugee Committee". From December 1943 to May 1944, the committee raised $118,529.27 for transportation, relief, and rehabilitation of refugees, many of them International Brigade veterans, throughout the world. The largest contributions went to Mexico, Portugal, and North Africa. The pamphlet includes photographs illustrating the impact of the committee's efforts (such as a photograph of Spanish refugee children delighted to be on a ship headed towards the "new world"; children studying at the Luis Vives Institute in Mexico; and a new hospital – opened by the committee – with a staff of Spanish Republican doctors). Anna Seghers wrote the first essay, praising the welcome she and so many other refugees received in Mexico, and the aid they were offered by the committee:

> *I give the most credit to this Committee not because it brought us over to America but because it helped us begin life anew. No type of care, no matter how unique, was beyond the realm of the Committee. In essence I might say that the Joint Anti-Fascist Refugee Committee not only saved us from fascism but helped us become strong again for the fight against fascism.*[57]

She concludes by looking forward to the victory over Nazi Germany, the day of "all freedom loving people" that was being brought closer by the "heroic Red Army and the armies of Great Britain, the United states and the other Allies."[58]

Constancia's article reiterates many of the points made in *In Place of Splendor*, and brings the situation of the Spanish refugees up to date – highlighting the roles of the Mexican government and the American run Joint Anti-Fascist Refugee Committee (JAFRC). She gives an account of the Falangist "victors" imprisonment and execution of more than half a million Republicans who had not been able to leave; and how those Spanish refugees who had returned to Spain after being cornered by Nazis in France had met a terrible fate. She praises Mexico and the JAFRC not only for helping the refugees get to Mexico, but also for enabling Spaniards to rebuild their lives. Their assistance " . . . aimed at helping college professors and workers, peasants and scientists, writers and school children . . . to follow once more their normal activities, to continue their studies, to write and publish their work – in other words, to live as free men and women."[59] The JAFRC contributed to medical relief, education – building schools and creating scholarships – and helping refugees find employment.

Despite her appreciation of Mexico, Constancia thought of it as a temporary home. She felt about Spain what Anna Seghers did about Germany: that she would soon be rebuilding her own free country:

> *the people of Spain along with all the other freedom loving nations will see the rebirth of democracy. When that time arrives thousands of able and useful citizens of all ages will return to their Spanish homeland to assist us in the great tasks of reconstruction, thanks to the generosity and brotherhood of the American people.*[60]

Her vision of the future was expressed in a letter she wrote to her daughter Luli (still in the Soviet Union) in May 1944.[61] At the time, she described her main activities at the Soviet Embassy in Mexico as editing and publishing a weekly Spanish language news bulletin. She reports that she is full of enthusiasm for this job, but confesses that she and Ignacio only think of getting back to Spain and taking Luli with them. She says that "the situation in Spain is changing rapidly and we don't want to get caught here, unable to leave; that's why we want to get out now and 'Papi' is doing everything possible to get this underway and I'm also going to do everything I can." Constancia's new optimism was based on news both she and Ignacio had received from their families in Spain. Ignacio's relatives had broken their ties with him even before the Spanish Civil War began. Their renewed interest in him led Constancia to hypothesize that they were afraid that the Franco regime might be crumbling:

> *Not only do they openly say who they are, but they all signed the letter with their full names and return address, and mention Papi's other brothers – one is Military Chief in one region and the other is Director of the General Military Academy in Zaragoza . . . My family, of course, is still writing to me and sending me money every month. As you are all probably aware of the new "Junta Suprema"[62] that has been created in Spain, you know how important these things are. Ignacio and I believe that his brothers – who are certainly aware of the existence of the Junta in Spain – want to know from someone they trust (like Papi) whether their lives and properties are going to be respected or if there will be reprisals, which is what they are terrified of. So, these are our main concerns. Of course, the most important one – because everything else depends on it – is Hitler's defeat.[63]*

Clearly both Ignacio and Constancia's families thought it prudent to establish a cordial relationship with their exiled Republican relatives as insurance against any changes the end of the war in Europe might bring. Constancia and Ignacio became optimistic that they were on the verge of returning to a Spain in which they would again be prominent figures and their Francoist families would be proven wrong. If Ignacio's brothers, who supported Franco, were seeking assurances from Ignacio in exile, it seemed that the tables must already be turning.

The Soviet Embassy in Mexico

In Place of Splendor had given Constancia the false reputation of being a great writer. After trying unsuccessfully to live up to this image by writing follow-up works, she turned her energy elsewhere and went to work at the

Soviet Embassy. Though officially Constancia held only a secretarial post, she was apparently Ambassador Constanin Oumansky's right hand collaborator.[64] Oumansky spoke English, but not Spanish, and Constancia translated everything for him, including his speeches. One of the few people to write about the role of the Soviet propaganda department in Mexico was Julián Gorkin, who was a vehement anti-Stalinist.[65] According to Gorkin, Oumansky was a charming and elegant representative of pure Stalinism. He had a large and expert group of people working under him, and while he spent a much time socializing and giving lavish receptions to win over public opinion, his staff and collaborators (many of them Soviet Secret Police agents) were busy infiltrating the government and the press. Many of the articles concerning the Soviet Union that appeared in the newspapers, signed by Mexicans, Spaniards, or unsigned, apparently came directly from the Soviet Embassy.[66] With her background in the Foreign Press Office and her feelings for the Soviet Union, where her daughter still was, Constancia was indispensable to the embassy's propaganda machine and probably was responsible for placing many of these articles.

A 1944 letter shows that Constancia was still working at the Soviet Embassy, and that she wished Luli could come and join her:

Dearest daughter, I'm talking to you about all these things as if you were my best friend. After all, these are the things we would talk about if we were together. These and a thousand more that I am overflowing with and can't hold back. Eight years is too long to put up with containing all my maternal affection . . . What we really need here is someone who can translate Russian to Spanish! Couldn't you do this job? That way we could work together.[67]

Constancia also maintained a friendship with Paul Patrick Rogers. Rogers, the professor from Oberlin College and member of the American Communist Party whom she had met in Spain during the war, made frequent trips to Mexico during World War II and at least until 1950.

An FBI informant suspected Rogers of being a courier for the Communist Party.[68] This conclusion was drawn from the fact that in October 1942 he stayed with Constancia and Ignacio at their 56, Avenida Veracruz residence in Mexico City. The informant claims that the couple were known to be supporting communist party causes and that Constancia was a "Spanish refugee writer and actively engaged in Russian War Relief Society".[69]

In another FBI report on Rogers dated January 24, 1949, it is alleged that in the summer of 1947 Rogers lived in Mexico City with Juan Vicens de la Llave, identified as a "Soviet Embassy employee". Vicens was an exiled Spanish librarian, who during the war had directed the Republican propaganda office in Paris.[70] According to writer Max Aub, Vicens and his great friend filmmaker Luis Buñuel worked in counterespionage in France during the civil war.[71] Vicens lived alternately at Paris 7, a boarding house run by the mother of the "communist artist" José Alfaro Siqueiros,[72] and Veracruz 56, home to many Spanish exiles including Constancia and Ignacio. These addresses were thought to corroborate his communism.

It is not clear whether Vicens met Constancia through his propaganda work during the war, or if they met in exile in Mexico, but the FBI informant observed that he was "very friendly" with Constancia, who this time is identified as an "employee of the Soviet Embassy in Mexico and probably very high up in the Soviet Hierarchy (sic)" and as the person who arranged to have Vicens hired at the embassy.[73] Constancia, Rogers, and Vicens were clearly associates in Mexico. Rogers traveled to Mexico frequently and "allegedly transferred confidential documents in 1943 to CP official and stated: 'We have a very good courier system out of Spain.'" His contacts were listed as members of the communist party and alleged Soviet secret police agents, Spanish loyalist refugees and employees of the Soviet Embassy in Mexico.[74]

Rogers' contacts in Mexico, including Vittorio Vidali, the staff at the offices of Alemania Libre, and Alvarez del Vayo, were also close to Constancia and Ignacio. The informant reports that Constancia was a "Soviet propagandist" according to the former Soviet Vice Consul in San Francisco, Gergory Kheifets.[75] The same report claims that Constancia was closely involved with a group of allegedly expelled Communists being organized in Mexico, though the informant does not indicate what the group was organizing.[76] The point of this particular report was that Rogers was planning, in the spring of 1950, to take a leave from Oberlin College and travel to Mexico and Europe. All of Rogers' subversive activity, according to the FBI, was connected to Spain: "it has been alleged he visited Spain during the Civil War in that country . . . " and he "has been active in many Communist front organizations, particularly those developed as a result of the Spanish Civil War."[77] Despite much suspicion and many allegations about Rogers and Constancia, the FBI seemed unable to produce concrete evidence of their activities or collaborative work.

Constancia was still working at the embassy when in January 1945 Ambassador Constantin Oumansky, his wife, and most of the Russian embassy staff were killed in a plane crash. *The Nation*'s Freda Kirchwey was in Mexico at the time, and cabled a story back which began, "It would be impossible in New York to imagine the emotion felt here at the horrible accident."[78] Constancia was not on the plane, but most of the people she worked with died:

*Although the immediate investigation ordered assumed that the tragedy was a
pure accident such as happens every so often in even the best-regulated air force or
airline, the plane that crashed was the personal plane of General Cárdenas, and
the pilot was rated the best in the force. The fact that Oumansky was traveling
in an army rather than a regular passenger plane was the combined result of his
own desire and the amiability of the Mexican government. At a Foreign Office
dinner he had recently expressed the wish that he could go direct to San José
without stopping en route, as he would have on a commercial flight. When
Cárdenas heard of Oumansky's remark, he immediately offered his own plane . .
. it was an act of courtesy characteristic of this generous people and of Cárdenas
in particular; that it ended in tragedy seems peculiarly cruel.[79]*

Kirchwey then goes on to explain the importance of Oumansky's presence in Mexico, offering a perspective on the ambassador Constancia worked
with that stands in contrast to Julian Gorkin's derisory portrait of a single-
minded propagandist:

*Everybody liked him, and his almost fabulous social success must have modified
considerably the fear of Russia that has long dominated upper-class groups here
as elsewhere. Critics of Oumansky imply that this was all deliberate diplomatic
strategy; if so, it should certainly be studied and emulated by other Allied
ambassadors.[80]*

Just a few days before his death, Kirchwey had dinner with the ambassador. He had impressed her with his views on the threat of fascism:

*He had no illusion that fascism would be ended by the impending defeat of
Germany. He had followed in minute detail developments all over Latin America
and was convinced that this hemisphere would be the scene of a terrific struggle
against fascist tendencies that are already well rooted. This conviction obviously
controlled his attitude toward other problems, including the future of Spain.[81]*

After the plane crash, nearly the entire staff of the Soviet Embassy in
Mexico had to be replaced. Tamara Pascual, the daughter of First Secretary
to the new ambassador, recalls that Constancia was no longer working at
the embassy after Oumansky's death. According to Pascual, Constancia had
only worked there because of her close personal friendship with Oumansky.
The Soviet Embassy had a position in the press department reserved for a
native Spanish speaker and non-Soviet citizen. The job was along the lines
of a press attaché, and involved daily analysis of the Soviet Union in the
Spanish language press, putting together a weekly news bulletin in Spanish,
and translating. This was similar to the work Constancia had done in the
press office in Spain. However, when the new ambassador arrived,

Constancia was replaced by Juan Vicens de la Llave. According to Pascual, Vicens was an older man, very reserved, extremely intelligent and fluent in Russian.[82] Vicens was a friend of Constancia's, and the FBI files said that she had helped him get this job at the embassy.

It is possible that, as Pascual says, her position had depended on her relationship with Oumansky, and that Vicens was more useful than Constancia because he spoke Russian. It is also possible that she distanced herself from the embassy out of fear. Almost all her co-workers and superiors had been killed. It was rumored that Oumansky, apparently a favorite of Stalin's, had long been a target of Trotsky's supporters who wanted to avenge his murder.

After leaving the Soviet embassy, Constancia continued to work on behalf of the Spanish refugees and prisoners in Spain. Dolores Ibárurri, better known as "Pasionaria", wrote in her autobiography, *Memorias de Pasionaria 1939–1977*, about the women in Unión de Mujeres Españolas, a reconfiguration of Mujeres Antifascistas. UME's objective in the 1940s was to support and collaborate with women in Spain and to encourage resistance against the Franco regime. The organization had offices in France, Northern Africa, Great Britain, the United States, and Argentina and amongst its key "freedom fighters" Pasionaria lists Victoria Kent, Irene Falcón, and Constancia.

UME held its first meeting in France in 1946. Many women attended the conference held in Toulouse and it was decided that UME should concentrate on making the situation in Spain known to the world and appealing to the United Nations; and to do everything possible to help Spanish political prisoners. For the latter task, funds needed to be raised, and it was decided that different groups of UME activists would "adopt" a specific prison as their charge.[83]

It is likely that Constancia attended this meeting in 1946. She made at least one trip to Europe because she met with her parents in Portugal.[84] She told Eladia de los Ríos that during this meeting, she and her father argued because he was furious at the way she had described the treatment of the peasants at La Mata, her family's estate in *In Place of Splendor*. He said that her characterization of the peasants' lives was untrue, and she defended her memoir's portrayal.[85]

Constancia's cousin, Carlos Semprún Maura, corroborates that she was in France in 1946. Carlos and his Republican family, including his brother the future writer Jorge, had fled to France during the war. He remembers that in 1945 or 1946 Constancia came to France and visited his family at Saint-Prix, and that she was "a real chatterbox and a real Communist." She told them that her mother was silly enough to try to lure her back to Spain by promising her land to set up a "koljos". Constancia wanted a revolution in Spain and was not interested in collective farming experiments on her family's land. Carlos remembered that her communism did not stop her from regularly receiving her income from the family estates, even in Mexico.[86]

Eladia de los Ríos also says that Constancia did not live on the sales of *In Place of Splendor* alone. Eladia took Constancia's allowance to Cuernavaca once a month. The money was sent by Constancia's father via a Catalan family her parents knew in Mexico City.[87] Whether her parents were motivated by love or duty towards Constancia or Luli, or a fear of reprisals if Franco was deposed in the aftermath of World War II, is not clear.

Cuernavaca became the home of many exiles from Europe and the United States. Nancy Johnstone, an English writer who had been in Spain during the war working with Quaker relief organizations, became a close friend of Constancia's. In her memoir of Mexico she describes why she, like so many other people, chose Cuernavaca because of its location and climate.[88] Cuernavaca was cheap, beautiful and became a cultural center for "expats" of all kinds including Leonard Bernstein and Martha Gellhorn.

Constancia built a house in Acapantzingo. The man who designed it was a Tarascan Indian from Morelos, Rodolfo Ayala. Ayala, nicknamed "El Loco", seems to have been the main person in Constancia's life after Ignacio. However, nobody knows exactly what kind of relationship they had. Though they were inseparable, there was a rumor that he was a homosexual. Fredericka Martin reported that "Connie never fell in love with anyone but had an affair with a eunich (sic) of a fellow named Rudolfo (sic) Ayala. These facts checked with several reliable sources."[89] Another close friend of Constancia's, Eladia de los Ríos, also says that Rodolfo had a sexual "congenital abnormality"[90] which made their relationship something of a mystery.

Nevertheless, Ayala and Constancia became very close and he was devoted to her. Though untrained, he was an intuitively great architect who understood the Mexican Colonial style, of which Constancia's house was an example.[91] The house was much admired by everyone and in 1957 it was used in the film *Tizoc*.

Aurora Arnaíz recalls that Constancia and the house complemented one another in a tribute to the essence of Mexican style.

her new house had beams, doors, and ironwork that Constancia had brought back from the most out of the way places. She had traveled over unpaved roads to find these things . . . and what I really remember about the house was its simplicity and its authentic mexicanidad. .. For several years Connie wore her hair parted down the middle, and with two braids with colored wool woven into them.[92]

Apart from the beauty of the house, Arnáiz doesn't remember much happiness in Constancia's life after Ignacio:

> *My husband and I went to Cuernavaca once and dropped in on Connie. She was still in the same house, but nothing else was the same. Ignacio's presence was definitely missing. It was a sad visit. I didn't get to meet "El Loco" Ayala, apparently he himself liked people to use this nickname, but we used to hear very sad stories about their life together . . . I used to wonder how this could have happened to her. I had always seen her as such a stable person, with great common sense, but sometimes even the strongest people can be sunk.*[93]

In the late forties, most probably in 1947, after growing progressively distanced from her political life, Constancia left the communist party. According to Eladia de los Ríos, Vicente Uribe, a leading figure of the Spanish communist Party (PCE), met with Constancia in Cuernavaca and they had a violent disagreement. After World War II, Uribe had become the second in command of the party, and in November 1947 in Moscow he, and another key party leader Fernando Claudín, set in motion a series of internal purges of the PCE. What transpired in his conversation with Constancia is not known, but she told de los Ríos that he had made her so angry that she wanted to have no more to do with the party.[94]

Uribe may simply have ejected Constancia from the party, and she, in order to save face might have told people that she had decided to leave. Did PCE leaders think that Constancia had become too *"aburguesada"* (bourgeois) and distanced from the party to be of any political use? Since Uribe was in charge of rejecting undesirables, it is possible that the substance of their meeting went along these lines.[95]

Although Constancia may not have known this, Ruth Mckenney and her husband Richard Bransten were cast out of the American Communist party in September 1946. They were accused of "petty-bourgeois radicalism", though they continued to declare themselves loyal members of the party.[96]

By the late forties, Constancia's political activities on behalf of refugees and prisons in Spain, and her contacts with other Spanish exiles seem to have diminished. Despite the allied victory, Franco's power in Spain remained secure, and this must have devastated the hopes she had held since 1939 of a return to democracy. It must be remembered that Constancia's initial role had been as a liaison between the Republican government and the British and Americans. She had pinned her hopes on the United States, especially, but their government had let Franco rule with tacit approval. A CIA report from 1947 reflects the American stance that, as far as priorities stood, security and stability far outweighed Democracy:

Under its present government, Spain provides no current threat to US security because however antithetic Franco's political philosophy may be toward Democracy, he must presently favor the Western Powers as the only alternative to the Eastern . . . The Franco Government, furthermore, is relatively secure for the time being; it controls all power in the state. Its downfall, solely as a result of political activity generated within Spain seems unlikely.[97]

Constancia's life became centered on Cuernavaca where she turned part of her house into a hotel for the foreigners who still came to meet the famous author of *In Place of Splendor*. Her house was so beautiful and original that the writer and architect Esther Mccoy wrote a piece on it. She employed a Mexican couple, Fidel and Delfina Moreno, as well as two Tarascan Indian maids. The Morenos admired Constancia and named their first daughter after her. She and Rodolfo Ayala were made Constancia Moreno's godparents.

Lini de Vries, an American woman who had been in Spain as a nurse during the war, arrived in Cuernavaca in 1949 with her daughter and describes Constancia's house:

We were expected at Constancia de la Mora's home in Acapantzingo, on the outskirts of Cuernavaca. I had never met her, but I knew of her. To all of us who had been in Spain, she was a legend. A refugee from Franco Spain, she had become a Mexican citizen. Her grandfather had been Prime minister to the King of Spain, but she worked hard for the Republic. I had read her book, In Place of Splendor. On a long chance, I wrote to her for advice on how to live and work in Mexico. She replied, offering me her home in exchange for work. . . . I wondered about the home to which I would be going. Constancia had written me she would soon be leaving for Guatemala as the guest of an American friend, but that there would be time before her trip to show me how to operate her small guest house, manage the servants . . . We approached the gates of what seemed to me a huge estate. Inside a handsome, brown-skinned man left his rake to take our luggage. In the attire of the proud Indian woman of the Isthmus of Tehuantepec, Constancia de la Mora came to the door to welcome us. When the gardener brought our bags into the room, Constancia introduced him, saying: "This is Fidel, my compadre . . . Following him came a three year old girl . . . And this is my godchild, Constancia Moreno."[98]

From Cuernavaca, Constancia took visitors on her special tours around the country and in late 1949, shortly after Lini de Vries' arrival, she set off on an extended tour of Mexico and Guatemala with a wealthy American woman from Minnesota, Mary O'Brien.

Adiós Connie – The Mary O'Brien Manuscript

Mary Wallner O'Brien was also living in Cuernavaca in the late 1940s. She says she had moved there for the climate, scenery, and culture. At the end of 1949, she met Constancia, about whom she had already heard a lot. The two women spent over a month traveling together, from Christmas 1949 until the end of January 1950.

Nearly three decades later, in 1976, O'Brien wrote a memoir about her brief but intense friendship with Constancia. She had made a deep impression on O'Brien, who had carefully kept a diary of their experiences together. Her unpublished manuscript is a unique account of Constancia's lifestyle at the end of 1949.[99] O'Brien was not a writer as her style and spelling demonstrate, yet her observations are detailed, and often perceptive. Overall, she gives the only portrait of Constancia during this period. In her preface, O'Brien admiringly describes Constancia's family, and is clearly impressed by her grand lineage. She praises *In Place of Splendor* which she calls "one of the most valuable historical documents of the social and political life of a Spanish period." She describes how in Mexico Constancia continued to fight for her ideals and says that "Constancia de la Mora was born a Spanish aristocrat, but of a very rare breed . . . (she) had lived and written with magnificent honesty, courage, and conviction . . . This is a simple narration describing the real Constancia as I knew her, a warm genuine, lovable person."[100] Ironically, Mary O'Brien, who knew Constancia for less than a couple of months, wrote more in tribute to her than anybody, including Ignacio or her other friends. Despite the important cultural and political differences between the two women, which often caused tension, the manuscript is a tribute to Constancia, who was probably the most fascinating person O'Brien ever met.

In O'Brien's memoir, Constancia, who had always had such determination and courage, seems to be thinking much more about the past than the present or future: "she never tired of telling her nostalgic stories."[101] The familiar image of Constancia the militant was replaced by that of a woman in exile who felt slightly disoriented, homesick, and at a loose end.

It is surprising that Constancia would spend her time traveling with O'Brien, with whom she really had nothing in common. It is unclear whether by 1949 Constancia had given up all her former political activities, or if she was simply concealing them from her new American friend. O'Brien gives several clues, although it seems that she did not really understand who Constancia was or what political beliefs she represented. Despite Constancia's falling out with Vicente Uribe, it is difficult to believe that she had completely abandoned her activism. During the trip the two women were about to take, she often seemed anxious and had a premonition that she was in danger.

O'Brien had first met Constancia at a party in Cuernavaca in December of 1949. The social life Constancia had now was a far cry from the earlier period spent with Ignacio and their friends Pablo Neruda and Tina Modotti, or Constantin Oumansky. Her new social circle is described by O'Brien:

> *A beautiful model from Greenwich Village huddled with two charming boys, while nearby a famous columnist was questioning the daughter of a former Mexican President. A sausage manufacturer from Milwaukee tried to stop his chubby blond wife from discussing their home life, while a Countess who had lost all but her title tried to get a word in somehow. In a far corner a Mexican movie star was hemmed in by a group of admiring females, while a pretty Mexican girl sat nearby on a foot-stool quietly hoping for some attention . . . This was a gay crowd, an international group, an assortment of people of strangely contrasting backgrounds.*[102]

Of Rodolfo Ayala, Constancia's companion, she writes:

> *A rather handsome Tarascan Indian who had spent many years barefoot, and later became a well known builder of Colonial homes, tried desperately to disprove his inferiority complex by becoming vulgarly boisterous. He made rude remarks about the "Gringos", telling shady jokes about the tourists who come to Mexico, forgetting that often the tourists return to live in Mexico, usually building new houses, always seeking a good Mexican architect.*[103]

O'Brien did not think much of Ayala, who did not seem worthy of the legendary Spanish Republican writer whose friendship she actively pursued. In fact, O'Brien did not seem interested in any of Constancia's friends and was only content when the two of them were alone together.

> *We met often after that and our friendship grew as we spent many late afternoons sitting on Constancia's cool terrazza (sic) sipping tequila out of tiny clay mugs. I loved to listen to her interesting tales of experiences in the Indian villages where she did most of her buying for a little shop she owned. Constancia had an attractive Colonial house on the street of Atlacomulco in the small village of Acapatcingo on the outskirts of Cuernavaca. It had been built for her by her friend the Tarascan architect, and each nook and corner was of intrinsic value in the way of Spanish Colonial architecture . . . In her little shop nearby she sold wonderful colored yarns, huipils, embroideries, hand woven materials, and many articles made by native artisans.*[104]

Constancia tolerated O'Brien, though later she was often impatient and disdainful of her new American friend, and even once told her that she was stupid.[105] Constancia remained enigmatic and rarely told O'Brien anything personal.

The two women, nevertheless, planned a trip to Guatemala financed entirely by O'Brien. Constancia complained that she did not have as much money as she had before the war in Spain, and seemed nostalgic for the life she had lost:

> *"But at least you have money", said Constancia "while I have had to fight my way ever since I left Spain. It has not been too easy, for I too once had all the luxuries of life, and I threw them away for an Ideal (sic). Now I struggle for a living and often feel like running away, knowing that I cannot run away from myself."*[106]

Before the trip she was despondent and restless, and according to O'Brien, the only thing that cheered her up was the idea of going to Guatemala.

Constancia laid down the conditions of their travels. She was in charge of the adventure, and was clearly contemptuous of her bourgeois companion. The experience would be rough, she warned O'Brien:

> *"We will take no jewelry, only a wrist watch and a pair of silver earrings for our pierced ears, no dressy clothes. Our Mexican cottons, a reboso, and a few necessities which we will carry in a pouch bag – and we will wear huaraches, our native Mexican sandals. We will travel in comfort with the average people, and we will never be taken for 'damas elegantes', and you will soon realize that this is for the best, because we will be sleeping in hammocks or on petates."*[107]

Constancia and O'Brien, dressed identically, were seen off by a huge group of Constancia's friends, including Rodolfo Ayala. Constancia was the center of attention, and O'Brien confesses to feeling a bit jealous: "Connie had many friends who loved her, and I felt very much left out of it all as I stood quietly aside. I felt the great difference of another race. They were an emotional people . . . yet I could not feel any closeness to any of them, such as I felt for Connie."[108] O'Brien often reveals an attachment to Constancia that seems to border on infatuation.

Constancia was oddly nervous about the trip. For the first time, she took out an insurance policy. Ironically, she bought air travel insurance for the flight to Merida, but none for the rest of the trip. Constancia made her friend Lena Gordon and her maid, Delfina Moreno, the beneficiaries of the insurance instead of her daughter Luli. O'Brien expressed her surprise, but Constancia stuck by her plan, and seemed unconcerned about Luli. Perhaps she had not yet come to accept Luli's marriage to Severiano Caraballo. Since he was so successful, she may have assumed that Luli would always be taken care of.

On the plane, Constancia told O'Brien more about her life and talked about *In Place of Splendor*: "This flight brings back my first plane trip [the day she met Ignacio] which I once wrote about . . . My life was interesting enough to write a book about it . . . ".[109] Mary had only been able to find a Spanish edition of the book, which she struggled through.[110]

When they arrived in Merida, Constancia was greeted at the airport by a different group of friends. This reception again made O'Brien jealous and she had a sense of being kept in the dark:

> *Entering the airport, Connie heard her name being paged over the loudspeaker, and suddenly a small reception committee greeted her effusively, offering their services . . . Connie appeared delighted, but I became puzzled. Not a word had been said about having any friends, or acquaintances in Merida.*[111]

O'Brien emphasizes many moments such as this one, in which she felt that Constancia was concealing things from her, but what she was excluded from is mysterious. She would later be hounded by the FBI about her friendship with Constancia.[112]

O'Brien copied her friends's Mexican style of dress and the two must have been quite a sight in their "Cuernavaca skirts, clean white blouses . . . hair bound in colorful yarns . . . huaraches."[113] They took a bus from Merida to Progreso where Constancia met another exiled Republican, someone she had known in Spain:

> *Connie met an elderly man whom she had known years ago in Spain. He greeted her with tears in his eyes, pointing proudly to the walls of his "tienda" . . . a small ice-cream parlor which had been decorated with many flags of Republican Spain . . . they spoke sadly of their lost Cause (sic), and of the many friends in Spain whom they would never see again. I heard the man say "There will come a day when we will rise again, and we will win, because in our hearts we know we are right." "Nunca. That is all past", said Connie. "I am now living in Mexico where I have found a new life. I find there is so much to live for, and now I am trying to forget the struggling times (sic) I spent in Spain."*[114]

Like all of the exiles, Constancia had to accept that Franco was in power for the foreseeable future. Her optimism about returning to Spain, which she had communicated in a letter to Luli five years earlier, had vanished. When Hitler's defeat in 1945 did not also bring about the fall of the Franco regime, many Republicans felt their cause was finally lost and the late 1940s was a period of real bitterness for many.

Constancia and O'Brien traveled back to Merida for New Year's Eve. On December 31, 1949 Constancia made a New Year's toast to O'Brien:

"To you . . . Salud! May you find happiness because you deserve it. Perhaps for me there will be no more, yet I have had so much of it in Spain – not with my family, but with my husband Ignacio. He was all the happiness in my life, and I have thrown it away."[115]

This incident corroborates Fredericka Marten's opinion that Constancia was heartbroken when Ignacio left and that she never recovered. However, Constancia still had a plan for the future. She told O'Brien that she was going to raise silkworms when she returned to Cuernavaca. Inspired by her friend Lena Gordon, she planned to weave beautiful silks and to become wealthy again. In her search for a raison d'être, she seems to have returned to the artesanal and entrepreneurial spirit embodied by Zenobia Camprubí in the early days of the Republic in Madrid.

They traveled by bus to Uxmal and the desolate villages reminded Constancia of Spain:

"Do you know, Mary, this reminds me of my childhood days, going into the peasants' houses, thinking it perfectly natural that they were living in filth and poverty, while we lived in luxury. The poor there also dipped their dishes into the stream to wash them, then washed their clothing, and later on washed themselves in the same water. Often the drinking water in the villages trickled from the corner in the churchyard near the many graves. When I pointed out to my father and rich uncles that the poor needed help, my aristocratic family would jump down my throat, calling me a stupid idealist."[116]

Throughout the trip, she lamented the terrible conditions of poverty people were forced to live in. By the sea, in Campeche, Constancia opened up to O'Brien about her desire to escape:

"Ay, Mary, if only I could be a bird and fly out there. Just across the water, Spain is so close I can feel it, and feel that I can almost touch it. Have you ever been to Málaga? Somehow, this takes me back to Málaga with its intoxicating colors, its cliffs and gardens rising out of the sea, and its lovely Moorish ruins. It was such a restful spot, yet I was never happy there, and never did I have the feeling of peacefulness I have right now, hearing the water and smelling the sea."[117]

The next morning Constancia told O'Brien she had had horrible dreams all night long, and "hours of lying awake thinking of all of the things I thought I had forgotten, and have tried so hard to forget."[118]

Despite being haunted by the past, Constancia still displayed her old toughness and an imposing take-charge attitude. She protected O'Brien from beggars and unwanted advances from men throughout their travels. She bartered prices with local vendors and kept all their Quetzales and dollars in a money belt: "Connie was in charge of all finances, relieving me of any responsibility."[119] On a bus to Chompoton, O'Brien was approached by a "rather handsome young man who appeared to be very intoxicated . . . "[120] The fellow came up close to her and started whispering "suggestive words in Spanish" until Constancia came to the rescue:

> As he continued to annoy me, Connie, who had been watching the disgraceful performance, flounced from her seat, grabbed the young man by the collar, then dragged him through the bus to the open door, and with ease, tossed him out to the ground. Then, as if she might have had years of experience in operating busses, she grabbed the lever slamming the door tightly shut.[121]

When a policeman came to insist that the young man, who was the son of the owner of the bus company, be let back on the bus, Constancia refused. She started a mini-revolution and got all the passengers on the packed bus to refuse to let the offensive drunk back on.

On the road to Guatemala, Constancia confided again in her new friend. She did not tell her very much, certainly not as much as O'Brien would have liked to hear. However, what she said made an impact:

> The time passed rapidly as Connie, in a very talkative mood, excitedly told of several incidents in her past life, of her birth into a politically famous family in Madrid, her childhood days and her education in England. Her words impressed me as a bitter review of the past, which she would like to forget. "Connie", I asked, "when you tell of the many trips and the fashionable resorts in Spain, don't you have the slightest desire to go back once more, and to live the life you once did?"[122]

Constancia responded, echoing her book, that she had no more interest in high society and described how she had rebelled against them. She said that she remembered exactly when she became a rebel, during a summer in Zarauz, where surrounded by aristocrats and courtiers she felt bored, stifled, and alienated. O'Brien asked about her family, but this query was less successful:

> "But your family, Connie, don't they miss you? Will you ever go back to visit them, and aren't there times when you think of your mother and father, and the sister Marichu of whom you wrote in your book? I can still picture your white haired grandfather when he was the Prime minister of Spain, and your description of Ignacio Cisneros (sic) sounded so romantically fascinating." Connie's habit of abruptly terminating a conversation was customary, so I was not sur-

prised at her sudden "Here we are" as we fastened our seatbelts for the landing . . . [123]

Her family was evidently a subject that was too painful to discuss.

In Guatemala, they went to visit the English writer Nancy Johnstone. Johnstone had been in Spain during the war. She had moved to Mexico and then to Guatemala. To O'Brien's dismay, Johnstone and Constancia refused to speak to each other in English, and instead chattered on in Spanish and French. Although Constancia and Johnstone may have been discussing private or political matters, it was not polite for them to speak French or Spanish together and O'Brien sensed this.

Nancy and Connie had been friends in Spain. Both had written books telling of their adventures . . . These impressing factors, and my lack of speaking French greatly subdued me . . . [124]

O'Brien repeatedly emphasizes being left out of these conversations. Later the FBI would be interested in Constancia's meetings with Johnstone, but O'Brien could tell them nothing because she had not understood. After a day of visiting coffee estates, O'Brien went to bed leaving Connie and Nancy alone together: "They continued speaking French, which I did not understand." (73) She was also irked by the fact that Constancia had to register with the authorities in Guatemala. Though Johnstone explained that all Spanish refugees were required to do this, O'Brien began to suspect for the first time that Constancia was a communist:

I recalled the joking conversation at the going-away party in Cuernavaca, when someone had said that all Communists and prostitutes had to register when entering Guatemala. At that time I thought it an invention of some jester's mind, laughing heartily with the others. But at this moment it raised a question over which to ponder, knowing that Connie's moral reputation was unquestionable. [125]

As they travelled around and she saw Constancia interact with other people, O'Brien caught a few more glimpses of her friend's militant side. In Guatemala City, they met a couple to whom Constancia had been introduced through a friend from Mexico. O'Brien was again reluctant to let anyone intrude on their time together, but Constancia prevailed as usual. The couple they met, who O'Brien refers to only as "Señor" and "Señora", arrived in an expensive Cadillac and were clearly very wealthy. The "Señora" was decked out in Parisian clothes and was quite surprised to meet the famous Constancia de la Mora dressed in her old huaraches and homsepun blouse and skirt. Constancia sat silently throughout the tea the four had together. She had been offended by their ostentatious display of wealth, especially in the context of Guatemala where she was very aware of the consequences of poverty. O'Brien remembered that on the ride back to Guatemala City, the situation worsened:

> *Comfortably seated for the return trip, the first question asked by the hostess was, "Please tell me, do you feel the terrible threat of Communism in Mexico?" I could feel Connie's back stiffen without looking at the back seat occupants. Anything but Politics or Religion at this moment, I thought, but the bomb had been thrown, so I sank lower in my seat wondering what the outcome of this conversation would be.*[126]

Constancia got into a heated debate:

> *"I do not know what you mean by Communist threat, Señora, and I am sure that the people in Mexico are happier than those I see here in Guatemala."*
>
> *What I mean", stammered the Señora, "is that we in Guatemala have been very conscious of Communist influences for some time, and it is a growing thing which cannot be easily controlled . . . it is all so deplorable . . . It is so bad for this country, especially after the church had spent so many years in helping the poor Indians to become civilized."*
>
> *"How has the church helped them?", exploded Connie. "Have they been educated, or fed by the church? Does religion feed an empty stomach? Can the many poor we have seen in your country help themselves? . . . yes, but up to now has there been any proof of the badness you speak of? What have we in this world but rich, or poor, sick, or well . . . and I think Guatemala needs a lot of pulling up by the bootstraps, and whoever does it well shall not be called bad."*[127]

The journey continued in silence. O'Brien was relieved to arrive at Nancy Johnstone's home. Afterwards Constancia continued to fume at how unpleasant and misinformed the Guatemalan couple was. Mary was startled by Constancia's reaction and her defense of communism, and it revealed something to her that she had not suspected from reading *In Place of Splendor*:

> *I returned to my room where I stood restlessly staring out of the window. A saying my mother often used came to my mind. "Things we do not understand, we must not judge." I think I understand, I thought. Yes I am beginning to understand.*[128]

After Guatemala City, O'Brien and Constancia no longer spent any time alone together. They continued to travel, but were joined by another American woman, identified only as Clara. She was a retired businesswoman from the Midwest and the three seemed to hit it off. Nancy Johnstone also decided to come along for the trip to Río Dulce. Constancia must have welcomed the company after spending so much time alone with O'Brien who was a clingy friend and an inexperienced traveler. They decided to head towards the Río Dulce, and hired a car with a driver and his assistant. Coincidentally, both the chauffeur and his colleague were from Spain:

> *The driver of the car, an agressive mannered person, and his assistant, wore berets jauntily draped over one eye. Connie was delighted when she discovered they were "Castilianos" (sic), both being refugees from Spain. Most of the trip was spent in re-living the Spanish Revolution, in questioning about her old friends, many of whom they seemed to know, and in discussing the Franco regime. All of them voiced hopes for the future.*[129]

The two refugees were making a living as tour guides and knew a great deal about Guatemala. They drove the party to Panacache from where they took a steamboat down the Rio Dulce. O'Brien pointed out the beauty of the water and the cliffs, which looked like "huge palaces from the distance" to which Constancia replied in a sad voice, "I have seen hills far more beautiful in Spain . . . and one day I hope to see them again."[130]

They arranged the next part of their trip to three villages on Lake Atitlan, at which point Clara left them and flew back to Mexico City. For some reason, Constancia, though still energetic enough to be bossy, had become gloomier:

> *Connie, who had started out on our vacation in a gay spirit, suddenly seemed less animated, sometimes becoming moody. I thought that she might be anxious to return to her home in Cuernavaca, or perhaps too much female companionship became tiring . . . as usual (she) had made all the reservations for the trip, after much investigation on the condition of the roads. With a large assortment of information on all tours, she finally made her decision.*[131]

As they set out, their party grew and they now shared a car with two other passengers who they didn't know, two men named Carlos and Enrique, a young woman, and the driver, Roberto. O'Brien provides little information about who these people were, or why they were included in the trip.

In Chichicastenango, Constancia, O'Brien, and Johnstone went to the famous church of Santo Tomás together. After their visit the guide requested that they please leave through the side door as "People arriving faced the altars and saints, and many of them backed out of the church, while others took the side exit when leaving, thus never turning their backs on the saints or the altars."[132] Always irreverent when it came to religion, Constancia paid no attention and turned around and walked straight out the front door.

As we left the side entrance I noticed an Indian shaking his fist in the air, cursing loudly at Connie. Paying the guide I asked him to please forgive my friend . . . With a stony expression (he) answered "It is a calumnia – a disaster. One does not turn one's back on God, or the Gods." Then he abruptly walked away.[133]

In retsopect, O'Brien seemed to see this as a bad omen. Constancia though nothing of the guide's comment, and left the church to walk around town look at the hand looms that she wanted to learn about for the weaving project she was planning as a future business. She filled her notebook with designs and colors which she planned on copying once she returned to Cuernavaca.[134]

But her enthusiasm for weaving did not keep her bad moods at bay for long. On January 27, the group got to Panajachel, and on their way to the Playa San Jorge, Constancia seemed more despondent than ever. When O'Brien asked her what was wrong, she answered:

"Forgive me, Mary, if I have been a bit melancholy. I will try to be gay, but tomorrow happens to be my birthday and for some unknown reason I always become sad and depressed on my birthday. A birthday always brings back memories of my home, my childhood, my parents, and Ignacio. It is a form of self-pity, I suppose, but this feeling grips me like a vice, and I simply cannot shake it."[135]

O'Brien told the others and they all made plans to buy champagne and celebrate. They got in the car to leave and Constancia, who until then always sat in the back seat because of O'Brien's carsickness, sat in the front. She seemed to have cheered up. She turned around to toss O'Brien a white orchid, saying "This is the first time we have ever put Mary in the back seat."[136]

They hadn't driven far when the car suddenly swerved to the left. Roberto, the driver, shouted that the brakes were not working and the car went head on into an embankment: "When the car hit the embankment, everything turned black."[137]

O'Brien came to and saw Nancy staggering towards her, crying with her face covered in blood:

I tried helplessly to bring her out of her complete state of shock, then pulling myself together as best I could, I went in search of the others. I found Carlos, Enrique, and the Señorita, all lying in an orderly row on the blood stained serapes. None of them had regained consciousness. One look and I screamed, "Connie. Where is Connie?" Rushing up to a man I had never seen before, I screamed "Connie está muerta. I know Connie is dead." I calmed down when I saw men carry Roberto across the sand, putting him gently down on a serape. After a frantic effort, the men had released him from beneath the steering wheel of the car which itself had

*buried itself deeply in a sand embankment. Other men worked stonily quiet, trying
to release Connie who was pinioned between the dashboard and the front seat. I
stood silently by, praying "Oh God, please don't let her die." When her body was
finally released, one look at her white face told me she was dead.*[138]

The others were taken to the hospital in Solola. Employees from the
nearby Hotel Tzanjuju had rushed to the scene to get everybody out of the
wrecked car. An eyewitness reported that the car had "crashed into the
mountainside, then turned over three times, nosing its way into the sand
at the bottom of an eighteen meter drop."[139] O'Brien was told that
Constancia had died without suffering. Her neck had been broken instantly
when the car hit the embankment.

O'Brien was overwhelmed by Constancia's death, in particular because
they had changed seats, and this made her feel that she should have died
instead. Back in Guatemala City, Constancia's body was embalmed and the
Mexican Consulate helped Nancy's husband, Ferdinand, with all the
arrangements:

*There was nothing left to do until word came from the family with instructions
for the burial. The burial law in Guatemala is the same as in Mexico, which
calls for the burial of a body within twenty-four hours after death. Connie's body
had been placed in a vault in the cemetery, a form of pseudo burial until she could
be shipped to Mexico . . . Waiting to hear from the family was maddening. One
night passed, then another, without word from anyone. Calling long distance had
been futile, and the telegrams sent had not been answered. A New York Times
reporter called on Nancy for details, which were later printed inaccurately with
most of our names misspelled. On the heels of the* Times *reporter came a delegation from the Tourist Bureau, insisting that the bad conditions of the roads must
not be mentioned in the newspapers. Nancy was furious.*[140]

Five days after the accident, word finally arrived from Mexico to ship
Constancia's body back. In the meantime, Luli had written a telegram to
Ignacio who was living in Warsaw: "Infinite sadness. Mamá died in an automobile accident."[141] O'Brien flew back to Mexico City with the coffin,
which was promptly taken to Constancia's house. In Cuernavaca her body
was put on view for one more day. Rodolfo Ayala had put the coffin on the
dining room table and surrounded it with flowers and candles. A large
crowd came to the house to pay their respects. Ayala was devastated and
blamed O'Brien for Constancia's death:

*"As I stepped out of the car a man rushed up to me, pointing his finger in my face,
glaring like a mad man shouting, "You killed her, you gringa you are the cause
of it all . . . You and your stinking money, if you had not taken her on this trip
she would still be alive."*[142]

The coffin was draped with the flags of Republican Spain and the Spanish Communist Party.[143] There were wreaths of flowers from the Labor Party, the Czechoslovakian Embassy's Cultural Delegation, and the *Daily Worker*. The details at last confirmed to O'Brien that Constancia had been a communist: "All these, so prominently displayed, seemed to answer many of the questions I had so often wanted to ask."[144]

Before taking the coffin to the cemetery, O'Brien was surprised that four friends of Constancia's, "all of the same Political Belief (sic)" stood rigidly by the coffin and "Extending their arms forward, looking straight ahead to the north, all uttered one word in unison, 'Comrade'."[145]

Constancia was buried in a beautiful spot, where she herself had said many times that she would liked to be buried:

The empty dug grave in Acapatzingo had been waiting to give the last sheltering rest under the great ahuhuete trees. In the valley the rice fields shimmered brightly in the sunshine. Off in the far distance the snowy tops of Popocatapetl and Ixtaccinatl could be seen in the afternoon shadows of cloulds. "Popo" looked down upon his legendary sweetheart who also slept, as Connie would be sleeping forever under the blue skies of the country she loved.[146]

Lini de Vries was also at her burial, and she later returned to the grave to bring flowers:

In place of splendor, she had chosen to be part of the Republic of Spain. She had lived with the splendor of her warm heart. Now she would lie under a great, spreading Indian laurel tree in the quiet cemetery of Acapantzingo, Morelos. Months later, on All Saints's Day, I returned to her grave. On her tomb I lay marigolds, the flower of the dead . . . Constancia lay peacefully in the Mexican soil that had given her refuge in 1940. For ten years she had known the vitality and wonder of Mexico; now its warm earth sheltered and embraced her.[147]

At the ceremony, Pablo Neruda read a eulogy he had written. He described Constancia as a disciplined warrior, and as the very core of a great collective fight. He said that she would live on through her book, and in the struggle of her people and the victory they still awaited. He vowed to keep Spain's struggle alive in memory of Constancia, and said that her legacy was the will to continue to fight and to hope.[148]

O'Brien again heard her friend referred to as "comrade" by Neruda, and became upset:

At last I was forced to face the truth to which I had stupidly closed my eyes. As I walked away from the grave, a well-known newspaper reporter came to my side, sneeringly remarking "If you play with pigs, you get dirty." I wanted to slap his face but calmly I answered "I knew her only as a generous lovable, kind hearted person, and so I shall remember her until the day I die." The realization dawned slowly on my befuddled mind. Had Connie returned with me, would our friendship have continued without any discussions? I am an American, and Connie's beliefs were contrary to my belief in Democracy.[149]

O'Brien's horror of Constancia's Communism is so powerful that she does not even allow herself to write the word.

In her postscript, O'Brien says that Constancia's companion Rodolfo Ayala came to her house the day after the funeral to demand that she give him money for the "cause". Though he never explained what the cause was, she clearly thought it was the Communist Party. He threatened that she would regret it if she didn't cooperate, and she called her chauffer Juan to scare him away.[150]

Though a decade had gone by since the success of her book in the United States, the *New York Times* published an obituary that reviewed Constancia's life and accomplishments. Whether the journalist knew that she had been a Communist or not, her affiliation is not mentioned. She is described as having been born into a "Spanish family of high estate" and is heralded for writing a book that "contrasted the worlds of aristocracy and democracy in the first part of the century", and for championing the cause of the Spanish Republic.[151]

The obituary of *Mundo Obrero* (the publication of the Spanish Communist Party in exile) presented a different portrait, that of a Communist heroine. In *The New York Times* Constancia was "Señorita de la Mora", and in *Mundo Obrero* she is "Camarada Constancia de la Mora". As "camarada", Constancia was described as a valuable member of the party's ranks. Despite being the granddaughter of the "sadly famous and hated Conservative leader Antonio Maura", she soon learned where her true place was and "resolutely joined the Communist Party of Spain." She was praised for having done all she could to help the people's struggle during the Civil War, and for continuing to work for the Republican cause while in exile. The death of "our beloved comrade" is lamented and she is remembered by all who knew her for her "intelligence, political commitment, and goodness".[152]

O'Brien was questioned repeatedly by the FBI after Constancia's death: "What people did Constancia see . . . Where did she go? . . . How much time did she spend away from me? . . . and a thousand more questions . . . Did I think Nancy was a Communist? Was I a sympathizer?" Finally, they gave up in exasperation after hearing my hundredth "I do not know".[153] If Constancia had political obligations during her travels with O'Brien, she discharged them discreetly. Just what the FBI suspected her activities were in Mexico and Guatemala, and how Nancy Johnstone was connected, is a mystery. Immediately after her death, there were rumours that she had been killed by the FBI. There was a large group of Americans in Cuernavaca at the time, most of them blacklisted writers or intellectuals, to whom her death was clearly a political murder carried out by the US government.[154] It is worth noting that there is no available FBI file on Constancia.

While there is no evidence that she was murdered by the FBI or any other organization, it cannot be ignored that her death was one of a series of mysterious deaths in her circle of associates in Mexico in the 1940s including those of Tina Modotti (1942) and Ambassador Oumansky (1945). It was widely suspected that Modotti did not die of natural causes, and the circumstances of Oumansky's death were also suspicious. Finally, though she was only forty-three, she seemed afraid of death before setting off on the trip to Guatemala, as Luli later noted in a letter to Ignacio:

Although I am by no means a fatalist, and this may seem absurd, it is strange that she seemed to have had a foreboding. She was convinced that she would die in a plane accident – in fact a few days before departing on the trip she went to Acapantzingo with a friend and showed her the spot where she wanted to be buried.[155]

Epilogue

Ignacio was in Poland when Constancia died. He received many letters from friends, including Wenceslao Roces and Pablo Neruda, as well as from Luli telling him about the accident and the funeral. From their letters it appears that for the last few years of her life Constancia had distanced herself from the people she had been close to in the first years of her exile in Mexico.

Roces had given the eulogy on behalf of the Spanish Communist party. He said it was the party's last goodbye to an old comrade. He praised her great talent, burning passion, and how she had sacrificed her ties to her family and class in order to join the party. He described her as an exceptional woman. Of her book, he said: "The story of her life, as she herself told it, is one of the great documents of contemporary Spain and will remain forever in the annals of the terrible epic of the Spanish people, as an example and an inspiration."[1] Though Eladia de los Ríos remembered Constancia leaving the Communist Party after an argument with Vicente Uribe, Constancia was buried as though she had remained a full-fledged party member until her death. Roces said that "During these long and hard years of exile, we've lost many brothers and sisters, but Constancia de la Mora remained loyal to the Spanish flags: those of the Republic and of her party. She was one of those who never lost the clear vision of the horizon . . . who knew who the Republic's enemies are (those who use Franco in order to take over our country) and who the true friends and allies of the Republic and the Spanish people are . . . ." Roces spoke of Constancia as part of the world that "marches forward in one giant step, along the path of democracy and peace; guided by Stalin's Soviet Union, by Dimitrov and Rakosi's popular democracies, by democratic China's Mao Tse Tsung, and by the glorious party of Dolores Ibárruri whose insignia accompanies, in this last tribute, the beloved comrade to whom we bid farewell."[2]

After the ceremony, Roces wrote a long letter to Ignacio. He said that Constancia had been invited on a trip by an American woman, and that shortly before the accident she had written to a friend in Cuernavaca saying that she was tired and longing to return home. He described the accident saying that Constancia was asleep, and that her death had been instant. The other passengers had all survived and the wealthy American woman

(O'Brien) was unscathed, though in shock for a few days. "Naturally it had to be poor Conny (sic), the Spanish refugee, who lost her life."[3]

News of Constancia's death reached the house in Cuernavaca by telegram, and caused quite a commotion. It took her friends some time to confirm the information, because at the time there was no telephone connection between Mexico and Guatemala. They got in touch with the Consul and soon made all the arrangements, which were expensive, and mainly covered by a couple called Nikiforov. Luli cabled Ignacio and Constancia's parents, who had already found out through the press. The Mexican papers *El Popular* and *El Nacional* had written about the accident and finally the *Excelsior* published what aimed to be a proper obituary, but had many mistakes. The article gave Ignacio's last name as "de los Cisneros" and claimed that after divorcing Constancia he had returned to Spain.[4] Over thirty friends, including Roces and his wife Carmen, had gone to the airport to wait for Constancia's coffin to arrive, and had gotten all the details of the accident from O'Brien, who Roces refers to as "la gringa del demonio" (that damned *gringa*). In his letter, he tried to console Ignacio:

> *We have thought of you a great deal and with so much affection during these days. We and all your close friends have been thinking of you constantly. What else can I tell you, dear Ignacio? Carmen and I are tremendously sad (you know how much Carmen loved Conny) and how deeply our feelings will always be tied to you and Conny. We have so many unforgettable emotions of good, and bad times, of the terrible lives we've had all these years. It's all over for Conny. Her impassioned and tormented life was like a blaze, that is now extinguished. Her daughter is from a different world. The true child that Conny has left behind is her book, in which she left the best of herself: the great example of her life. She leapt over many hurdles to join the fight and the Party; and at the root of that was her undying bond with you, and the connection you both had to all that is greatest in our people. After a long silence on my part, I regret, Ignacio, that this is the letter I have to write to you.*[5]

Roces' affection for Constancia seems tied more to past than recent experiences. A year before, Roces had written Ignacio an exceptionally long letter updating him about events and people in Mexico and had not even mentioned Constancia.

Concha Mantecón also wrote to Ignacio. Her letter shows that his close friends knew how much Ignacio still cared for Constancia:

> *I never thought writing to you would ever be such a sad task as it is today . . . I know that Wences has written you with the details of the accident . . . All I can say is that everything was taken care of as she would have liked . . . We got to her house in the evening and Luli and Severiano were there, and her servants, and*

her very loyal friends . . . Carmen Roces, Regina Lago, her close friend Elena Gordon, Lila Diaz, Juan Vicens, Clarita Porset, and me . . . At dawn a group of women from the village came, and barefoot Indians – all the people she had helped and who loved her. All day, until 6:00 in the evening when we went to the cemetery, people poured in from Mexico City and Cuernavaca, all of her friends. Her comrades from the Party – Arconada, Wences, Castellote, Moret, and many more led the vigil. Luli was in a stupor and barely knew what was happening. Afterwards she was extremely upset and devestated . . . she'll stay in the house a few days, but she's not alone . . . she's got Severiano who loves her as intensely as the day they were married, and above all she's got her two daughters who are the center of her world and who absorb her completely.[6]

Pablo Neruda wrote a beautiful description of the cemetery for Ignacio, with its tombstones gaily painted in blue, white, and yellow; surrounded by great old ficus and gum trees and mountains. The coffin was lowered into the grave wrapped in the Republican flag. Neruda described the tremendous sorrow everyone felt at the cemetery and during the trip back to Mexico City, which he made with Roces, Concha Mantecón, and Eladia de los Ríos. It wasn't until after the funeral that Neruda found out that there had been talk of sending Constancia's remains back to Spain. Ostensibly, her family had suggested this at some point.[7]

Luli

On March 3, Luli also wrote a letter to Ignacio, who she still called *Papi*, about her mother's death:

We were already here (in Colima) when the terrible tragedy occurred. You can imagine that I do not want to remember the whole ordeal, though I can think of nothing else; I'll do it for you. Poor Mami flew to Guatemala on a plane with an American woman, a millionaire, who had asked her to accompany her on an all expenses paid trip. My mother was happy about the idea, although just before leaving she had second thoughts. Finally she had postponed it so many times that she thought it would be rude to say no . . . After touring the Yucatán and taking some beautiful trips through Guatemala with this American woman and Nancy Johnstone (who divorced Archie . . . after which he stayed in the USSR and became a Soviet Citizen) . . . they were passing through a village and they decided to stop and buy a very good wine they make there to celebrate her birthday the next day. It was late and they were approaching the hotel when the car was going along some curves and went over the precipice because it didn't have any brakes. IMAGINE HOW HORRIBLE AND STUPID EVERYTHING IS!!![8]

Luli hoped that at least her mother had not suffered. She reported that Nancy Johnstone was recovering, and that the American woman had not been injured, "NOT AT ALL."

I was worried that you might find out from someone else before me, and I thought I should be the first to tell you . . . My grandparents[9] had already heard before receiving my telegram. We spoke to them on the phone. You can imagine . . .

Luli also gave Ignacio a brief report on other aspects of her life. Ironically, Luli wanted nothing more than to be a mother. While Constancia had given her life over to politics, defying her own parents and spending years apart from her daughter, Luli, weaned on revolutionary ideals in the Soviet Union, wanted only to settle down and have children:

We like Colima and I am content here. Luckily, I am very happy in my marriage, and this and my two daughters are my consolation. Should I be embarrassed that I seem to have been born merely to be a mother? . . . The ocean is divine here. The other day I took Lulita (the eldest) to the beach for the first time, and first she was afraid of the waves but then she was thrilled. She's only twenty-one months old . . . Severiano has a fifty-acre coconut grove here and thirty more acres that aren't planted yet. We sold the place in Cuernavaca . . .

Finally, she signs off warmly: "What I really wanted to say is that I am thinking of you very much, perhaps now more than ever. I always remember you with great affection."

Ignacio

Ignacio, who had been in touch with his brother, Paco, in Spain for a few years, wrote to him in May 1950. In the letter he expressed his feelings about Constancia's death:

Connie's death was a terrible blow. Though we were apart, we still had a great friendship and, as you say in your letter, I'll never be able to forget the kinds of things we went through together. She died in a car accident in Guatemala. The brakes failed on a steep hill. Her body was taken to Mexico and she was buried in Acapantzingo near Cuernavaca in a tiny cemetery full of flowers and enormous trees at the foot of the volcanoes. Connie told me a number of times that she would like to be buried in this cemetery near the house where we first lived when we arrived in Mexico.[10]

Ignacio never lost his Communist fervor. In the same letter to Paco, he claimed that his enthusiasm for the Soviet Union was growing. Perhaps fraternal ties really overrode politics in the Hidalgo de Cisneros family, if not Ignacio would not have been so open to a Franco supporter in Spain:

> *I am getting to know these countries where a new life is being born. It is fasci-nating to see the way life improves day by day, and the enthusiasm and joy you see everywhere. I fear you will think this is propaganda, so I will stop at that, but the surprise for the non-believers will be huge when they discover what is really going on in these places.*[11]

He also confessed that he missed Spain profoundly, but his Communism made it impossible for him to return. In October, 1954 at the Fifth Conference of the PCE, he was elected to be a candidate member of the Central Committee.[12] Between the fall of 1962 and the winter of 1965 Ignacio gave regular broadcasts on Radio España Independiente, which was the only uncensored radio station. He spoke on many different subjects, which he varied according to what was happening in the world on any given day, including: the role of the military in contemporary society, the American bases in Spain, the trial and execution of Julián Grimau, the mili-tary coups in Latin America, and the war in Vietnam.[13]

His work for the party had obliged Ignacio to move from country to country. In addition to Mexico and Poland, he spent time living in Paris, Switzerland, Denmark, Germany, and finally in Romania. Although the party took care of his essential needs, he was forced to live a spartan life. In one of his radio broadcasts, he declared his commitment to the party above all else:

> *I've been called a "snob", but I've been a member of the Communist Party of Spain for nearly thirty years, and despite the important and complicated events that have taken place during this period, every day I am more convinced that I am on the right path. Of course, I have no cars, nor estates, nor servants. But the lack of these – which for some people are the supreme ideal – is compensated for by the wellbeing and peace one feels when fighting for a just cause. That just cause – the triumph of democracy – is knocking on Spain's doors.*[14]

Ignacio had close friends in exile. He stayed in touch with Pablo Neruda, and saw a great deal of Manuel Sánchez Arcas, who had been responsible for hiring Constancia as a press censor back in 1937. He spent the last years of his life writing his two-volume autobiography, *Cambio de Rumbo* (Bucarest, 1964). In it, he describes his aristocratic background and conversion to Communism. He says nothing about the twenty-five years he spent in exile between 1939 and the year his memoirs were published. He says very little about Constancia in his book. In fact, aside from the anecdote about how they joined the Communist party, and their dinner with Stalin, he writes nothing about her that is not already in *In Place of Splendor*. Historian Herbert Southworth remembered meeting Ignacio at a lecture in Paris shortly after the publication of *Cambio de Rumbo*. Southworth had worked closely with his friend Jay Allen on behalf of the Spanish Republic, and had often seen Constancia at Allen's house in 1939. But Ignacio did not want to reminisce about Constancia with Southworth: "After the lecture, I asked Don Ignacio to sign a book or two, and remarked that I had known Constancia in New York. He did not react."[15]

In 1966, when he was seventy-two years old, Ignacio died suddenly of a heart attack in Bucharest. He was given a full military funeral with highest honors, and his coffin – like Constancia's – was draped in both the flag of the Spanish Republic and that of the Communist party. On his tombstone, under his name, was inscribed "Airforce General" and below "Hero of the Spanish People".

To the surprise and dismay of Ignacio's friends, his brother Paco's son – Ignacio Hidalgo de Cisneros Alonso – brought his remains back to Spain in 1994. Ignacio is now buried in the family mausoleum in the Santa Isabel Cemetery in Vitoria. The second burial, which was officiated by a Catholic priest and took place on October 29, 1994, was attended by a strange mix of people: Ignacio's conservative, aristocratic family shared the stage with a multitude of members of the Spanish Communist Party who arrived on busses.[16]

Casa de las Moras

Constancia had taken out insurance in the case of accidental death in a plane, but not for automobile accidents so her maid, Delfina Moreno, inherited nothing. The Morenos had adored Constancia who had encouraged their daughter Constancia – her goddaughter – to become a teacher, which she did. Constancia Moreno grew up hearing many stories about her godmother, and says that her parents always spoke of her generosity and felt that she was a part of their family. One of the last things Constancia wrote was a postcard addressed to the Morenos from Guatemala saying that she missed them and was ready to come home.[17]

The well-known blacklisted Hollywood screenwriter Gordon Kahn moved in to Constancia's house with his family. His son, James, had never met Constancia but was so impressed with what people said about her that in 1958 he wrote an award-winning high school essay entitled "Constancia". Kahn's short piece shows the mythical status she had acquired. He describes her house as the "legendary abode of the late, beloved

Constancia de la Mora . . . the magnificent, imposing home of the Spanish refugee who sought and found her freedom in Mexico."[18] He says that it is not the house that is special, but that

> *It is Constancia herself. People say that the house is haunted by the ghost of this woman. In a way they are right, for Constancia still lives – for those who were her neighbors. In every room of the house there is something to remind one of her – something to make one sense her presence – something to cause one to stop and wonder about the noble "inmigrante" who shared everything she had with the "peones" in the wooden huts, which lie at the foot of her rambling mansion.*

He praises her for renouncing her privileges for her ideals and says that "Up until the day of her death, she continued helping hundreds upon hundreds of her fellow countrymen to find refuge in Mexico when her own country was finally overcome."

There have been few public memorials for Constancia. It was not until twelve years after her death on August 25, 1962 that her family published a commemorative obituary in the newspaper *ABC* requesting prayers for their mother, who died just weeks after Constancia, their father, and their sister Teresa. Finally, last on the list, is Constancia's name.[19] For many years, Fredericka Martin looked after Constancia's grave, but today the tombstone designed by Ayala has mysteriously vanished from the spot under the tree chosen by Constancia. Fredericka Martin, who knew more than most people about Constancia's life, read O'Brien's manuscript and tried to help her find an editor. Martin thought that the "Least we can do for Connie's memory is try to get the poignant story of her death on record",[20] but the memoir was never published.

In August 1975, only a few months before Franco's death, a new Italian edition of *In Place of Splendor* came out with an introduction by Vittorio Vidali and a poem by Rafael Alberti, "Constancia de la Mora, hoy".[21] Vidali's short essay reveals nothing new about Constancia, and some of his facts are wrong: he claims that her father was Miguel Maura, that she went into exile with Ignacio in 1930, that she had written and completed *In Place of Splendor* by March 1939. But Alberti's poem celebrates her courage in choosing a difficult path, says that she died a militant, and considers her symbolic value as Spain, after nearly forty years, finally began its transition to democracy:

> *Constancia de la Mora, compañera constante*
> *reapareces ahora cuando más te deseamos*
> *tu mano fiel, tu impulso para la reconquista*
> *de aquella libertad que perdimos entonces.*

Asciende hasta la luz, levanta tus banderas
espejos de una vida que al viento han de mirarse.
Los vivos con los muertos de ayer unidos cantan.
No es el retorno, es algo futuro que se inicia.[22]

Alberti links Constancia to the image of a new country in which there is freedom after Franco, and in which the memory of the banished, imprisoned, and dead Republicans can be revealed and coexist with new generations of Spaniards. In 1977, the Spanish translation of *In Place of Splendor*, *Doble esplendor*, was at last published in Spain.

Nearly three decades later, the recovery of the history and stories from the Republican side during the war and the post-war is still very incomplete, and continues to provoke controversy and resistance at every step. It is within this ongoing process that the life of Constancia de la Mora, as well as the lives of many, many other Republicans have a timely and poignant value today.

Notes

Introduction

1 And what became . . . of Hidalgo de Cisneros/Constancia de la Mora . . . /What became/of all those distant ghosts? *Coplas a la muerte de mi tía Daniela*. Barcelona: Editorial Laia, 1984.

2 Interview with Milton Wolff.

3 Interview with Moe Fishman.

4 Norma Barzman, *The Red and the Blacklist* (New York: Thunder's Mouth Press/Nation Books, 2003), p. 66.

5 José Ramón Gómez Fouz (*Clandestinos*, Oviedo: Pentalfa ediciones-Biblioteca Asturianista, 1999), <http://helicon.es/dig/499/fouz04.pdf>.

6 Mario Mengs' interview with Eusebio Cimorra, April 20, 1994. Ignacio Hidalgo de Cisneros Papers, Mario Mengs.

7 Vittorio Vidali. Introduction to (Italian edition of *In Place of Splendor* translated by Giuseppe Garritano) *Gloriosa Spagna* (Roma: L'Unità Editori Riuniti, 1976), p. 16.

8 Shirley Mangini, *Memories of Resistance: Women's Voices from the Spanish Civil War* (New Haven and London: Yale University Press, 1995), p. 61.

9 <http://www.crossings.org/thursday/Thur022306.htm>.

I Old Spain: Portrait of a Family

1 *The New York Times*, November 19, 1939.

2 Constancia de la Mora, *In Place of Splendor* (New York: Harcourt Brace & Company, 1939), p. 25. Hereafter cited by author name only.

3 De la Mora, p. 6.

4 De la Mora.

5 De la Mora.

6 De la Mora, p. 26.

7 Letter dated July 12, 1920. Fundación Antonio Maura.

8 Letter dated October 10, 1920. Fundación Antonio Maura.

9 Letter dated December 8, 1920. Fundación Antonio Maura.

10 De la Mora, p. 49.

11 Undated letter from Saint Mary's Convent. Fundación Antonio Maura.

12 Letter dated October 2, 1924. Fundación Antonio Maura.

13 De la Mora, p. 52.

14 *ABC*, Thursday, February 4, 1926, Morning edition, p. 32.

15 *ABC*, Tuesday, March 24, 1925, Morning edition, p. 13.

16   De la Mora, p. 88.
17   De la Mora, pp. 84–5.
18   De la Mora, p. 88.
19   One of the great ironies of Constancia's story was that her first husband's brother, Luis Bolín, would later become her propaganda counterpart during the war on the Nationalist side. In addition to his propaganda work for Franco, Bolín was key in preparing the uprising and securing arms from Italy. For more on Bolín's role, see Southworth, *Guernica! Guernica!*
20   Conversation with Regina de la Mora.
21   De la Mora, p. 95.
22   *ABC*, Tuesday, February 9, 1926. Morning edition, p.16.
23   *ABC*, Tuesday, April 27, 1926. Morning edtion, p. 14.
24   De la Mora, p. 101.
25   De la Mora, p. 102.
26   De la Mora, p. 105.
27   De la Mora, p. 112.
28   De la Mora, p. 113.
29   De la Mora, p. 115.
30   De la Mora, p. 118.
31   De la Mora, p. 122.
32   De la Mora, p. 127.
33   In *The Spanish Civil War* Hugh Thomas [hereafter cited as Thomas] says of Miguel Maura: "A son of Antonio Maura, and brother of the Duque de Maura, who had been a member of the King's last cabinet until 14 April. Miguel was regarded as the black sheep of this remarkable Jewish-Catholic family until his niece, Constancia de la Mora y Maura, married the republican air chief Hidalgo de Cisneros, and became a communist," pp. 32–3.
34   De la Mora, p. 138.
35   De la Mora, p. 139.
36   "Madrid, October 1934. JA to Jr.", p. 1. From the Collection of Michael Allen.
37   De la Mora, p. 144.
38   Extractos de la correspondencia entre la Ilma. Sra. doña María Rúspoli Caro con su marido Ilmo. Sr. don Mariano del Prado O'Neill, condes de Buelna del 18 al 22 de junio, 1931. Fundación Antonio Maura.
39   The female vote in Spain was a contentious subject, even amongst women. Nelken and Kent, for example, were opposed and worried about the effects of the female vote on Spain's political future. They knew that the power of the church combined with a lack of education would make most women vote for the right. See Rosa María Capel, "La mujer en España: De la Belle Epoque a la Guerra Civil" in *El voto de las mujeres 1877–1978* (Madrid: Editorial Complutense, 2003); Mangini, *Memories of Resistance*, and Nash, *Defying Male Civilization*.
40   De la Mora, p. 148.
41   Ignacio Hidalgo de Cisneros, *Cambio de Rumbo* (Vitoria: Ikusager Ediciones,

2001), pp. 216–17. Previously published in Spanish in Bucharest (1964), in Paris (1977), and Barcelona (1977). (All quotations from *Cambio de Rumbo* are my translations). Hereafter cited by author name only.

42   Hidalgo de Cisneros, p. 263.

43   Hidalgo de Cisneros, p. 300.

44   Thomas, p. 97.

45   Hidalgo de Cisneros, p. 328.

46   PS Madrid, Caja 344, número 162, pp. 345–6. Archivo General de la Guerra Civil, Salamanca.

47   *Ibid.*, p. 347.

48   Hidalgo de Cisneros, p. 331.

49   Hidalgo de Cisneros, pp. 335–6.

50   PS Madrid, Caja 344, número 162, p. 354.

51   PS Madrid, Caja 344, número 162, p. 351.

52   Hidalgo de Cisneros, p. 337.

53   Hidalgo de Cisneros, p. 342.

54   Ignacio remembered only his last name, Comyn.

55   Hidalgo de Cisneros, p. 355.

56   Hidalgo de Cisneros, p. 347.

57   Hidalgo de Cisneros.

58   De la Mora, p. 191.

59   De la Mora, p. 192.

60   De la Mora, p. 192.

61   De la Mora, p. 191.

62   Helen Graham, *The Spanish Republic at War 1936–1939* (Cambridge: Cambridge University Press, 2002), p. 58.

63   Though Constancia offers little description of the Albertis's charm, they had a distinctly glamorous communist style. The following passage from the memoir of Jaime Salinas, son of the poet Pedro Salinas, gives a more vibrant portrait of the couple when they finally returned to Madrid from this same trip. It shows their tremendous appeal, and the resentment that María Teresa, as a militant woman and mother, could inspire in other women: "When I opened the door I was dazzled by the most attractive couple I had ever seen. They were Rafael Alberti and María Teresa, just back from Russia . . . María Teresa . . . told my mother about their trip to the Soviet Union: how they had visited schools, orphanages, training camps. She kept repeating: My little Russian children, those Russian children, they are the most handsome little children. That evening, at dinner, I heard my mother tell *Tata* Andrea: 'María Teresa would be better off looking after her real children, instead of talking about "her Russian children"'." Jaime Salinas, *Travesías* (Barcelona: Tusquets, 2003), p. 22.

64   Quintanilla was indeed arrested for being a part of the Revolutionary Committee and held in the Cárcel Modelo of Madrid. André Malraux, Ernest Hemingway, and John Dos Passos all rallied to have him released. He was held

until June 10, 1935. During the war he led troops in combat and was later put in charge of Intelligence on the French side of the Basque country. See (son) Paul Quintanilla's website devoted to the artist and his life: <http://www.lqart.org/index.html>.

65   Jay Allen, "Madrid, October 1934" (JA to Jr.), p. 1. Papers of Jay Allen.

66   *Ibid.*, p.2.

67   De la Mora, p. 195.

68   De la Mora, p. 197.

69   The German radio network in Spain would become an important propaganda instrument. Thomas notes: "in December 1936 a huge Lorenz radio transmission plant arrived in Vigo from Hamburg, three times larger than any other in Spain. Henceforward, the voice of Salamanca and Burgos could be clearly heard throughout not only nationalist but Republican Spain as well." Thomas, p. 504.

70   Hidalgo de Cisneros, p. 384.

71   Hidalgo de Cisneros, p. 386.

72   De la Mora, p. 200.

73   Hidalgo de Cisneros, p. 394.

74   De la Mora, p. 207.

75   De la Mora, pp. 211–12.

76   De la Mora, p. 209.

77   De la Mora, p. 209.

78   De la Mora, p. 215.

79   De la Mora, p. 216.

80   See Thomas, p. 194 and De la Mora, p. 219.

81   De la Mora, p. 219.

II   The War, 1936–1939: Fighting Fascism from the Press Office

1   *The Secret Diary of Harold L. Ickes* (New York: Simon & Schuster, 1954), p. 388.

2   De la Mora, p. 240.

3   De la Mora, p. 241.

4   The engagement of "the charming señorita Constancia de la Mora y Maura, granddaughter of the unforgettable statesman" to Manuel Bolín was announced on Tuesday, February 9, 1926; the May 17, 1926 wedding of the "most beautiful señorita Constancia de la Mora y Maura" was announced on April 27, 1926. *ABC* Archives, Madrid.

5   *Frente Rojo*, nº 424, p. 3, June 4, 1938.

6   *Frente Rojo*, nº 544, p. 4, October 26, 1938.

7   *Ibid.* My translation.

8   "Epilogue" in Mary Nash, *Defying Male Civilization: Women in the Spanish Civil War* (Denver: Arden Press, 1995).

9   Herbert Southworth, *Conspiracy and the Spanish Civil War: The Brainwashing of Francisco Franco* (London and New York: Routledge, 2002), p. 1.

10   Ignacio Hidalgo de Cisneros, *Cambio de Rumbo* (Vitoria: Ikusager Ediciones, 2001), p. 504.

11 De la Mora, p. 228.

12 De la Mora, p. 233.

13 Ramón Sala Noguer, *El cine en la España Republicana durante la guerra civil (1936–1939)* (Bilbao: Mensajero, 1993), p. 336.

14 Sala Noguer, *El cine en la España Republicana*, cites Thorold Dickinson's article "Spanish ABC" published in *Sight and Sound*, Vol. 7, 25, Spring 1938, p. 30. Sala Noguer, p. 337.

15 De la Mora, p. 242.

16 De la Mora, p. 266.

17 De la Mora, p. 267.

18 Kowalsky, *Stalin and the Spanish Civil War* (e-book), <http://www.gutenberg-e.org>, Chapter 7.

19 Mangan had gone to Spain looking for her German lover, Jan Kurzke (whose real name was Hans Robert Kurzke). He was a Marxist painter who fled the Nazi regime in 1933 and lived as a refugee in Spain. He fought in the Spanish civil war as a volunteer with the International Brigades. "Biography", Jan Kurzke Papers, Archives of the International Institute for Social History, Amsterdam. Mangan and Kurzke co-wrote the unpublished memoir *The Good Comrade*.

20 Kate Mangan and Jan Kurzke, *The Good Comrade* (unpublished manuscript, Jan Kurzke Papers, International Institute for Social History, Amsterdam), p. 82.

21 Secret certificate signed S. Miller and V. Ovchinnikova, October 24, 1944. Comintern Archive. File of Luli Hidalgo de Cisneros.

22 Hidalgo de Cisneros, pp. 462–3.

23 Burnett Bolloten, *The Spanish Civil War: Revolution and Counterrevolution*, Foreword by Stanley G. Payne (Chapel Hill, NC: University of North Carolina Press, 1992), p. 838, n. 18. Bolloten knew Constancia from his work as a correspondent for United Press during the war. Hidalgo de Cisneros told Bolloten that he has joined the party in January 1937, but according to *Cambio de Rumbo* it must have been earlier because the *Neva* came to Alicante in the early fall of 1936, by which time both he and Constancia were already members.

24 Irene Falcón, *Asalto a los cielos*, p. 194. (My translation).

25 Hidalgo de Cisneros, p. 235.

26 Zenobia Camprubí, *Diario I (1937–1939)* (Alianza Editorial/ Editorial de la Universidad de Puerto Rico, 1991), p. 40. (All quotes from Camprubí are my translations).

27 Camprubí, *Diario I*, p. 111.

28 Camprubí, *Diario I*, p. 152.

29 De la Mora, p. 268.

30 De la Mora.

31 De la Mora, p. 268.

32 Archivo General de la Guerra Civil Española. Fuentes Orales México. Libro no. 35, p. 242.

33 De la Mora, p. 278.

34 After Constancia's marriage to Ignacio, he was generally considered Luli's father, even on official documents.

35 Ronald Radosh and Mary Habeck, eds., *Spain Betrayed: The Soviet Union and the Spanish Civil War* (New Haven: Yale University Press, 2001), p. 114.

36 De la Mora, p. 281.

37 Louis Fischer, *Men and Politics*, p. 457.

38 Hidalgo de Cisneros, p. 504.

39 De la Mora, p. 283.

40 De la Mora, p. 284.

41 De la Mora, pp. 288–9.

42 Louis Fischer, *Men and Politics*, p. 457.

43 Kate Mangan and Jan Kurzke, *The Good Comrade*, p. 62. Hereafter cited by author names only.

44 Mangan and Kurzke, p. 223.

45 *Ibid.*, p. 244.

46 Mangan renamed many of the people she knew and worked with in Spain, and her daughter, Charlotte Kurzke, is still in the process of identifying the real identities of many of the "characters" in the memoir, including that of "Poppy".

47 Mangan and Kurzke, pp. 244–5.

48 Kellt may have been Otto Katz, the Comintern agent who had assumed responsibility for pro-Republican propaganda.

49 Rudolf Selke was a former editor of the *Frankfurter Zeitung*.

50 Mangan and Kurzke, p. 246.

51 Ibid., p. 365. For a contrasting and largely unsubstantiated view of Oak as an innocent victim persecuted by communists, see Stephen Koch's *The Breaking Point: Hemingway, Dos Passos, and the Murder of José Robles* (New York: Counterpoint, 2005).

52 One of the great ironies of Constancia's story was that her first husband's brother, Luis Bolín, would be her propaganda counterpart during the war on the Nationalist side. In addition to his propaganda work for Franco, Bolín was key in preparing the uprising and securing arms from Italy. For more on Bolín's role, see Southworth, *Guernica! Guernica!*

53 Mangan and Kurzke, p. 295.

54 *Ibid.*, p. 259.

55 *Ibid.*

56 Mangan adds that after a time of being ordered about by Rubio, and made to re-write Azaña's long speeches in English, Auden "got fed up with the politics and intrigues in Valencia and went to the front as a stretcher-bearer and one could not blame him", p. 261.

57 Coco Robles was the sixteen-year old son of José Robles, a professor of literature at Johns Hopkins University. As Coco had been raised in the United States, he spoke English fluently.

58 See Thomas, *The Spanish Civil War*, pp. 370–80.
59 Mangan and Kurzke, p. 295.
60 *Ibid.*, p. 416.
61 *Ibid.*, p. 419.
62 Mangan and Kurzke, p. 429.
63 Arturo Barea (1997–1957) is the author of the famous three-volume autobi-
    ography *La forja de un rebelde* (Buenos Aires: Losada, 1951).
64 Barea, *La forja de un rebelde*, p. 611. My translation.
65 *Ibid.*, p. 719.
66 *Ibid.*, pp. 730–1.
67 *Ibid.*, p. 732.
68 *Ibid.*, p. 733.
69 Louis Fischer, *Men and Politics*, p. 456.
70 *Ibid.*, p. 324.
71 At the point when Luli was living in Russia with Uritzky and his family.
72 Fischer, *Men and Politics*, p. 456.
73 Indalecio Prieto, "María: Una mujer excepcional", <http://www.bermemar.
    com/personaj/marpriet.htm> (Página de María Lejárraga de Martínez Sierra)
    reproduced from *Le socialiste*, jeudi, 22 fevrier, 1962, pp. 1–2.
74 Burnett Bolloten, *Revolution and Counterrevolution*, p. 539.
75 Bolloten worked with Constancia as the correspondent for Associated Press
    during the war.
76 Bolloten, *Revolution and Counterrevolution*, p. 539.
77 Fischer, *Men and Politics*, p. 457.
78 Helen Graham, *The Spanish Republic at War 1936–1939* (Cambridge:
    Cambridge University Press, 2002), p. 333. Constancia also told Bolloten (in
    their interview shortly after the war) that "Prieto hated me . . . because he
    believed that I had influenced Ignacio to join the communist party," Bolloten,
    p. 540.
79 Fischer, *Men and Politics*, p. 460.
80 Bolloten, *Revolution and Counterrevolution*, p. 540.
81 Fischer, *Men and Politics*, p. 461.
82 Even after the end of the war Fischer would serve as an unofficial liaison
    between Negrín and the United States government, where he also had many
    friends.
83 Bolloten, *Revolution and Counterrevolution*, p. 540.
84 The Soviet Intelligence Service.
85 Bolloten, *Revolution and Counterrevolution*, p. 500.
86 *Ibid.*, p. 501.
87 *Ibid.*
88 See Graham, *The Spanish Republic at War 1936–1939*, pp. 286–7. On the ques-
    tion of the role of the police, Graham furthermore says that: "To expect the
    'old' police or military mentality to have drawn a distinction between
    different sorts of anti-governmental rebellion in wartime is unrealistic – espe-

cially when the left was, anyway, a target with which many policemen were not comfortable. If we look again at what was happening, a much older and more deeply ingrained political culture than Stalinism begins to be apparent behind police zeal," p. 287.

89 De la Mora, p. 301.
90 Hidalgo de Cisneros, p. 503.
91 Thomas, *The Spanish Civil War*, p. 431.
92 *Ibid.*, p. 432.
93 De la Mora, p. 301.
94 Graham, *The Spanish Republic at War 1936–1939*, p. 306.
95 Langston Hughes. *I Wonder as I Wander. An Autobiographical Journey* (New York: Hill and Wang; Farrar, Straus, and Giroux), 1956).
96 Philip Jordan. *There Is No Return* (London: Cresset Press, 1938), pp. 287–8.
97 Mangan and Kurzke, p. 419.
98 This is the same women's prison that Mangan visited with journalists. See p. 19.
99 Diary (August 8–August 24, 1937). Paul Patrick Rogers Papers. Harry Ransom Humanities Research Center at the University of Texas at Austin.
100 Undated Correspondence. Paul Patrick Rogers Papers. Harry Ransom Humanities Research Center at the University of Texas at Austin.
101 Margaret Hooks, *Tina Modotti: Photographer and Revolutionary* (Cambridge, MA: Da Capo Press, 2000), p. 229.
102 Albers, Patricia, *Shadow, Fire, Snow: The Life of Tina Modotti* (Berkeley: University of California Press, 2002), p. 300.
103 Albers, *Shadow, Fire, Snow*, p. 301.
104 Hooks, *Tina Modotti*, p. 230.
105 Letter of July 1, 1938 from Tina Modotti, "María", to Alvarez del Vayo. Sent from the Socorro Rojo de España Offices in Barcelona (Calle Caspe 59). Archivo MAE. Sección de la Subsecretaría de Propaganda.
106 Hooks (p. 232) quotes Luisa Viquiera (niece of Tina's colleague Matilde Landa) as saying that Tina *"Se enteró e informaba"* (She found out and informed).
107 Hooks, *Tina Modotti*, p. 232.
108 Mangan and Kurzke, 430–1.
109 Robles' disappearance has been investigated in Ignacio Martínez de Pisón's *Enterrar a los muertos* (Barcelona: Seix Barral, 2005). Stephen Koch also explores the episode in *The Breaking Point: Hemingway, Dos Passos, and the Murder of José Robles* (New York: Counterpoint, 2005).
110 Martínez de Pisón, *Enterrar a los muertos*, p. 19 (all quotes from Martínez de Pisón are my translations).
111 Martínez de Pisón, *Enterrar a los muertos*, p. 30.
112 Mangan and Kurzke, 248.
113 Martínez de Pisón, *Enterrar a los muertos*, p. 35.
114 *Ibid.*, p. 33.
115 John Dos Passos, "Spain: Rehearsal for Defeat" in *The Theme is Freedom*.

Freeport, New York: Books for Libraries Press. 1970. (Originally published in 1956), pp. 128–9.

116 Dos Passos, *ibid.*

117 Martínez de Pisón, *Enterrar a los muertos*, p. 162.

118 De la Mora, p. 296.

119 De la Mora.

120 Mangan and Kurzke, p. 420.

121 Martínez de Pisón, *Enterrar a los muertos*, p. 170.

122 *Ibid.*

123 "Poppy" was Milly Bennett (Mildred Bremler), who worked in Spain for the London *Times*, Associated Press and United Press. See letter from A. Tom Grunfeld on Bennett in *The Volunteer*, Vol. XXXVI, No. 4, December 2004, p. 20.

123 *Ibid.*, p. 166.

124 Mangan and Kurzke, p. 420

125 Herbst, Josephine, *The Starched Blue Sky of Spain* (New York: Harper Collins, 1991), pp. 154–5.

126 Constancia's impressions show that she considered Herbst *de confianza*: "Josephine Herbst came when we were still in Valencia. She was especially interested in the people. I remember taking her to a big mass meeting on a Sunday morning. Pasionaria was one of the speakers and Jo Herbst seemed very impressed by the great love that Dolores Ibárruri inspired in her audience", *In Place of Splendor*, p. 297.

127 Martínez de Pisón, *Enterrar a los muertos,* p. 84.

128 *Ibid.*, p. 85.

129 There was in fact no proof that Orlov orchestrated Nin's fate. See Graham, *The Spanish Republic at War*, p. 288.

130 Helen Graham, *The Spanish Republic at War*, "War, Modernity, and Reform: The Premiership of Juan Negrín" in *The Republic Besieged: Civil War in Spain 1936–1939*. Edited by Paul Preston and Ann L. Mackenzie (Edinburgh: Edinburgh University Press, 1996), p. 191.

131 Wilebaldo Solano. "La larga marcha por la verdad sobre Andreu Nin". Página web de la Fundación Nin, <http://www.fundanin.org/solano8.htm>.

132 Solano, ibid.

133 Pierre Broué. "Acerca de *"Queridos Camaradas"*, *Iniciativa Socialista*, número 58, Otoño 2000.

134 Wildebaldo Solano explains that the failure to extract a confession from Nin through torture led to his being murdered. Solano cites a letter written by Orlov to his superiors on July 24, 1937 in which he states that Nin was killed by himself and four other men: Jusik (also of the NKVD) and three Spaniards whose initials he gives as L., A. F., and I. L. Also present were the Hungarian Erno Gerö (aka *Pedro*) and his chauffeur mentioned only as "Victor". Further analysis of Nin's murder can be found in *Le POUM: Révolution dans la guerre d'Espagne* (Paris: Syllepse, 2002) and in the 1992 documentary *Operacíon Nikolai* shown on TV3 Catalana.

135 De la Mora, pp. 317–18.
136 Fischer to Negrín, 9 November 1937. Louis Fischer Papers, Seeley G. Mudd Manuscript Library, Princeton University.
137 De la Mora, p. 368.
138 Archivo del Ministerio de Asuntos Exteriores (MAE). Sección de la Subsecretaría de Propaganda.
139 K. Scott Watson is probably the "unidentified reporter for the *Star* whose message about Guernica was one of the first printed and the most widely quoted" and the "unidentified 'Special Correspondent" who Herbert Southworth says sent a telegram to the Labour Party's *Daily Herald* about the bombing of Guernica in late April, 1937. Southworth cites Vicente Talón who identified "a man named Watson" as the correspondent for both the *Star* and the *Daily Herald*.
140 May 30, 1938 letter from K. Scott Watson to Alvarez del Vayo. Archivo del MAE. Subsecretaría de Propaganda.
141 Memorandum from Constancia to Berbeito. June 3, 1938. Archivo del MAE. Subsecretaría de Propaganda. Lobo's 'Open Letter to the Editor of The Times' [(concerning the Spanish Catholic church and the Spanish Civil War), by Father Leocadio Lobo, June 1938, Barcelona. p. 4. Typescript] is in the Spanish Civil War collection of the British Library of Political and Economic Sciences.
142 De la Mora, p. 345.
143 De la Mora, p. 356.
144 De la Mora, p. 362.
145 De la Mora, p. 365.
146 Kowalsky, Daniel. *Stalin and the Spanish Civil War* (e-book) <http://www.gutenberg-e.org>, Chapter 3.
147 Graham, *The Spanish Republic at War*, p. 391, n. 4–5.
148 Hidalgo de Cisneros, p. 547.
149 Irene Falcón. *Asalto a los cielos: mi vida junto a la Pasionaria* (Madrid: Temas de Hoy, 1996), p. 166.
150 My interview with Dolores Ruiz.
151 Hidalgo de Cisneros, p. 548.
152 Enrique Castro Delgado, *Hombres made in Moscú* (Barcelona: Luis de Caralt, 1963), p. 636. My translation. The names preceding the dialogue have been added for clarity.
153 Marcelino Pascua was the Republican ambassador to Moscow during the Civil War. For an account of the challenges he faced in this position, see Daniel Kowalsky, *Stalin and the Spanish Civil War*.
154 *Spain Betrayed*, p. 512.
155 Gerald Howson, *Arms for Spain* (New York: St. Martin's Press, 1998), p. 244.
156 Kowalsky, *Stalin and the Spanish Civil War*, chapter 10.
157 David Wingeate Pike, *In the Service of Stalin* (Oxford: Oxford University Press), 1993. p. 15.

158 De la Mora, p. 414.
159 Mangan and Kurzke, p. 436.
160 "Information about Ignacio Hidalgo de Cisneros", September 13, 1943. Signed Belov/Blagoeva. Hidalgo de Cisneros file, Comintern Archive.

III Mission to New York: Propaganda and Diplomacy

1 De la Mora, *In Place of Splendor*, p. 415.
2 Margaret Hooks, *Tina Modotti: Photographer and Revolutionary* (Da Capo Press, 2000), p. 239.
3 The collection of these sculptures was abandoned in a barn for decades, and was finally purchased by the High Museum in Atlanta, Georgia in 2005.
4 De la Mora, p. 366.
5 Alice Graeme, "Loyalist Leaders in Sculpture Presented at Whyte Gallery". *The Washington Post*, January 8, 1939. Proquest Historical Newspapers.
6 Dorothy Parker. Catalogue of the Jo Davidson Exhibit For Benefit of Spanish Children's Milk Fund. Reproduced in Jannis Conner and Joel Rosenkranz, *Rediscoveries in American Sculpture: Studio Works 1893–1939* (Austin: University of Texas Press, 1989).
7 *Ibid.*
8 From Martha Dodd's file in the KGB archives. Quoted in *The Haunted Wood* by Allen Weinstein and Alexander Vassiliev (New York: Random House, 1999), p. 51.
9 *The Haunted Wood*, p. 63.
10 Letter from J. D. LeCron to Jay Allen, March 16, 1939. Papers of Jay Allen.
11 Letter signed "Blank" from the National Labor Relations Board to Jay Allen, March 25, 1939. Papers of Jay Allen.
12 According to documents in his Comintern file, Ignacio arrived in the USSR from Paris in May 1939, with "other Spaniards". He was given a three-month residence permit (memorandum from K. P. Sukharev to comrade Smodorinskii, May 13, 1939. Ignacio Hidalgo de Cisneros file, Comintern Archive). The information on Ignacio's "Application for Nonimmigrant Visa" form dated September 4, 1939 (signed in Paris) shows the chaos his life was plunged into during the first year of exile. He stated that he planned on traveling to New York on September 23/24th. He gave his former fixed domicile as 24, avenue Charles Floquet, Paris; his US address as c/o Jay Allen, 21 Washington Square North, New York City; and his future fixed domicile as Gran Hotel, Mexico City. As references he listed Lawrence Braymer, Honey Holow Farm, Lahaska Pennsylvania; and Don Juan Negrín, 24 avenue Charles Floquet, Paris. This visa allowed him a maximum stay in the United States of one month which gave him enough time in the States to join Constancia and then continue on to Mexico together. In the epilogue to new edition of *Cambio de Rumbo* (Vitoria: IKUSAGER Ediciones, 2001) Ignacio's nephew, Ignacio Hidalgo de Cisneros Alonso, says that after the war ended his uncle remained in Paris and then went straight to the Soviet Union until 1945. This

is incorrect, and in keeping with his determination in his epilogue to mini-
mize Ignacio's relationship with Constancia.

13   The date is deduced by the fact that she wrote to Eleanor Roosevelt on May
      18 1939 that "I am sorry to trouble you again about the same question, but
      Dr. Negrín will stay here for at least another week and I thought I would let
      you know" (FDR Library). And that Ignacio's travel plans for September were
      being discussed. Constancia was only in the States from February until
      December of 1939.

14   "Don Juan" was the Republican Premier, Dr. Juan Negrín.

15   Archivo Histórico del Partido Comunista de España. Legajo Ignacio Hidalgo
      de Cisneros.

16   On July 9, 1939 a message signed Soslov was sent to Soledad Sancha
      announcing a new request from Constancia: "Hidalgo de Cisneros' wife wants
      to come [to the Soviet Union] for two months and go back to the USA with
      him. She is asking whether they can go to the Spanish people." This would
      seem to mean that she wanted to go to Moscow to spend the summer with
      Luli and Ignacio, and find a way to make a trip to Spain. Soslov is sympathetic
      to this request and points out that Ignacio was an honest, modest, bourgeois
      anti-fascist and that he missed his family. This same message also mentions
      Mikhail Koltsov, who was soon to be executed: "He [Ignacio] often sees
      Koltsov's wife, Maria Osten . . . she says that Koltsov will be freed soon."
      Soslov to Sancha, July 9, 1939. Ignacio Hidalgo de Cisneros' file, Comintern
      Archive.

17   Irene Falcón. *Asalto a los cielos: mi vida junto a la Pasionaria* (Madrid: Temas de
      Hoy, 1996). My translation.

18   These appearances, and others, are all listed in the "Events Today" sections of
      the *The New York Times* in May and June 1939. *New York Times (1857–Current
      File)*. Proquest Historical Newspapers.

19   This is what Vittorio Vidali claims in his Introduction to (the Italian edition
      of *In Place of Splendor*) *Gloriosa Spagna* (Rome: L'Unitá-Editori Riuniti, 1976)
      His other recollections regarding the writing of Constancia's book are not reli-
      able, but it is very likely that it was Jay Allen who came up with the idea of
      a book signed by Constancia to turn American attention to Spain.

20   Isabel de Palencia, *Smouldering Freedom: The Story of the Spanish Republicans in
      Exile* (New York: Longmans, Green and Co., 1945), p. 214. De Palencia's
      earlier book, *I Must Have Liberty*, was also published by Longmans, Green and
      Co. in 1940. She had been Minister Plenipotentiary for Republican Spain to
      Finland and Sweden from 1936–1939. After the war she lived in exile in
      Mexico.

21   Vittorio Vidali. Introduction to *Gloriosa Spagna*, p. 16.

22   The Cuban Julio Antonio Mella was famous for being the young, charismatic
      creator of the Anti-imperialist League (*Liga Antimperialista*) and one of the
      founders of the Cuban Communist Party. He and Tina became lovers in
      Mexico where on January 10, 1929 he was assassinated in front of her.

23   Christiane Barckhausen-Canale, *Verdad y leyenda de Tina Modotti* (La Habana: Casa de las Américas, 1989), p. 300. My translation.
24   My interview with Eileen Bransten.
25   Obituary of Jerome Chodorov. *Variety*, September 13, 2004.
26   My italics.
27   Martha Dodd had just published an autobiographical account of her political "awakening" in Germany, *My Years in Germany* (New York: Harcourt, Brace & Co., 1939). It should be noted that Harcourt, Brace & Co. published McKenney, Dodd, and Constancia's memoirs.
28   Undated letter from Constancia to Jay Allen. Probably written in the summer of 1939. From the Papers of Jay Allen.
29   McKenney and Bransten were ousted by the Communist party in 1946 for their "petty-bourgeois radicalism" and for " . . . conducting a factional struggle against the party line and its national leadership". See article in the *The Daily Worker*, September 12, 1946 and follow-up in *The New York Times*, September 13, 1946.
30   "Students Protest Spanish Embargo". *The New York Times*, February 25, 1939, p. 7.
31   My correspondence with Eileen Bransten, daughter of Ruth McKenney.
32   Ruth McKenny and her husband Richard Bransten were ousted from the Communist Party in 1946. Their daughter, Eileen Bransten, says that her mother never talked about being blacklisted, but McKenney's name appears in *Blacklisted: The Filmlovers Guide to the Hollywood Blacklist* (Palgrave Macmillan, 2003). Her sister Eileen's fatal crash with Nathaniel West was not the last tragedy in her life. On McKenney's forty-fourth birthday, November 18, 1955 her husband killed himself. She died in New York in 1972 at age sixty.
33   De la Mora, p. 288.
34   De la Mora, p. 136.
35   See n. 28.
36   McKenney writes about the Westport house in the last chapter of *The McKenney's Carry On* (New York: Grosset & Dunlap with Harcourt Brace & Co., 1937).
37   Clara Sancha is the sister of Soledad Sancha (who worked at the Mexican embassy in Moscow) and the widow of the sculptor Alberto Sánchez Pérez. He also taught (drawing) at one of the schools (#7) for the Spanish children in Moscow.
38   My interview with Clara Sancha, January 2006.
39   De la Mora, p. 373.
40   Kate Mangan and Jan Kurzke, *The Good Comrade*, Archives of the International Institute of Social History, Amsterdam.
41   Malcolm Cowley, "Disillusionment." *The New Republic*, June 14, 1939.
42   Letter to Jay Allen. Undated, but probably written in early July 1939 in Westport, Connecticut.

43   John Dos Passos, "The Death of José Robles," *The New Republic*, July 19, 1939.
44   Dos Passos, "The Death of José Robles."
45   *Ibid.*
46   Milly Bennett appears as "Poppy" in Kate Mangan's memoir.
47   Milly Bennett. Letter to *The New Republic*, July 19, 1939.
49   De la Mora, p. 423.
50   Ibarruri, *El unico camino*, p. 461.
51   De la Mora, p. 425.
52   De la Mora, p. 426.
53   Letter to Van Golden. Elizabeth Whitclmb Houghton Collection, Marquette University Archives.
54   Corrected typescript of *In Place of Splendor*. Elizabeth Whitcomb Houghton Collection, Marquette University Archives.
55   Feld, Rose. "A Patrician in Republican Spain". November 19, 1939.
56   Barrish, Mildred. "Spanish Republican Retains Persevering Loyalty". *The Los Angeles Times*, January 14, 1940.
57   "Gossip of the Rialto", *The New York Times*, October 12, 1941.
58   My interview with Germán de la Mora.
59   Constancia discusses Flynn on pp. 297–8. The news of the lawsuit appeared in *The New York Times*, September 5, 1940.
60   Constancia and Concha Prieto had worked together at the children's colonies and in the hospitals in Alicante. At the time, Indalecio Prieto was the Minister of Air and Marine. He was worried about Concha and ordered her to leave Spain. Constancia never forgave him and wrote: " The women of Madrid were fighting beside their men . . . while the guns roared. We were comparatively safe, doing work . . . that was absolutely necessary. Why should the Minister of Air consider his daughter above the women of Madrid? I have never believed that because a man has power in the government he should not share the suffering of his country . . . " (De la Mora, pp. 268–70)
61   Leigh White, "Spanish Testament: *In Place of Splendor: the Autobiography of a Spanish Woman*" (Review), *The Nation*, December 23, 1939, pp. 713–14.
62   Frida Kirchway was the Editor of *The Nation*.
63   Letter from Constancia to Jay Allen, December 31, 1939. From the papers of Jay Allen.
64   Mildred Adams wrote for the *New York Times* and many other publications. She worked on behalf of the Spanish Republican refugees and in the spring of 1940 became a member of the executive board of the Spanish Refugee Relief Campaign. Her papers are at the Immigration History Research Center, University of Minnesota.
65   Mildred Adams, Letter published in *The Nation*, January 13, 1940, p. 56.
66   De la Mora, p. 258.
67   De la Mora, p. 286.
68   On January 8, 1940 Leonard Lyons announced in his "New Yorker" column in the *Washington Post* that "William Carney, who covered the Franco side

during the Spanish war, is preparing a suit against Constancia de la Mora and her publishers because of references to him in her book, "In Place of Splendor".

69   Letter from Constancia to Jay Allen, December 31, 1939. Papers of Jay Allen.

IV   Refugee Crisis: From the White House to the Blacklist

1   Rey García, Marta, *Stars for Spain: La Guerra Civil en los Estados Unidos* (A Coruña: Edicios do Castro, 1997), pp. 384–5.

2   Letter from Department of State to Jay Allen, March 25, 1939. Rauner Special Collections Library, Dartmouth College.

3   Letter from Stanley M. Isaacs to Jay Allen, June 19, 1940. Rauner Special Collections Library, Dartmouth College.

4   Letter from J. D. LeCron to Jay Allen, June 18, 1940. Rauner Special Collections Library.

5   Letter from Martha Gellhorn (San Francisco de Paula, Cuba) to Eleanor Roosevelt, March 8, 1939. Eleanor Rooosevelt Collection, Series 100. From the holdings at the Franklin D. Roosevelt Library.

6   Blanche Wiesen Cook, *Eleanor Roosevelt, Volume 2. 1933–1938* (New York: Viking, 1999), p. 506

7   Letter from Constancia (21 Washington Square North, New York City) to Eleanor Rooosevelt, April 12, 1939. Eleanor Rooosevelt Collection, Series 100.

8   Letter from Eleanor Roosevelt to Constancia, April 21, 1939. Eleanor Roosevelt Collection, Series 100.

9   Letter from Constancia to Eleanor Roosevelt, May 7, 1939. Eleanor Roosevelt Collection, Series 100.

10   On April 12, President Roosevelt held a press conference at which he made clear that the United States would not remain indifferent to Hitler and Mussolini's actions in Europe. See "President's Views" by Felix Belair, Jr., *The New York Times*. April 12, 1939. p. 1.

11   Letter from Negrín to Claude Bowers, Paris, April 17, 1939. Fischer's corrections added by hand. The Louis Fischer Papers. Series 2, Subject Correspondence. Seeley G. Mudd Manuscript Library, Princeton University.

12   Letter from Constancia to E. Roosevelt, May 18, 1939, and reply from May 22, 1939. Eleanor Roosevelt Collection, Series 100.

13   Letter from Claude Bowers to Negrín. St. Jean de Luz, April 20, 1939. Louis Fischer Papers. Correspondence. Seely G. Mudd Manuscript Library, Princeton University.

14   The fact that Constancia mentions Bergamín is, according to Burnett Bolloten, because of Bergamín's " . . . intimate association with the Spanish Communists by whom he was surrounded when he emigrated to Mexico in 1939 . . . " and that "His importance to the Communists can be gauged by a letter sent by Constancia de la Mora, a member of the PCE, to Eleanor Roosevelt in July 1939 praising Bergamín's cultural activities in Mexico." Burnett Bolloten, *Revolution and Counterrevolution*, p. 892, n. 18.

15 Letter from Constancia to Eleanor Roosevelt, July 17, 1939. Eleanor Roosevelt Collection, Series 100.

16 Letter from E. Roosevelt to Constancia, July 22, 1939. Eleanor Roosevelt Collection, Series 100.

17 Letter from Sumner Welles to Eleanor Roosevelt, July 24, 1939. Eleanor Roosevelt Collection, Series 70.

18 *Comité International de Coordination et d'Information pour l'Aide à l'Espagne Républicaine*

19 *The Nation*, August 5, 1939.

20 Letter from Constancia to Malvina Thompson, secretary to Mrs. Roosevelt, August 9, 1939. Eleanor Roosevelt Collection, Series 100.

21 This positive reaction is mentioned in a letter from Constancia to Eleanor Roosevelt "I want to tell you how pleased I was to know that you have liked my book and how grateful I am to you for mentioning it as one of the three books that you have most enjoyed reading during the past year." December 5, 1939. The new letterhead shows that sometime in late November or early December 1939 Constancia had moved from Jay Allen's house on Washington Square to 340 East 57th Street. Eleanor Roosevelt Collection, Series 100.

22 Letter from Adolf A. Berle Jr. to Herman F. Reissig, December 20, 1939. Eleanor Roosevelt Collection, Series 70.

23 Memorandum for Mrs. Roosevelt from Adolf A. Berle Jr., December 20, 1939. Eleanor Roosevelt Collection, Series 70.

24 This is clearly not how Berle viewed the struggle of the Spanish Republicans.

25 Memorandum for Mrs. Roosevelt from Adolf A. Berle. Op. Cit.

26 Letter from Eleanor Roosevelt to Constancia, December 28, 1939. Eleanor Roosevelt Collection, Series 70.

27 The first address Constancia gives in Mexico is "La Casona" in Cuernavaca.

28 Letter from Constancia to Eleanor Roosevelt, December 25, 1939. Eleanor Roosevelt Collection, Series 100.

29 Letter from Constancia to Felice Clark, Spanish Refugee Relief Campaign (North American Committee), December 25, 1939. Spanish Refugee Relief Organization Collection. Pt. B, Box 20. Rare Book and Manuscript Library, Columbia University.

30 Letter from Constancia to Felice, Spanish Refugee Relief Campaign (North American Committee), December 25, 1939.

31 Letter from Constancia to Herman Reissig, Spanish Refugee Relief Campaign (North American Committee), January 9, 1940. Spanish Refugee Relief Organization Collection. Pt. B, Box 20. Rare Book and Manuscript Library, Columbia University.

32 Letter from Herman Reissig to Constancia, Spanish Refugee Relief Campaign (North American Committee), January 16, 1940. Spanish Refugee Relief Organization Collection. Pt. B, Box 20. Rare Book and Manuscript Library, Columbia University.

33 She was translating *In Place of Splendor* into Spanish.

34   Letter from Constancia to Jay Allen, January 14, 1940. Papers of Jay Allen.

35   David Wingeate Pike, *In The Service of Stalin* (New York: Oxford University Press, 1993), p. 39.

36   Letter from Constancia to Eleanor Roosevelt, February 19, 1940. Eleanor Roosevelt Collection, Series 100.

37   Letter from Eleanor Roosevelt to Constancia, February 29, 1940. Eleanor Roosevelt Collection, Series 100.

38   After returning from Spain, the Veterans of the Abraham Lincoln Brigade (the North American division of the International Brigades) continued their political activism on behalf of Spanish Republicans for decades. Today their organization, in collaboration with the Abraham Lincoln Brigade Archives, supports and promotes the study of the role of the United States in the Spanish Civil War, and still publishes the magazine that Constancia wrote for, *The Volunteer.* See <http://www.alba-valb.org>.

39   *Volunteer for Liberty*, Volume II., no. 1, January, 1940. Convention Issue, p. 10.

40   Letter from Adolf A. Berle., Jr. to Melvina Thompson (secretary to Mrs. Roosevelt) Eleanor Roosevelt Collection, Series 70.

41   The 6,000 left behind, unfit to serve or work, faced an uncertain fate. Most refugees had been incorporated into the *Compagnies des travailleurs étrangers*, or had otherwise been incorporated into the workforce, and approximately 15,000 had joined the Foreign Legion or the Bataillons de marche. David Wingeate Pike, *In The Service of Stalin*, p. 4.

42   Letter from Constancia to Melvina Thompson, Secretary to the First Lady, April 18, 1940. Eleanor Roosevelt Collection, Series 100.

43   Letter from Eleanor Roosevelt to Constancia, April 18, 1940. Eleanor Roosevelt Collection, Series 100.

44   Letter from Constancia to Eleanor Roosevelt, June 18, 1940. Eleanor Roosevelt Collection, Series 100.

45   Letter from Mrs. Roosevelt to Constancia, June 27, 1940. Eleanor Roosevelt Collection, Series 100.

46   Letter from Constancia to Eleanor Roosevelt, September 12, 1940. Eleanor Roosevelt Collection, Series 100.

47   Letter from Constancia to Eleanor Roosevelt, December 6, 1940. Eleanor Roosevelt Collection, Series 100.

48   Letter from Eleanor Roosevelt to Constancia, December 11, 1940. Eleanor Roosevelt Collection, Series 100.

49   The Molotov–Ribbentrop pact was signed on August 23, 1939 and came as such a shock to Communist party members and sympathizers that many believed it was a forgery. Pike, *In the Service of Stalin*, p. 21.

50   "The Inside History of the Spanish Refugee Relief Campaign", p. 11 April 12, 1940. Documentación de Archivo. Fundación Pablo Iglesias. Alcalá de Henares.

51   The majority members of the committee's Executive Board were: Samuel Guy Inman (Chairman), Jay Allen, Eleanor Copenhaver Anderson, Roger N.

Baldwin, Clark M. Eichelberger, Miguel Garriga, Paul Kellogg, W. W. Norton, Joseph Schain, Mrs. Vincent Sheean, Guy Emery Shipler, Maxwell S. Stewart, Leland Stowe, Mrs Caspar Whitney, and Roy Wilkins.

52 The minority members – who were asked to resign – were: Dr. Edward Barsky, Professor Lyman Bradley, professor T. C. Scheirla, Katherine Terrill, and Dr. Jesse Tolmach.

53 "The Inside History of the Spanish Refugee Relief Campaign", p. 10, April 12, 1940. Documentación de Archivo. Fundación Pablo Iglesias. Alcalá de Henares.

54 Letter from Jay Allen to Louis Fischer, July 9, 1962. Papers of Jay Allen.

55 "The Inside History of the Spanish Refugee Relief Campaign", April 12, 1940, p. 11. Documentación de Archivo. Fundación Pablo Iglesias.

56 "The Inside History of the Spanish Refugee Relief Campaign", April 12, 1940. Documentación de Archivo. Fundación Pablo Iglesias. p. 11.

57 "The Inside History,"p. 12.

58 "The Inside History," p. 13.

59 *Ibid.*

60 Letter from Jay Allen to Amaro del Rosal Diaz, May 7, 1940. Documentación de Archivo, Fundación Pablo Iglesias.

61 *Ibid.*

62 Letter from Jay Allen to Louis Fischer, July 9, 1962. Papers of Jay Allen.

63 Veterans Milt Wolff, Jerry Cooke, and Fred Kelley were amongst the fifty one protesters. They were arrested and taken to Rikers Island. *Volunter for Liberty*, Vol. II, no. 3, May 1940.

64 *Ibid.*

65 "An Open Letter to Jay Allen" by Constancia de la Mora. Documentación de Archivo, Fundación Pablo Iglesias.

66 *Ibid.*

67 "The Fifth Avenue Riot" (Editorial). *The Nation*, March 30, 1940.

68 David Wingeate Pike, *Jours de gloire, jours de honte* (Paris: Sedes, 1984), p. 9.

69 *Ibid.*

70 Letter from Hemingway to Jay Allen, February, 1940. Papers of Jay Allen.

71 Letter from Hemingway to Luis Quintanilla, undated. Papers of Luis Quintanilla.

72 Letter from Jay Allen to Louis Fisher, July 9, 1962. Papers of Jay Allen.

V   Mexico, 1940–1950: Exile

1 Letter from Constancia to Jay Allen, January 14, 1940. Papers of Jay Allen.

2 Sebastian Faber, *Exile and Cultural Hegemony: Spanish Intellectuals in Mexico*. (Nashville: Vanderbilt University Press, 2002), p. 14.

3 *Ibid.*, p. 16.

4 *Ibid.*, p. 17.

5 Constancia to Jay Allen, January 14, 1940. Papers of Jay Allen.

6 Aurora Arnáiz, *Retrato hablado de Luisa Julián* (Madrid: Compañía Literaria. 1996), p. 243. My translation.

7   *Ibid.*, p.244.

8   *Ibid.*, p. 244.

9   *Ibid.*, p. 245.

10 *Ibid.*, p. 246.

11 Interview with Aurora Arnaíz, October 29, 2004.

12 Arnáiz, *Retrato hablado de Luisa Julián*, p. 245. Arnáiz's description of Constancia's "aristocratic" background is a common misnomer. Constancia was the granddaughter of the politician Antonio Maura and had grown up in a wealthy family, but her background was not aristocratic. Her image as an aristocrat was fuelled in part by *In Place of Splendor*, but she may have also cultivated this myth in person.

13 They divorced in Huamantla, Tlaxcala on March 15, 1941. The certificate is in the Ignacio Hidalgo de Cisneros file, Archivo Historico del Partido Comunista de Espana.

14 Mario Mengs' interview with Fernando Hernández Franch. Collection of Mario Mengs.

15 Mario Mengs' interview with Fernando Hernández Franch.

16 Mario Mengs' interview with Fernando Hernández Franch.

17 Mario Mengs' interview with Santiago Carrillo. Collection of Mario Mengs. Clara Sancha also recalls Ignacio complaining that Constancia had left him for someone else, and his disbelief because this person was, according to Ignacio, so inferior to him in every way. This may have been the Tarascan architect Rudolfo Ayala, who Constancia lived with later in Cuernavaca.

18 Letter from Fredericka Martin to Alvah Bessie, August 21, 1976. Fredericka Martin Collection. Tamiment Library/Robert F. Wagner Laber Archives. New York University. Martin was Chief nurse and administrator of the North American medical units in Spain during the Civil War.

19 My interview with Dr. Ignacio Luque.

20 A certificate in Ignacio's Comintern file says that he left for America on May 5, 1947. This probably means that he went to Mexico, but it is unclear how long he stayed, or whether he saw Constancia.

21 See bibliography for references to translated editions.

22 Patricia Albers, *Shadows, Fire, Snow: The Life of Tina Modotti* (Berkeley: University of California Press), p. 323.

23 My interview with Kate Condax Decker.

24 Kerr's letter is quoted in a letter from Constancia to the Condaxes dated August 29, 1940. Papers of John and Laura Condax.

25 Constancia was not physically "far away" – she was in Mexico. However, though she found her adopted country fascinating, in 1941 she was naturally more concerned and involved with what was happening in Franco Spain and the rest of Europe.

26 Letter to the Condaxes, dated July 2, 1941. Papers of John and Laura Condax.

27 Christiane Barckhausen-Canale, *Verdad y Leyenda de Tina Modotti* (La Habana: Casa de las Américas, 1989), p. 308.

28   Margaret Hooks, *Tina Modotti: Photographer and Revolutionary* (Cambridge, MA: Da Capo Press, 2000), p. 253.

29   Headlines from *La Prensa* are quoted in Barckhausen-Canale, *Verdad y Leyenda de Tina Modotti*, p. 309.

30   Letter dated April 29, 1942. Papers of John and Laura Condax.

31   David Wingeate Pike, *In the Service of Stalin* (New York: Oxford University Press, 1993), p. 53.

32   My interview with Kate Decker Condax.

33   Barckhausen-Canale, *Verdad y Leyenda de Tina Modotti*, p. 291.

34   *Ibid.*, p. 306. The author also says (quoting Vidali) that Constancia died soon afterwards when she in fact died nine years later, and that she was killed in a plane crash. Russian Ambassador Constantin Oumansky, who Constancia worked with, was killed in a plane crash, but Constancia in fact died in a car accident.

35   Modern Age catalogue, 1941. Papers of John and Laura Condax.

36   Interview with Kate Decker Condax. The photographs and Constancia's text are in the collection of John and Laura Condax.

37   "Fete of Guadalupe in Mexico", December 7, 1941.

38   Constancia de la Mora, "Young Spain in the USSR" in *Soviet Russia Today*, July 1942, pp. 13–15.

39   *Ibid.*, p. 13.

40   *Ibid.*, p. 14.

41   *Ibid.*, p. 15.

42   O'Brien's unpublished manuscript *Adiós Connie* is in the ALBA Vertical File, Robert F. Wagner Labor Archives at the Tamiment Library, New York University, hereafter cited as O'Brien.

43   Telegram to Ignacio, via Soledad Sancha, July 9, 1939. Ignacio Hidalgo de Cisneros file, PCE Historical Archive.

44   See Daniel Kowalsky, *Stalin and the Spanish Civil War*, "The Evacuation of Spanish Children to the Soviet Union", Part II, 5. <http://www.gutenberg-e.org/kod01/main.html>.

45   Even the documents that say her father is Bolín, conflate Constancia's two husbands, for they have *Bolín* as the chief of the Republican airforce and say he lives in Mexico with Constancia.

46   Secret certificate signed S. Miller and V. Ovchinnikova. October 24, 1944. Comintern Archive. File of Luli Hidalgo de Cisneros.

47   Comintern Archive. File of Luli Hidalgo de Cisneros. 495, 220, 623.

48   *Ibid.*

49   The message is from Comrade Belov to Comrade Bogdanov (Ufa).

50   The message is from Comrade Belov to Comrade Mytirev of the National Committee of Health Services. File of Luli Hidalgo de Cisneros, Comintern Archive.

51   "Information about Ignacio Hidalgo de Cisneros", September 13, 1943. Signed Belov/Blagoeva. Hidalgo de Cisneros file, Comintern Archive.

52 The date of her departure is confirmed by an information sheet in Luli's Comintern file, dated May 13, 1946 and signed L. Fyodorov.
53 Interview with Hernández Franch. Collection of Mario Mengs.
54 Interview with Hernández Franch.
55 The groups involved included: the Spanish Democratic Union, the Giuseppe Garibaldi International Alliance, the Polish Association, Free Germany, International Democratic Action, Free Hungary, Free France. See Betty Kirk, *Covering the Mexican Front: The Battle of Europe Versus America* (Norman:University of Oklahoma Press, 1942)
56 Kirk.
57 "Anna Seghers and Constancia de la Mora Tell the Story of the Joint Anti-Fascist Refugee Committee." New York, 1944, p.4.
58 *Ibid.*, p. 5.
59 *Ibid.*, p. 8.
60 *Ibid.*, p. 10.
61 Letter from Constancia to Luli, May 1944. Legajo de Ignacio Hidalgo de Cisneros. N.45. Archivo Histórico del Partido Comunista de España.
62 The Junta Suprema de Unión Nacional (JSUN) was created in 1943 as a clandestine coalition of anti-Franco groups within Spain. Though it included communists, it was at odds with the traditional and exclusive party line of the Spanish communist party (PCE). See Carlos Fernández, "Madrid, ciudad clandestina comunista" in *Cuadernos de Historia Contemporánea*, 2004, Universidad Complutense de Madrid, vol. 26, págs 161–180.
63 Letter from Constancia to Luli, May 1944.
64 My interview with Eladia de los Ríos.
65 For more about Gorkin's anti-Stalinism, see Herbert Rutledge Southworth's "*El gran camuflage*": Julián Gorkin, Burnett Bolloten y la Guerra Civil Española" in *La República asediada*, Paul Preston, ed. (Barcelona: Península, 1999), pp. 417–491.
66 Julián Gorkin. "La muerte en México de Victor Serge.". Marxists Internet Archive, 2001. Digital Edition from the Fundación Andreu Nin.
67 Letter from Constancia to Luli, May 1944.
68 FBI File No. 100-13807. Report dated April 28, 1944. Title: "Dr. Paul Patrick Rogers"
69 *Ibid.*
70 Vicens's wife, Elena Huerta de Arenal, also appears in the FBI report as a librarian in the Rusian-Mexican Exchange Institute in Mexico City.
71 <http://www.redaragon.com/trebede/oct2000/articulo2.asp>.
72 Siqueiros, along with Vittorio Vidali, was involved in the 1940 attempt on Trotsky's life.
73 FBI File no. 100-13807. Report dated January 24, 1949. Title: Dr. Paul Patrick Rogers, p. 3.
74 FBI File no. 100-13807. Report dated September 26, 1949. Title: Dr. Paul Patrick Rogers, p. 1.

75 FBI File no. 100-13807, p.4
76 FBI File no. 100-13807. Report addressed to the Director, FBI, dated January 25, 1950. Re: Dr. Paul Patrick Rogers, p. 2
77 FBI File no. 100-13807, pp. 2–3
78 Freda Kirchwey, "Constantin Oumansky", *The Nation*, February 3, 1945, pp. 115–16.
79 *Ibid.*, p. 116.
80 *Ibid.*
81 *Ibid.*
82 My interview with Tamara Pascual.
83 Pilar Domínguez Prats, p. 247.
84 My interview with Eladia de los Ríos.
85 Interview with Eladia de los Ríos.
86 Carlos Semprún Maura, *Recuerdos 4. Bataillon, Nelken y Otros*, Libertad Digital.Com.
87 Interview with Eladia de los Ríos.
88 Nancy Johnstone, *Sombreros are Becoming* (New York: Longmans, Green & Co., 1941).
89 Fredericka Martin.
90 My Interview with Eladia de los Ríos.
91 Interview with Eladia de los Ríos.
92 My interview with Aurora Arnáiz.
93 Interview with Aurora Arnáiz.
94 Interview with Eladia de los Ríos.
95 My interview with Juan Haro and María Sánchez Arcas de Haro.
96 "Two Writers Ousted by Communist Party", *The New York Times*, September 13, 1946, p. 4.
97 "The Political Future of Spain". NARA; pound; NN3-263-92-005. 12/5/1947, p. 1.
98 Lini de Vries, *Please God, Take Care of the Mule* (Mexico, D.F.: Editorial Minutiae Mexicana, S.A., 1969), p. 6.
99 O'Brien.
100 O'Brien, i.
101 O'Brien, p. 39.
102 O'Brien, p. 10.
103 O'Brien.
104 O'Brien, p. 12.
105 O'Brien, p. 97.
106 O'Brien, p. 15.
107 O'Brien, p. 19.
108 O'Brien, p. 21.
109 O'Brien, p. 24.
110 *In Place of Splendor* was published in Spanish as *Doble Esplendor*, México: Atlante, 1944.

111 O'Brien, p. 24.

112 In a letter to Alvah and Sylviene Bessie (December 1, 1977) Fredericka Martin, who got to know O'Brien in Cuernavaca alludes to Mary's desire to avoid political subjects in her memoir. Martin says that Mary 'does not elaborate on the FBI', and 'For Mary who just tried to get away from the FBI, there is no story.' Fredericka Martin Papers.

113 O'Brien, p.25

114 *O'Brien*, p. 31.

115 O'Brien, p. 35.

116 O'Brien, p. 39.

117 O'Brien, p. 65. Málaga was where Constancia had spent the first unhappy years of her marriage to Luis Bolín.

118 O'Brien, p. 64.

119 O'Brien, p. 90.

120 O'Brien, p. 64.

121 O'Brien, p. 65.

122 O'Brien, p. 67.

123 O'Brien

124 O'Brien, p. 68.

125 O'Brien, p. 72.

126 O'Brien, p. 117.

127 O'Brien, p. 118.

128 O'Brien, p. 118.

129 O'Brien, p. 127.

130 O'Brien, p. 132.

131 O'Brien, p. 144.

132 O'Brien, p. 163.

133 O'Brien, p. 164.

134 O'Brien.

135 O'Brien, p. 166.

136 O'Brien, p. 167.

137 O'Brien, p. 168.

138 O'Brien, p. 169.

139 O'Brien, p. 170.

140 O'Brien, p. 177.

141 Telegram sent from Luli to Ignacio on January 31, 1950. Addressed to Ignacio c/o the "Legation de la Republique Espagnole", Hotel Polonia, Warsaw. Legajo de Ignacio Hidalgo de Cisneros. Archivo Histórico del Partido Comunista de España.

142 O'Brien, p. 180.

143 Mary O'Brien did not notice the PCE flag, but Concha de Mantecón mentions this in her letter to Ignacio of February 2, 1950. Legajo de Ignacio Hidalgo de Cisneros. Archivo Histórico del Partido Comunista de España.

144 O'Brien, p. 182.

145 O'Brien.
146 O'Brien, p. 183.
147 Lini de Vries, *Please God, Take Care of the Mule*, p. 9.
148 "Palabras de Pablo Neruda en el entierro de Constancia de la Mora" Legajo de
    Ignacio Hidalgo de Cisneros. Archivo Histórico del Partido Comunista de
    España.
149 O'Brien, p. 183.
150 O'Brien, p. 184.
151 "Señorita de la Mora Killed in Guatemala". *The New York Times*, January 28,
    1950.
152 "Ha muerto la camarada Constancia de la Mora". *Mundo Obrero* (Paris),
    February 9, 1950.
153 Interview with Tony Kahn.
154 O'Brien, p. 183.
155 Letter from Luli Bolín de Caraballo to Hidalgo de Cisneros, March 3, 1950.
    Archivo Histórico del Partido Comunista de España. Legajo Hidalgo de
    Cisneros.

Epilogue

1 Palabras de Wencesalo Roces en el entierro de Constancia de la Mora, Archivo
   Histórico del Partido Comunista de España. Legajo Ignacio Hidalgo de
   Cisneros.
2 Palabras de Wencesalo Roces en el entierro de Constancia de la Mora.
3 Letter from Wenceslao Roces to Ignacio Hidalgo de Cisneros, February 2,
   1950. Archivo Histórico del Partido Comunista de España. Legajo Ignacio
   Hidalgo de Cisneros.
4 Letter from Roces, February 2, 1950.
5 Letter from Roces, February 2, 1950.
6 Letter from Concha Mantecón to Ignacio, February 2. 1950. Archivo
   Histórico del Partido Comunista de España. Legajo Ignacio Hidalgo de
   Cisneros.
7 Letter from Pablo Neruda, February 1, 1950. Archivo Histórico del Partido
   Comunista de España. Legajo Ignacio Hidalgo de Cisneros.
8 Letter from Luli Bolín de Caraballo to Ignacio Hidalgo de Cisneros, March 3,
   1950. Archivo Histórico del Partido Comunista de España. Legajo Ignacio
   Hidalgo de Cisneros.
9 Luli is referring to Constancia's parents here and calls them, affectionately "los
   abuelitos".
10 Letter from Ignacio Hidalgo de Cisneros to Francisco (Paco) Hidalgo de
   Cisneros, May 22, 1950. Papers of Mario Mengs.
11 *Ibid.*
12 This information is in a "Certificate" with information provided by T. P.
   Ivanova and approved by Bogomolov, October 30, 1954. Ignacio Hidalgo de
   Cisneros file, Comintern Archive.

13 Vicente García Dolz, "Hidalgo de Cisneros, un heterodoxo", Aéroplano. (Madrid: Ministerio de Defensa, 1996), p. 53.

14 *75 años de la radio en España, 1941–1977. Radio España Independiente. Madrid: Grupo Municipal de Izquierda Unida* (Madrid: Ayuntamiento de Madrid, 2000), p. 9.

15 Letter from Herbert Southworth to Mary O'Brien, October 28, 1980. Fredericka Martin Collection.

16 Video of Ignacio Hidalgo de Cisneros's burial. Collection of Mario Mengs.

17 (Undated) postcard from Constancia de la Mora. From Delfina Moreno.

18 "Constancia", published in *Oracle*, p. 5. Collection of James Kahn.

19 *ABC*, 25 de Agosto, 1962.

20 Letter from Fredericka Martin to Alvah Bessie, August 21, 1976. New York University Archives. Fredericka Martin file.

21 *Gloriosa Spagna* (Roma: L'Unità-Editori Riuniti, 1976). First published in Italian by Edizioni Rinascita in 1951, translated by Giuseppe Garritano.

22 Constancia de la Mora, constant companion/You reappear now, when we most need/Your loyal hand, your drive to reconquer/That freedom we lost then./Ascend towards the light, raise your flags,/Mirrors of a life reflected in the wind./The living and the dead of yesterday sing together./There is no return, but a future is beginning. *Glorious Spagna*, p. 10.

Bibliography

Primary Sources

Archives
Archivo General de la Guerra Civil Española (Salamanca).
Archivo Histórico del Partido Comunista (Madrid).
Archivo del Ministerio de Asuntos Exteriores (Madrid).
Franklin D. Roosevelt Library (Hyde Park, NY).
Fundación Pablo Iglesias (Madrid).
Harry Ransom Humanities Research Center, University of Texas at Austin.
Hemeroteca Municipal (Madrid).
International Institute of Social History (Amsterdam).
Rare Book and Manuscript Library, Columbia University (New York).
Rauner Special Collections, Dartmouth College (Hanover, NH).
RGASPI (Moscow).
Seeley G. Mudd Manuscripts Library, Rare Books & Special Collections, Princeton
    University (Princeton, NJ).
Tamiment Library/Wagner Labor Archives, New York University (New York, NY).

Newspapers

ABC (Madrid).
Ahora (Madrid).
Frente Rojo (Valencia/Barcelona).
Mundo Obrero (Madrid).
The New York Times (New York).

Unpublished Sources

Mangan, Kate and Kurzke, Jan. *The Good Comrade.* International Institute of Social
    History (Amsterdam).
O'Brien, Mary. *Adiós Connie.* Tamiment Library/Wagner Labor Archives, New York
    University (New York, NY).

Published Sources

Abellán, José Luis, director. *El exilio español de 1939.* Madrid: Taurus, 1977.
Albers, Patricia. *Shadow, Fire, Snow: The Life of Tina Modotti.* University of California
    Press, 2002.
Alberti, Rafael. *La arboleda perdida.* Barcelona: Seix Barral, 1975.

Aranzueque, Gabriel. "Paul Ricouer" memoria, olvido, y melancholía" entrevista, *Revista de Occidente*, n. 198, Madrid, Noviembre 1997.

Aznar Soler, Manuel, ed. *El exilio español de 1939. Actas del congreso internacional (bellaterra, 27 de noviembre–1 de diciembre 1995)*, 2 vols. Barcelona: Gexel-Cop d'Idees, 1988.

Barea, Arturo. *La forja de un rebelde*. Buenos Aires: Losada, 1951.

Barckhausen-Canale, Christiane. *Verdad y leyenda de Tina Modotti*. La Habana: Casa de las Américas, 1989.

Barzman, Norma. *The Red and the Blacklist*. New York: Thunder's Mouth Press/Nation Books, 2003.

Blanchot, Maurice. *L'espace littéraire*. Paris: Gallimard, col. Folio essais, 1988.

Bolloten, Burnett. *The Spanish Civil War: Revolution and Counterrevolution*, Foreword by Stanley G. Payne, Chapel Hill, NC, University of North Carolina Press, 1992

Camprubí, Zenobia. *Diario I* (1937–1939). Alianza Editorial/ Editorial de la Universidad de Puerto Rico. 1991

Capel, Rosa María, ed. *El voto de las mujeres 1877–1978*. Madrid: Editorial Complutense, 2003

Carnés, Luisa. *El eslabón perdido*. Madrid: Renacimiento, Biblioteca del Exilio n. 9, 2002.

Castro Delgado, Enrique. *Hombres made in Moscú*. Barcelona: Luis de Caralt, 1963.

Caudet, Francisco. *Hipótesis sobre el exilio republicano de 1939*. Madrid: Fundación Universitaria Española, 1997.

Conner, Jannis and Rosenkranz, Joel. *Rediscoveries in American Sculpture: Studio Works 1893–1939*. Austin: University of Texas Press. 1989.

Domínguez Prats, Pilar. *Voces del exilio. Mujeres españolas en México (1939–1950)*. Madrid: Comunidad de Madrid, Dirección General de la Mujer, 1994.

Dos Passos, John. *The Theme is Freedom*. Freeport, New York: Books for Libraries Press, 1970.

Faber, Sebastiaan. *Exile and Cultural Hegemony: Spanish Intellectuals in Mexico, 1939–1975*. Nashville: Vanderbilt University Press, 2002.

Falcón, Irene. *Asalto a los cielos: mi vida junto a la Pasionaria*. Madrid: Temas de Hoy. 1996.

Ferrán, Ofelia. "Cuanto más escribo, más me queda por decir: Memory, Trauma, and Writing in the Work of Jorge Semprún." *Modern Language Notes 116*, 2001.

Fischer, Louis. *Men and Politics*. New York: Duell, Sloan, and Pearce, 1941.

Gómez Fouz, José Ramón. *Clandestinos*. Oviedo: Pentalfa ediciones (Biblioteca Asturianista), 1999.

Graham, Helen and Labanyi, Jo (eds). *Spanish Cultural Studies: An Introduction: The Struggle for Modernity*. Oxford: Oxford University Press, 1995.

Graham, Helen. *The Spanish Republic at War: 1936–1939*.Cambridge: Cambridge Univerity Press, 2002.

Guillén, Claudio. "On the Literature of Exile and Counter-Exile." *Books Abroad* 50 (1976): 271–80

———. *El sol de los desterrados: literatura y exilio*. Barcelona: Quaderns Crema, 1995.

Herbst, Josephine. *The Starched Blue Sky of Spain.* New York: HarperCollins, 1991.

Hertzberger, David K. *Narrating the Past: Fiction and Historiography in Postwar Spain.* Durham: Duke University Press, 1995.

Hidalgo de Cisneros, Ignacio. *Cambio de Rumbo.* Vitoria: Ikusager Ediciones, 2001.

Hooks, Margaret. *Tina Modotti: Photographer and Revolutionary.* Da Capo Press, 2000.

Hughes, Langston. *I Wonder as I Wander. An Autobiographical Journey.* New York: Hill and Wang (Farrar, Straus, and Giroux), 1956.

Ickes, Harold. *The Secret Diary of Harold L. Ickes.* New York: Simon & Schuster, 1954.

Iglesias Rodríguez, Gema. "Las Misiones Pedagógicas. Un intento de democratización cultural." In *Comunicación, cultura, y política durante la II República y la Guerra Civil.* Ed. Carmelo Garitaonandía, José Luis de la Granja, and Santiago de Pablo. Vol. 2 *España (1931–1939),* 337–65. Bilbao: Universidad del País Vasco, 1990.

Karátson, André and Bessière, Jean. *Déracinement et littérature.* Lille: Université de Lille III, 1982.

Kirk, Betty. *Covering the Mexican Front: The Battle of Europe Versus America* Norman: University of Oklahoma Press, 1942.

Kenwood, Alun, ed. *The Spanish Civil War: A Cultural and Historical Reader.* Providence, R.I., Oxford: Berg, 1993.

Koch, Stephen *The Breaking Point: Hemingway, Dos Passos, and the Murder of José Robles.* New York: Counterpoint, 2005.

Kowalsky, Daniel. *Stalin and the Spanish Civil War* (e-book) <http://www.gutenberg-e.org>.

León, María Teresa. *Memoria de la melancolía.* Madrid: Editorial Castalia, 1998.

Llorens, Vicente *Memorias de una emigración.* Barcelona: Ariel, 1975.

Macdonald, Nancy. *Homage to the Spanish Exiles: Voices from the Spanish Civil War.* New York: Insight Books, 1987.

MacMaster, Neil. *Spanish Fighters: An Oral history of Civil War and Exile.* New York: St. Martin's Press, 1990.

Mangini, Shirley. *Memories of resistance: Women's Voices from the Spanish Civil War.* New Haven & London: Yale University Press, 1995.

Marra-López. *Narrativa española fuera de España 1939–1961.* Madrid: Guadarrama, 1963.

Martínez de Pisón, Ignacio. *Enterrar a los muertos.* Barcelona: Seix Barral, 2005.

Mártinez-Gutiérrez, María José. *Escritoras españolas en el exilio. México 1939–1995.* Ph.D. diss., University of California San Diego, 1995.

Medio, Dolores. *Atrapados en la ratonera: Memorias de una novelista.* Madrid, Editorial Alce, 1980.

Mistral, Silvia. *Exodo (diario de una refugiada española).* México: Editorial Minerva, 1941.

Mora, Constancia de la. *In Place of Splendor: Autobiography of a Spanish Woman.* New York: Harcourt, Brace and Company, 1939.

———. *Doble esplendor*. México: Atlante, 1944; Barcelona: Grijalbo, 1977; Madrid: Gadir, 2004.

———. *Doppelter Glanz: Lebensgeschichte einer Spanischen Frau*. Berlin: Dietz Verlag, 1949.

———. *Fière Espagne: souvenirs d'une republicaine*. Paris: Editions Hier et Aujourd'hui, 1948.

———. *Gloriosa Spagna*. Roma: L'Unità – Editori Riuniti, 1976. Giuseppe Garritano, transl.

———. *Mîndra Spanie: amintirik unei republicane*. Bucuresti: Editori Politica, 1963.

Naharro-Calderón, José María. "¿Y para qué la literatura del exilio en tiempo destituído?" In *El exilio literario español de 1939. Actas del Primer Congreso Internacional*, ed. Manuel Aznar Soler, vol. 1, 63–83. Barcelona: Gexel, 1998.

Nash, Mary. *Defying Male Civilization: Women in the Spanish Civil War*. Denver, Colorado: Arden Press, 1995.

Palencia, Isabel de. *Smouldering Freedom: The Story of the Spanish Republicans in Exile*. New York: Longmans, Green and Co., 1945.

Pike, David Wingeate. *In The Service of Stalin*. New York: Oxford University Press, 1993.

———. *Jours de gloire, jours de honte*. Paris: Sedes, 1984.

Preston, Paul. *Doves of War*. Boston: Northeastern University Press, 2002.

Preston, Paul and Mackenzie, Ann L. *The Republic Besieged: Civil War in Spain 1936–1939*. Edinburgh: Edinburgh University Press, 1996.

Rey García, Marta. *Stars for Spain: La Guerra Civil en los Estados Unidos*. A Coruña: Edicios do Castro, 1997.

Radosh, Ronald an Habeck, Mary R. *Spain Betrayed: The Soviet Union in the Spanish Civil War*. New Haven: Yale University Press. 2001.

Rubio, Javier. *La emigración de la guerra civil de 1936–1939*. 3 vols. Madrid: San Martin, 1977.

Ruiz-Vargas, José María (ed.), *Claves de la memoria*. Madrid: Editorial Trotta, 1997.

Said, Edward. *Reflections on Exile and Other Essays*. New York: Vintage, 1994.

Sala Noguer, Ramón. *El cine en la España Republicana durante la guerra civil (1936–1939)*. Bilbao: Mensajero, 1993.

Salinas, Jaime. *Travesías*. Barcelona: Tusquets. 2003.

Sánchez Barbudo, Antonio. "La adhesión de los intelectuales a la causa popular." *Hora de España* 7 (1937): 70–5.

Sanz Villanueva, S. *El exilio español de 1939*. vol. IV., *Cultura y literature*. Madrid: Taurus, 1977.

Semprún, Jorge. *Autobiografía de Federico Sánchez*. Barcelona: Planeta, 2002

———. *L'écriture ou la vie*. Paris: Folio, 1994.

Sicot, Bernard. *Exilio, memoria e historia en la poesía de Luis Cernuda*. Madrid: Fondo de Cultura Económica de España, S.L., 2003.

Southworth, Herbert. *Conspiracy and the Spanish Civil War: The Brainwashing of Francisco Franco*. London and New York: Routledge, 2002.

———. *Guernica! Guernica! A Study of Journalism, Diplomacy, Propaganda, and History.* Berkeley and Los Angeles: University of California Press, 1977.

Stein, Louis. *Beyond Death and Exile: The Spanish Republicans in France, 1939–1955.* Cambridge, MA: Harvard University Press, 1979.

Suleiman, Susan Rubin, ed. *Exile and Creativity: Signposts, Travelers, Outsiders, Backward Glances.* Durham and London: Duke University Press, 1998.

Tadié, Jean Yves and Marc. *Le sens de la mémoire.* Paris: Gallimard, 1999.

Torres Nebrera, G. *Los espacios de la memoria: La obra literaria de María Teresa León.* Madrid: Ediciones de la Torre, 1996.

Ugarte, Michael. *Shifting Ground: Spanish Civil War Exile Literature.* Durham: Duke University Press, 1989.

Usandizaga, Aránzazu. *Ve y cuenta lo que pasó: Mujeres extranjeras en la Guerra civil: una antología.* Barcelona: Planeta, 2000.

Vries, Lini de. *Please God, Take Care of the Mule.* Mexico, D.F.: Editorial Minutiae Mexicana, S.A., 1969.

Weinstein, Allen and Vassiliev, Alexander.*The Haunted Wood* by. New York: Random House, 1999.

Zapatero, Virgilio, director. *Catálogo de la exposición Exilio.* Madrid: Fundación Pablo Iglesias con la colaboración del Museo Nacional Centro de Arte Reina Sofía, 2002.

Index

The following abbreviations are used:
CM – Constancia de la Mora
IHC – Ignacio Hidalgo de Cisneros

ABC newspaper, 9, 11, 33, 176, 181*n*
Abraham Lincoln Brigade, 1, 92, 95, 136
  see also Veterans of the Abraham Lincoln
    Brigade
Acapantzingo
  CM's burial, 1, 167, 169, 173
  CM's house, 138, 153, 155, 157
Acción Nacional, 16
Acción Popular, 16
Adams, Mildred, 103–4, 191*n*
Adventures of a Young Man (Dos Passos), 96
Aguirre, Nacho, 140
Aid Fund for the Antifascist Spanish
    Resistance, 88
Alberti, Rafael, 19, 24–5, 42–3, 176–7,
    180*n*
  portrait with IH, *plate, 23*
Albornoz, Alvaro de, 20
Alcalá de Henares, 18, 21, 74
Alcalá Zamora, Niceto, 14, 28
Alemania Libre (Free Germany), 146, 150,
    198*n*
Alfonso XIII, King of Spain, 9, 13, 14, 15,
    23–4
  with Maura (1918), *plate, 2*
Alicante children's colonies, 36–7, 191*n*
Allen, Jay
  anti-fascism, 4
  arrested, 25
  Bolloten's book on Spanish Civil War,
    135
  break-up of friendship with CM, 130,
    131, 133
  CM moves in, 90

CM's flat in Madrid, 15, 93–4
CM's job at Foreign Press Office, 42
CM's letters from Mexico, 103, 123,
    137
critical reviews of *In Place of Splendor*,
    103, 104–5
disappearance of Robles, 96, 98, 99
influence on *In Place of Splendor*, 3, 89,
    91, 92, 94, 189*n*
list of death sentences, 135
portrait (1939), *plates, 10, 11*
refugee crisis, 87, 106–7, 127–8, 130,
    131, 194*n*
sheltering of fugitive Republicans, 25
as supporter of Spanish Republic, 15,
    87, 89, 106, 175
US embargo on munitions, 32
working for Negrín, 89
Alomar, Gabriel, 22
Alonso, Carmen, 16
Altoalaguirre, Manuel, 18
Alvarez del Vayo, Julio
  appeal to League of Nations in Geneva,
    62, 77
  as cabinet minister (1937), 64
  close working with CM, 75–6, 150
  CM's appointment at Press Office, 43
  contacts with IHC, 18
  Davidson's exhibition, 84
  disappearance of Robles, 70, 73, 96, 97,
    98, 99
  as friend of Rubio Hidalgo, 46, 49
  Hemingway on, 133
  leaves Spain (1939), 100

refuge in Allen's apartment, 25
refugee crisis, 129
Robles family, 72
and Tina Modotti, 67
Alvarez del Vayo, Luisy, 43, 89
America Magazine, 76
American Friends Service Committee, 124
"American Gothic", 85
American League for Peace and Democracy,
    89
Amlie, Hans, 98
anarchists
    disappearance of Robles, 70, 97, 98, 99
    Seville general strike, 19
Anderson, Eleanor Copenhaver, 194n
Anti-imperialist League, 189n
Anti-Nazi-Fascist Federation of Foreign
    Residents in Mexico, 146
Aragón, Luis, 89
Araquistaín, Luis, 18, 25
Arcas, Manuel Sánchez, 34, 43, 79, 174
Arden Gallery, 84, 85
Arnáiz, Aurora, 135–7, 138, 153–4
Arnal, Manuel, 77
Arriluce, 12
Arte Popular, 12, 13, 15–16, 27, 137
Asturias rebellion, 24, 25, 26
Atlantic Monthly Press, 139
Aub, Max, 150
Auden, W. H., 47, 183n
Ayala, Rudolfo
    CM's death, 166
    CM's departure for Guatemala, 158
    CM's house, 153
    CM's tombstone, 176
    demands money from O'Brien, 168
    as godparent, 155
    O'Brien's views on, 157
    relationship with CM, 153, 154, 196n
Ayuda, 67
Azaña y Díaz, Manuel, 28, 29–30, 59,
    183n
    Davidson's exhibition, 84
    exodus to France, 82
    Military Attaché post in Mexico, 22
    on Negrín, 65
    on political committee, 14
    relations with Fischer, 62

Baldwin, Roger N., 194n

Barbeito, Andrés, 67, 75–6
Barcelona, celebration of Soviet Union, 38
Barcelona strikes, 24
Barea, Arturo, 49–59
    views on CM, 58, 59, 64
Barea, Ilsa, 58–9
Barrish, Mildred, 102
Barsky, Dr. Edward, 194n
Barzman, Ben, 1–2
Barzman, Norma, 1–2
Bataillons de marche, 194n
Battleship Potemkin, 21
Belov, Comrade, 145–6
Bennett, Milly, 98, 99
Berenguer, Dámaso, 14
Bergamin, José, 109, 136, 192n
Berle Jr., Adolf A., 111–20, 125
Berlin, 26–7
Bernstein, Leonard, 91, 153
Bessie, Alvah, 138
Besteiro, Julian, 99, 100
Bolín de la Mora, Constancia María
    Lourdes (Luli), 11, 28
    arrives in Mexico (1946), 146
    in a children's home, 37
    CM gains custody, 20–1
    CM's death, 166, 169, 170, 171, 172–3
    CM's insurance policy, 158–9
    portrait (1945), *plate, 20*
    portrait with CM (1929), *plate, 6*
    portrait in Soviet Union, *plate, 14*
    portrait in Soviet Union (1943), *plate,
        15*
    in Rome, 22, 24
    in Soviet Union, 41–2, 59, 76, 88, 143,
        144–6, 148
Bolín, Luis, 179n, 183n
Bolín y Bidwell, Germán Manuel, 10–11,
    12, 13, 32, 33, 181n
Bolloten, Burnett, 182n, 184n, 192n
    book on Spanish Civil War, 135
    IHC's membership of Communist Party,
        39
    on the NKVD, 62–3
    Prieto's order suppressed by CM, 60
    views on CM, 62, 63–4
Bolsheviks, 21
Bonnet, Georges, 111
Bowers, Claude, 25, 108–9
Brace, Donald, 104–5

Bradley, Lyman, 195*n*
Bransten, Eileen, 92–3, 190*n*
Bransten, Richard, 92, 154, 190*n*
Braun, Madeleine, 110–11
Braymer, Lawrence, 188*n*
Britain, non-intervention policy, 35, 37, 77
Broué, Pierre, 74
Buñuel, Luis, 136, 137, 150

Calle Alcalá, 18
Cambio de rumbo (Hidalgo de Cisneros), 2, 34, 174–5, 182*n*
Cambridge, 8–9
Campeche, 160
Campoamor, Clara, 17
Campos, Matilde, 33
Camprubí, Zenobia, 160
    Arte Popular shop, 12, 13, 15–16, 27, 137
    background, 11–12
    CM's changing view of, 29, 40
    CM's Republicanism, 30
    Diario, 39–40
    disapproval of revolutionary ideas, 39–40
    first meeting with CM, 11–12
    friendship with CM, 11–12, 19, 39–40
    leaves Spain (1936), 39, 40
Caraballo, Severiano, 146, 159, 171, 172, 173
Cárcel de Extranjeros, 68
Cárdenas, Amalia, 134
Cárdenas, Lázaro, 134, 139, 151
Carlists, 17
Carlos María Isidro de Borbón (Don Carlos), 17
Carlos (traveller), 164, 165
Carney, William, 104–5, 191*n*
Carrillo, Santiago, 2
Casado, Segismundo, 99, 100
Casares Quirogo, Santiago, 14
Castro Delgado, Enrique, 80
Catalonia, 24, 74
Catalonian Left Party, 28
Catholic Sisters of Charity, 9, 10
CEDA see Confederación Española de Derechas Autónomas (CEDA)
"Charito", 42
Checa, Angelita, 136

Checa, Pedro, 136
checkas, 67
Chicago Daily Tribune, 15
Chichicastenango, 164–5
Chodorov, Edward, 102
Chodorov, Jerome, 91, 102
Christian Science Monitor, 45
Chrysler Motor Car Company, 12
Clara (American traveller), 163, 164
Claudín, Fernando, 154
CNT, 67–8
CNT-FAI, 45
Collins, Richard, 102
Comden, Betty, 91
Comintern
    CM's usefulness, 123
    dissident communists, 63, 74
    Mexico as base of operations, 123
Comintern Archives
    CM's communist affiliation, 38
    CM's mission to New York, 82
    IHC's arrival in Soviet Union (1939), 188*n*
    lack of file for CM, 144
    Luli's file, 144
Comité Nacional de Mujeres Antifascistas, 33, 88, 152
Commission of Women's Aid to the Ministry of Defense, 33
Communism
    American wariness of, 5
    CM's affiliations, 2, 3, 36, 38–9, 40, 60–1, 144, 163, 167–8, 170
    IHC's affiliation, 3, 38–9, 173–4, 182*n*
    lack of mention in *In Place of Splendor*, 3, 36, 38–9, 49, 66, 100, 102
    links to SERE, 120
    Prieto's hostility towards, 41, 60–1
    Seville general strike, 19
    see also PCE (Spanish Communist Party)
Compagnies des travailleurs étrangers, 194*n*
Companys, Lluís, 28
Condax, John, 139, 140, 141, 142
Condax, Laura, 139, 140, 141
    portrait (1939), *plate*, 13
Confederación Española de Derechas Autónomas (CEDA), 16, 24, 26, 28
Contreras, Carlos *see* Vidali, Vittorio
Convento de la Pasionaria, 65–6
Cooke, Jerry, 195*n*

Cowley, Malcolm, 96
Cuatro Vientos revolt (1930), 14,
    17–18
Cuban Communist Party, 189*n*

Daily Express, 45
Daily Herald, 76, 187*n*
Daily Worker, 167
Daladier, Edouard, 129, 132
Davidson, Jo, 84–5
Davis, Richard Harding, 93
December 1930 revolt, 14, 17–18
Diario (Camprubí), 39–40
Diáz, Jose, 69
Diaz, Lila, 172
Dickinson, Thorold, 35, 36
Dimitrov, Georgi, 170
Dodd Stern, Martha, 80, 86–7, 92, 101,
    190*n*
Domecq wine company, 137
Domingo, Marcelino, 21, 22
Don Carlos, 17
Dorronsoro de Roces, Carmen, 41–2, 171,
    172
Dos Passos, John
    Adventures of a Young Man, 96
    disappearance of Robles, 69–70, 71,
        72–3, 96–8, 99
    Journeys Between Wars, 96
    Quintanilla's arrest, 180*n*
    "The Spanish Earth", 69, 70, 95

Eichelberger, Clark M., 194*n*
Einstein, Albert, 84
Enrique (traveller), 164, 165
Ernesto, 136
Excelsior, 171

FAI, 46, 64
Falcón, Carmen, 79
Falcón, Irene, 33
    CM and IHC's communist affiliations,
        38
    exile in USA, 88–9
    Republican exodus to France, 79
    Unión de Mujeres Españolas, 152
    views on CM, 36
Falcón, Kety, 36, 79
fascism, 3, 4, 22–4, 151
    Catalonia, 74

Joint Anti-Fascist Refugee Committee
    (JAFRC), 146–7
Mujeres Antifascistas, 33, 88, 152
    in POUM, 103
    in PSUC, 103
FBI
    CM's funeral, 1
    questioning of O'Brien, 159, 162, 168
    report on CM, 150, 152, 168–9
    report on Rogers, 149, 150
Feld, Rose, 101–2
Felipe, León, 68
Fernández Colino, Manuel, 90–1
"Fete of Guadalupe in Mexico" (Mora), 142
Fields, Joseph, 91
Fischer, Louis
    Allen's letter, 130
    CM's appointment, 43
    CM's dismissal, 60–1
    CM's re-instatement, 61–2
    friendship with Negrín, 61, 62, 184*n*
    meeting with Uritsky, 42, 59
    Negrín's letter to Bowers, 108
    Rubio Hidalgo replaced by CM, 76
    views on CM, 42, 59–60, 62, 84
    views on IHC, 42
Flynn, Errol, 102, 105
*Fondo de Ayuda a la Resistencia Antifascista
    Espanola*, 88
Foreign Legion, 194*n*
Foreign Press Office, 2, 42–82
    CM applies for job, 42–3
    CM appointed Director, 34, 75
    CM fired, 41, 60–1
    CM's re-instatement, 61–2
    CM's role, 34–6, 43–4, 46–8, 49,
        58–66, 67–8, 75–7, 79, 82
    relocation to Barcelona (1937), 74–5
    set up in Perpignan, 82
    weekly meetings, 67–8
Fosse, Bob, 91
France
    CM's visit (1946), 152–3
    invasion by Germany (1940), 126
    refugee crisis, 106, 110–11, 124–5,
        128–33
    Republican exodus, 79–82
    SERE issue, 111–20
    Soviet arms shipments, 79–81
Franch, Hernández, 137–8

Franco, Francisco, 2, 102, 137
  Asturias strikes, 24, 26
  Political Responsibilities Law, 87,
    99–100
  and POUM, 63
  refugee crisis, 125
  security of power (late 1940s), 154–5,
    159
  support from Germany, 27, 44, 99, 100,
    102, 106, 107, 109
  support from Italy, 44, 99, 109
  US position, 109, 135, 154–5
Franco, Ramón, 27–8
Free France, 198*n*
Free Germany (*Alemania Libre*), 146, 150,
    198*n*
Free Hungary, 198*n*
Frente Rojo, 33, 36

Gandhi, Mahatma, 84
García Lorca, Federico, 18, 109
Garrett, Betty, 91
Garriga, Miguel, 194*n*
Gellhorn, Martha, 87, 107, 153
German radio network, 27, 181*n*
Germany
  CM in, 23, 26–7
  intentions towards Spain, 26–7, 30, 31,
    35, 77
  invasion of France (1940), 126
  support for Franco, 27, 44, 99, 100,
    102, 106, 107, 109
Gerö, Erno, 186*n*
Giral, José, 61, 63
Giuseppe Garibaldi International Alliance,
    198*n*
Godoy, Manuel de, 15
Golden, Nan, 101
Gordon, Lena, 158, 160, 172
Gorkin, Julián, 149, 151
Graham, Helen, 61, 63, 65, 78,
    184–5*n*
Green, Adolph, 91
Grimau, Julián, 174
Guardias de Seguridad y Asalto, 33
Guatemala, 155, 158, 161–6, 172
Guernica, 187*n*

Harcourt, Alfred, 104–5
Harcourt, Brace, & Co., 91, 99, 190*n*

Harper's Weekly, 93
Hemingway, Ernest, 107, 131
  disappearance of Robles, 72, 96
  on *In Place of Splendor*, 5, 102
  petition to re-instate CM, 61
  Quintanilla's arrest, 180*n*
  relationship with CM, 1, 5, 87, 127–8,
    133
  relationship with Dos Passos, 70, 72
  "The Spanish Earth", 69, 70, 95
Herbst, Josephine, 72–3, 186*n*
Hernández, Jesús, 66–7, 69
Hidalgo de Cisneros Alonso, Ignace, 175
Hidalgo de Cisneros, Baltasar, 17
Hidalgo de Cisneros, Ignacio, 6, 17–19
  Arnáiz's views on, 136
  in Berlin, 26–7
  Cambio de rumbo, 2, 34, 174–5, 182*n*
  CM's death, 166, 170, 171–2, 173–5
  CM's divorce from Bolín, 20–1
  CM's Republicanism, 30
  as Commander in Chief of Air Force,
    34–5
  communist affiliation, 3, 38–9, 173–4,
    182*n*
  coup (1939), 99
  death of, 175
  December 1930 revolt, 14
  dispute with Largo Caballero, 64
  divorce from CM, 137, 138, 160, 196*n*
  exodus to France, 79–82
  family relationships, 148
  first meeting with CM, 19
  illness, 76
  leaves Spain (1939), 100
  marriage to CM, 21, 32
  in Mexico, 101, 121, 135–6, 137–8
  Military Attaché post in Mexico, 21–2
  Modotti's death, 141
  Nin's murder, 74
  portrait (1929), *plates, 7, 8*
  portrait with friends, *plate, 23*
  portrait with Neruda, *plate, 24*
  portrait in Poland, *plate, 22*
  Prieto's escape, 25–6
  and Ramón Franco, 27–8
  remains in France (1939), 82, 84
  return to Spain (1934), 24, 25
  return to Spain (1935), 27
  in Rome, 3, 22–4, 26

in Soviet Union (1939), 188*n*
Uritsky's interest in, 42
US visa application, 87, 188*n*
Valencia radio station incident (1936), 30
visits to Soviet Union, 76, 77–9
Hidalgo de Cisneros, Paco, 173
Hidalgo, Miguel, 142
High Museum, Atlanta, 188*n*
Hitler, Adolf, 2, 86
    defeated (1945), 159
    pact with Stalin, 128
    Roosevelt's press conference, 108, 192*n*
    support for Franco, 44, 99, 100, 102, 106, 107
    support of western elites, 4
Hooks, Margaret, 67
Howson, Gerald, 81
Hughes, Langston, 65
Hull, Cordell, 111

I Must Have Liberty (Palencia), 189*n*
Ibárruri, Amaya, portrait in Soviet Union, *plate, 14*
Ibárruri, Dolores (*Pasionara*), 17, 33, 35, 79, 170
    CM's views on, 36
    Davidson's exhibition, 84
    Hemingway on, 133
    leaves Spain (1939), 100
    Luli's references, 144
    Memorias de Pasionara, 152
    Paul's views on, 86
    son in Soviet Union, 103
    speeches, 34, 69, 186*n*
Ickes, Harold L., 32
In Place of Splendor (Mora), 1, 2–4, 84, 89–105
    advertising campaign, 5
    Allen's influence, 3, 89, 91, 92, 94, 189*n*
    CM's pre-war experiences, 5–12
    CM's Republicanism, 30
    Condaxes view of, 139
    copy sent to Mrs. Roosevelt, 111, 193*n*
    disappearance of Robles, 71
    donation of original manuscript, 101
    February elections (1936), 28
    and Hemingway, 5, 102
    Italian translation, 176

lack of mention of communism, 3, 36, 38–9, 49, 66, 100, 102
McKenney's influence, 3, 91–5, 101, 105, 139, 140
Nin's death, 74
O'Brien's praise for, 156
POUM party, 74
praise for Negrín, 64–5
praise for Soviet Union, 41
references to Prieto, 26
reviews, 101–5
Robles family, 70–1
Soviet visits, 76, 77–8
Spanish Civil War (1936-1939), 34–5, 36, 38, 64–5
Spanish translation, 121, 122, 138, 177
Industrial Valley (McKenney), 91, 92
Inman, Samuel Guy, 194*n*
Intergovernmental Committee on Refugees, 110
International Brigades, 95
International Co-ordinating Committee, 132
International Democratic Action, 198*n*
International Red Aid (*Socorro Rojo*), 66, 67, 90
Isaacs, Stanley M., 107
Isabella II, Queen of Spain, 17
Italy
    CM in, 22–4, 26
    intentions towards Spain, 31, 35, 77
    support for Franco, 44, 99, 100, 102, 106, 107, 109
Ivens, Joris, 69, 73, 95

Jaén, 16
JAFRC (Joint Anti-Fascist Refugee Committee), 146–7
Jiménez, Juan Ramón, 11, 19, 21, 39, 40
Johnstone, Ferdinand, 166
Johnstone, Nancy
    CM's accident in Guatemala, 165, 166, 169, 172, 173
    friendship with CM, 153, 162, 163, 164
    Quaker relief organizations, 153
    residence in Guatemala, 162
Joint Anti-Fascist Refugee Committee (JAFRC), 146–7
Jordan, Philip, 65
Journeys Between Wars (Dos Passos), 96

Juan (chauffeur), 168
Junta Suprema de Unión Nacional (JSUN), 45, 148, 198*n*
Jusik (of NKVD), 186*n*

Kahn, Gordon, 175
Kahn, James, 175–6
Kalinin, Mikhail Ivanovich, 78
Keller, Helen, 127
Kelley, Fred, 195*n*
Kellogg, Paul, 194*n*
Kellt, 46
Kent, Victoria, 17, 152, 179*n*
Kerr, Chester, 139
KGB, 2
Kheifets, Gergory, 150
Kirchway, Freda, 89, 103, 150–1, 191*n*
Koch, Stephen, 68
Koltsov, Mikhail, 189*n*
Kowalsky, Daniel, 77–8
Kulcsar, Ilsa, 58–9
Kurzke, Jan, 82, 182*n*

Lago, Regina, 172
Largo Caballero, Francis, 61, 64
The League of American Writers, 101
League of Nations, 46, 77
LeCron, J. D., 107
Left Republican Party, 28
Lejárraga García, María, 17
Lemmon, Jack, 91
Lenin, Vladimir Ilich, 144
León, María Teresa, 19, 24–5, 42–3, 59, 180*n*
Lerroux, Alejandro, 24, 28
Liga Antimperialista, 189*n*
Liga de Intelectuales Antifascistas, 59
Lion d'Or Café, 18
Líster, Enrique, 82
Lobo, Father Leocadio, 76
Loewenstein, Helga, 127, 146
Los Angeles Times, 102
Louise (Mangan's roommate), 45
Luis Vives Institute, 147
Luli *see* Bolín de la Mora, Constancia María Lourdes (Luli)
Lyons, Leonard, 191*n*

Mccoy, Esther, 155
Machado, Antonio, 109

McKenney, Eileen, 91
McKenney, Ruth, 96, 100
    communist affiliation, 92, 190*n*
    ejected from American Communist party, 154
    Industrial Valley, 91, 92
    influence on *In Place of Splendor*, 3, 91–5, 101, 105, 139, 140
    The McKenney's Carry on, 92
    Mexico is Theirs draft, 140
    My Sister Eileen, 91, 92, 93
The McKenney's Carry on (McKenney), 92
Madrid children's colonies, 36–7
Madrid strikes, 24
Málaga, 47–8, 160, 200*n*
Malraux, André, 180*n*
Mangan, Kate, 44–9
    celebrations in Barcelona, 38
    on CM, 46–7, 60, 65, 68
    and Coco Robles, 69, 71
    disappearance of Robles, 71, 72, 96
    and Kurzke, 82, 182*n*
    leaves Spain, 82
    Press Office weekly meetings, 67–8
Mangini, Shirley, 3
Manhattan Center, 89
Mann, Heinrich, 146
Mantecón, Concha, 136, 137, 171–2
Mantecón, Ignacio, 136, 137
Mao Tse Tsung, 170
María Isabel, 9, 12
"María" of *Socorro Rojo see* Modotti, Tina
Martin, Fredericka, 138, 153, 160, 176, 196*n*, 199–200*n*
Martinez Barrio, Diego, 28
Martínez de Pisón, Ignacio, 68, 70, 71–2, 73
Marx, Karl, 144
La Mata del Pirón, 7, 8, 11
Maura, Antonio, 2, 6–7, 10–11, 32, 61, 196*n*
    giving a speech (1917), *plate, 1*
    with King Alfonso XIII (1918), *plate, 2*
Maura, Carlos Semprún, 152–3
Maura, Constancia, *plate, 3*
Maura, Estefania, *plate, 3*
Maura, Gabriel, Duke of, 7, 15
Maura, Jorge, 152
Maura, Margarita, *plate, 3*
Maura, Miguel, 14, 15, 179*n*

Maurois, André, 127
Medical Bureau, 106
Mejías, Ignacio Sánchez, 18
Mella, Julio Antonio, 90, 189*n*
Memorias de Pasionara (Ibárruri), 152
Ménard, Jean, 125, 129, 130, 131, 132
Merida, 159, 160
Mexico, 121–33
  anti-fascist movement, 146
  CM in, 3, 101, 121–4, 127, 133,
    134–42, 147
  as communist base of operations, 123
  IHC in, 101, 121, 135–6, 137–8
  Luli arrives, 146
  Military Attaché post, 21–2
  Soviet Embassy, 138, 148–52
  Spanish republican exiles, 134
  see also Acapantzingo
Mexico is Theirs (Mora), 139–40, 142
  advertisement, *plate, 18*
Meyer, Hannes, 140
Miaja, José, 84
Mikoyan, Anastas Ivanovich, 78
Millán Astray, Carmen, 66
Minton, Bruce, 92
MJB Coffee Company, 92
Modern Age, 140, 142
Modotti, Tina, 67, 88, 157
  CM's views on, 141
  death of, 66, 140–1, 169
  manuscript of *In Place of Splendor*, 90
  and Mella, 90, 189*n*
  in Mexico, 138–9, 140
  relationship with CM, 1, 66
Molotov, Vyacheslav, 77, 80
Montálban, Manuel Vázquez, 1
Montseny, Federica, 17
Mora, Constancia de la
  background, 5–12, 196*n*
  charity work, 9–10, 36–7
  childhood letters, 8
  communist affiliation, 2, 3, 36, 38–9,
    40, 60–1, 144, 163, 167–8, 170
  Davidson's exhibition, 84–5
  death of, 1, 165–9, 170–1
  divorce from Bolín, 20–1, 32
  divorce from IHC, 137, 138, 160,
    196*n*
  family relationships, 32–3, 152–3,
    161–2

"Fete of Guadalupe in Mexico", 142
first marriage to Bolín, 10–11, 32, 33,
    181*n*
  letters from Cambridge, 8–9
  Mexico is Theirs, 139–40, 142
  portrait (1923), *plate, 4*
  portrait (1925), *plate, 5*
  portrait (1939), *plate, 12*
  portrait (1943), *plate, 17*
  portrait (1944), *plate, 16*
  portrait with Laura Condax (1939),
    plate, 13
  portrait with Lini de Vries (1949), *plate,
    21*
  portrait with Luli (1929), *plate, 6*
  portrait in Mexico, *plate, 18*
  propaganda articles, 34, 44–5, 75–6,
    142–8
  school days, 8
  second marriage to IHC, 21, 32
  separation from Bolín, 12–13
  trial of Miguel Maura (1931), *plate, 9*
  "Young Spain in the USSR", 142–4
Mora, Marichu de la, 7, 9, 29, 30, 161
Mora, Regina de la, 9, 10, 17, 29
Mora, Teresa de la, 176
Moreno, Constancia, 155, 175
Moreno, Delfina, 155, 158, 175
Moreno, Fidel, 155, 175
Mortera, Gabriel, Count of, 7, 15
Moscow Institute of Energy, 144
Mujeres Antifascistas, 33, 88, 152
Mundo Obrero, 168
Mussolini, Benito
  Roosevelt's press conference, 108, 192*n*
  support for Franco, 44, 99, 100, 102,
    106, 107
  victory in Albania, 132
My Sister Eileen (McKenney), 91, 92, 93
My Years in Germany (Dodd), 190*n*

El Nacional, 171
Nash, Mary, 33
The Nation, 103, 110, 132, 150
National Labor Relations Board, 87
National Republican Party, 28
Nationalist uprising (1936), 32–3, 35
Nazis, 23, 26–7, 86
Negrín, Juan
  Allen works for, 89

Negrín, Juan *(continued)*
  becomes Prime Minister (1937), 64
  CM and IHC in USA, 87–8
  CM on, 64–5, 103
  CM's re-instatement, 61
  communist links, 120
  contacts with IHC, 18
  correspondence with Bowers, 108–9
  coup (1939), 99
  in France, 107
  friendship with Fischer, 61, 62, 184*n*
  IHC's US visa application, 87, 188*n*
  leaves Spain (1939), 100
  meeting with Mrs. Roosevelt, 108, 109
  refuge in Allen's apartment, 25
  refugee crisis, 129
  requests for Soviet aid, 77, 78–9,
    80–1
  Rubio Hidalgo replaced by CM, 76
Nelken, Margarita, 17, 33, 179*n*
Neruda, Pablo, 136, 157
  CM's death, 170, 172
  eulogy to CM, 1, 142, 167
  friendship with IHC, 19, 174
  IHC's job at Domecq wine company,
    137
  portrait with IH, *plate*, 23, 24
Neva, 37, 38, 41, 182*n*
The New Masses, 92
The New Republic, 96, 98, 99
New York
  CM at the Dodd Sterns, 86–9, 101
  CM returns to (1939), 100–1
  CM's mission (1939), 2, 82–3, 84
  Davidson's sculpture of CM, 84–6
New York Post, 72
The New York Times, 5, 85, 101–2, 104,
    142, 168
New Yorker, 91
Nikiforov couple, 171
Nin, Andreu, 62–3, 73–4, 186*n*
NKVD, 62–3, 67, 73, 86
Non-Intervention Pact, 37, 77, 109
North American Committee for Spanish
    Refugee Relief, 106
North American Committee to Aid
    Spanish Democracy, 106
Norton, W. W., 194*n*
Nuestro ejercito, 67

Oak, Liston
  disappearance of Robles, 97, 98
  Foreign Press Office, 45–6, 47, 48, 65,
    75
  leaves Spain, 70
O'Brien, Mary Wallner, 155, 156–69,
    170–1, 176, 199–200*n*
Orlov, Alexander, 73, 186*n*
Oumansky, Constantin, 157
  at Soviet Embassy in Mexico, 138, 149
  death of, 150–1, 169, 197*n*
  and Stalin, 152

Palencia, Isabel de, 89, 189*n*
Pan-American Conference, 123–4
Panacache, 164
Panajachel, 165
Panhellenic groups, 89
Parker, Dorothy, 85
Pascua, Marcelino, 18, 78, 81, 187*n*
Pascual, Tamara, 151, 152
Pasionara see Ibárruri, Dolores (*Pasionara*)
The Path of Life, 21
Paul, Elliot, 70–1, 89
  views on CM, 85–6
PCE (Spanish Communist Party), 2, 123
  Bolloten's disillusionment with, 62
  CM leaves, 154, 170
  CM's allegiance to, 60–1, 134
  CM's membership, 3, 38–9, 40, 144,
    168
  CM's obituary, 168
  disappearance of Robles, 97
  eulogy to CM, 170
  IHC's membership, 3, 38–9, 174
  Negrín's commitment to resistance, 79
  and the SRRC, 128
  support for Negrín, 64
Pérez, Alberto Sánchez, 190*n*
Pike, David, 132–3
Pindyck, Miss, 101
Playa San Jorge, 165
Polish Association, 198*n*
Political Responsibilities Law, 87, 99–100
Poppy, 45, 69, 72, 96
El Popular, 146, 171
Popular Front, 28, 29
Porset, Clarita, 172
POUM, 45, 46, 62–3, 64, 73–4, 103
Prado y O'Neill, Mariano del, 16

Prieto, Blanca, 41
Prieto, Concha, 37, 40–1, 191*n*
Prieto, Indalecio
  CM fired from Press Office, 41, 60–1
  CM and IHC's wedding, 21
  CM's first divorce, 20
  CM's views on, 26, 41, 103, 191*n*
  escape to France, 25–6
  friendship with IHC, 18, 60
  hostility towards communism, 41, 60–1
  IHC's diplomatic posting, 22
  Nazi plans, 27, 30, 31
  on Negrín, 65
  on political committee, 14
  relations with Fischer, 62
  removal of Concha, 40–1
  return to Spain (1935), 28
  views on CM, 64
Primo de Rivera, José Antonio, 29, 30
Primo de Rivera, Miguel, 9, 13–14, 32
propaganda
  articles by CM, 34, 44–5, 75–6, 142–8
  and Mangan, 45
  Prieto's order, 60
  Soviet Embassy in Mexico, 148–52
  Soviet materials, 38
PSOE, 62
PSUC, 45, 103
Publisher's Weekly, 91
Puerto de Hierro club, 9, 33

Quakers, 124, 128, 130, 153
Queipo de Llano, Gonzalo, 66
Quintanilla, Luis, 25, 72, 133, 180–1*n*
Quintanilla, Paul, 181*n*
Quiroga, Casares, 29–30, 31

Radical Party, 17
Radical Socialist Party, 17
Radio España Independiente, 174
Rakosi, Matyas, 170
refugee crisis, 106–33
  Allen's efforts to help, 87, 106–7,
    127–8, 130, 131, 194*n*
  CM's efforts to help, 106, 109–10, 111,
    121–6, 130–3, 146–7, 154
  and France, 106, 110–11, 124–5,
    128–33
  Mexico's policy, 134
  and Mrs. Roosevelt, 109–10, 120, 121,
    125–6
  and United States, 106–7, 109–10,
    111–26
  see also Spanish Refugee Relief
    Campaign (SRRC)
Reissig, Herman F., 111–20, 121, 122,
  123, 129–30
Renn, Ludwig, portrait (1944), *plate, 16*
Republican Union, 28
Republicanism, CM's commitment to, 6,
  14–17, 30
Río Dulce, 163–4
Ríos, Eladia de los, 141, 153, 154, 170,
  172
Ríos, Fernando de los, 18
Roberto (driver), 164, 165
Robeson, Paul, 146
Robles, Coco, 68, 183*n*
  disappearance of his father, 69, 71, 73,
    97, 98
  fall of Málaga, 47, 48
  in Foreign Press Office, 47, 48, 69,
    70–2
Robles, Gil, 16, 26, 27
Robles, José, 68–70, 71–3, 96–9, 183*n*
Robles, Márgara, 68, 70, 71–2, 73
Robles, Miggie, 68, 98
Roces, Wenceslao, 170, 171, 172
Rodriguez, Benigno, 79, 135
Rodriguez Mata brothers, 136
Rogers, Paul Patrick, 65–6, 149, 150
Rome, 3, 22–4, 26
Roosevelt, Eleanor
  CM introduced to, 107
  CM's letter on Pan-American
    Conference, 123–4
  receives copy of *In Place of Splendor*, 111,
    193*n*
  refugee crisis, 109–10, 120, 121, 125–6
  relationship with CM, 1, 3, 86–7, 94,
    107–8, 109–10, 111, 123–7, 131,
    133, 137, 188–9*n*
  SERE issue, 120
  as supporter of Republic, 107
Roosevelt, Elliot, 126–7
Roosevelt, Franklin D., 84, 108, 127, 192*n*
Rosal, Amaro del, 130
Rubio Hidalgo, Luis
  and Auden, 183*n*
  Barea and Ilsa's jobs in Madrid, 59

Rubio Hidalgo, Luis (*continued*)
  Barea on, 58
  death of José Robles, 69
  disliked by CM, 58
  distrust of, 58
  in Foreign Press Office, 43, 46, 47, 48, 49, 58
  incompetence of, 65
  relations with CM, 43
  replaced by CM, 75
Rúspoli y Caro, María, 16, 24
Russell, Rosalind, 91
Russian Revolution, 21

St. Jean de Luz, 8, 12
Saint Mary's Convent, Cambridge, 8–9
Salinas, Jaime, 180*n*
Salinas, Pedro, 180*n*
Sancha, Clara, 94–5, 190*n*, 196*n*
Sancha, Soledad, 87, 144, 189*n*, 190*n*
Sánchez, María, 145
Sánchez Román, Felipe, 28
Sanjurjo, José, 19–20
Schain, Joseph, 194*n*
Scheirla, T. C., 195*n*
Schenker, David, 105
Sección Femenina del Comité de Ayuda a España Republicana, 33
Seghers, Anna, 1, 146–7
  portrait (1944), *plate, 16*
Selke, Rudolf, 46, 183*n*
Sénder, Ramón J., 68
Servicio de Evacuación de Refugiados Españoles (SERE), 111–20, 125
The Seventh Cross (Seghers), 146
Sevilla coup (1932), 19–20
Sheean, Mrs. Vincent, 122, 194*n*
Sheean, Vincent, 5, 89
Shipler, Guy Emery, 194*n*
Shumilov, M. S., 81
Siqueiros, José Alfaro, 150
Smith, Francis G., 110
Smodorinskii, Comrade, 188*n*
Smouldering Freedom (Palencia), 89
Socialist Party, 17, 128
Socorro Rojo, 66, 67, 90
Solano, Wilebaldo, 74, 186*n*
Solola, 166
Soslov, Comrade, 189*n*

Southworth, Herbert, 34, 175, 187*n*
Soviet Russia Today, 142, 145
Soviet Union, 21
  celebration in Barcelona, 38
  CM and IHC's visits, 76, 77–9
  CM's work for, 134, 138, 148–52
  Embassy in Mexico, 138, 148–52
  IHC's arrival (1939), 188*n*
  IHC's enthusiasm for, 173–4
  Luli's residence in, 41–2, 59, 76, 88, 143, 144–6, 148
  Non-Intervention Pact, 37
  praise in CM's memoir, 41
  propaganda materials, 38
  Spanish evacuee children, 142–4
  supplies of food and aid, 37–8, 77–81, 134
"Spanish ABC", 35–6
Spanish Children's Milk Fund, 85
Spanish Civil War (1936-1939), 32–83
  CM's work in the children's colonies, 36–7
  July 1936 Nationalist uprising, 32–3, 35
  Soviet supplies of food and aid, 37–8, 77–81
  see also Foreign Press Office
Spanish Communist Party (PCE) *see* PCE (Spanish Communist Party)
Spanish Democratic Union, 198*n*
"The Spanish Earth", 69, 70, 95
"Spanish Portraits", 84
Spanish Refugee Relief Campaign (SRRC), 89, 111, 121–3, 127–30, 133
  communist links, 128, 130
SRRC *see* Spanish Refugee Relief Campaign (SRRC)
Stalin, Josef, 67, 170
  dinner with CM, 1, 32, 77, 78, 80, 146, 174
  memorandum from Voroshilov, 81
  and Oumansky, 152
  pact with Hitler, 128
Stalinism, 2, 149
Star, 187*n*
Stern, Albert Kaufman, 86, 88
Stewart, Maxwell S., 194*n*
Stowe, Leland, 5, 102, 194*n*
Sukharev, K. P., 188*n*
Syndicalists, 98

Taborda, Elvira, 33
Talón, Vicente, 187*n*
Terrill, Katherine, 195*n*
Thomas, Hugh, 179*n*, 181*n*
Thompson, Malvina, 121, 125–6
Times, 76
Tizoc, 153
Tolmach, Dr. Jesse, 195*n*
Tournier, 9
Tresca, Carlo, 70, 141
Trotsky, Leon, 136, 152
Trumbo, Dalton, 146

UGT, 45, 61, 67–8
Unamuno, Miguel de, 109
Unión de Mujeres Españolas (UME), 152
unionisation, 67–8
United Press, 62, 182*n*
United States
  CM refused visa (1940), 127
  Franco's regime, 154–5
  non-intervention policy, 35, 102,
    111–20
  refugee crisis, 106–7, 109–10, 111–26
  see also New York
Uribe, Vicente, 69, 154, 156, 170
Uritsky, Corps Commander, 42, 59
Uxmal, 160

Valencia radio station, 30
Valle-Inclán, Ramón, 68
Velilla (communist at Ministry of State),
  49–58
Veterans of the Abraham Lincoln Brigade,
  124, 194*n*

see also Abraham Lincoln Brigade
Vicens de la Llave, Juan, 136, 149–50,
  152, 172
Victor (chauffeur), 186*n*
Vidali, Vittorio, 66–7, 150
  CM's book, 90, 91, 176, 189*n*
  Mexico is Theirs, 142
  Modotti's death, 140–1
  relationship with CM, 1
Vinogradov, Boris, 86
Volunteer for Liberty, 124
Voroshilov, Kliment, 42, 77, 78, 80, 81,
  146
Vries, Lini de, 155, 167
  portrait with CM (1949), *plate, 21*

Wallace, Henry A., 87
Washington, D.C., 85
The Washington Post, 85, 191*n*
Watson, K. Scott, 76, 187*n*
Watt, Colonel George, 92
Welles, Sumner, 110
West, Nathaniel, 91
White, Leigh, 103–4, 105
Whitney, Mrs. Caspar, 194*n*
Whyte Gallery, 85
Wilkins, Roy, 194*n*
Wolff, Milton, 1, 195*n*
Women's Day, 91
Wood, Grant, 85

"Young Spain in the USSR" (Mora), 142–4

Zarauz, 161